THE HIDDEN ART
—— OF ——
HOLLYWOOD

THE HIDDEN ART
—— OF ——
HOLLYWOOD

In Defense of the
Studio Era Film

John Fawell

PRAEGER

Westport, Connecticut
London

Library of Congress Cataloging-in-Publication Data

Fawell, John Wesley, 1959–
    The hidden art of Hollywood : in defense of the studio era film / John Fawell.
        p. cm.
    Includes bibliographical references and index.
    ISBN: 978–0–313–35692–6 (alk. paper)
    1. Motion pictures—California—Los Angeles.   2. Motion pictures—United States—Aesthetics.
I. Title.
    PN1993.5.U65F36   2008
    791.4309794′94—dc22   2008028423

British Library Cataloguing in Publication Data is available.

Library of Congress Catalog Card Number: 2008028423
ISBN: 978–0–313–35692–6

First published in 2008

Praeger Publishers, 88 Post Road West, Westport, CT 06881
An imprint of Greenwood Publishing Group, Inc.
www.praeger.com

Printed in the United States of America

The paper used in this book complies with the
Permanent Paper Standard issued by the National
Information Standards Organization (Z39.48–1984).

10 9 8 7 6 5 4 3 2 1

To Yvette, Ted, and Charlie

Contents

Contents

Introduction

The purpose of this book is to explain why films as seemingly light in content and as commercial in orientation as those of the classic Hollywood era have been, and should continue to be, taken so seriously by film scholars. This may seem like an unnecessary task, seeing how much ink has been spilled on Hollywood by film scholars already. The number of books on Hitchcock alone has to supersede that of many a venerated writer. But despite all that has been written on Hollywood, I still see a general disconnect between the film scholar's attitude—and that of the general public—toward classic Hollywood.

For example, I teach a core curriculum program of art and literature into which we slip a small adjunct survey of film history. I have been struck by how difficult it is for the average college freshman or sophomore to easily see the merit of the classic Hollywood studio films we show them in this program. Ironically, classes on these films, which are introduced in many ways as a lively respite from drudgery of core humanities, are often the most difficult classes to teach. It's easy to sell a college freshman on the necessity of studying Marcus Aurelius, less so John Ford's *Stagecoach*, which the majority of them find, on first viewing, laughably antique.

Ford is actually easier to teach them than some of the other Hollywood filmmakers. Once you freeze-frame a shot from *Stagecoach* the visual care of the film is apparent. Teaching a director who is not so obviously visually striking, a Preston Sturges or an Ernst Lubitsch, is much more of an exercise in frustration. The virtues of these films are subtler, having to do with rhythm, pacing, allusive and sophisticated dialogue, and charm—never easy virtues to translate in core curriculum. Even students who tend to like this kind of filmmaking still often find it dated, quaint, more of an historical curiosity than something relevant to them. As one student asked me, in an earnest desire to understand, "Are these films good in themselves or just good for their time?" (It was clear he was tending toward the latter alternative.) It's this question that this book seeks to answer. And the answer it offers is unequivocal: these films were good then, and they are good now. The best of classical Hollywood filmmaking represents a high point in film history, a model of good filmmaking.

That said, I am utterly sympathetic to the students' confusion as to why they should take these films seriously. The classic Hollywood film lacks much that typically marks art as serious. These films are, for example, rarely socially relevant. Sam Goldwyn's famous quip, "If I wanted a message I'd call Western Union," is an accurate epigram for the era. This is devoutly unserious art. Students studying Hollywood for the first time experience an almost palpable sense of relief when they are shown a film from the latter part of the classical era, when Hollywood began vying with Europe in "high seriousness," something with social or historical relevance, like Stanley Kramer's *Judgment at Nuremberg* and Elia Kazan's *On the Waterfront*, even though the professor may be feeling, at the same time, that much of what represents the glory of Hollywood has been drained out of such didactic exercises.

Moreover, the classic Hollywood film lacks many of the virtues students have come to identify with successful cinema. After the airing out of cinema in the 1960s and 1970s, Hollywood studio films seem hopelessly unrealistic and hemmed in by stagy, artificial sets. And the naturalism in acting that seemed to breeze into film with exterior landscapes, makes the classic Hollywood actor seem stiff, wooden, and also a product of the stage. Schooled, as the modern audience is, in the clever hijinks of the European art film and the overpowering stimuli of the modern Hollywood special effect, the old Hollywood film can seem primitive in technique, slow and static, too much like filmed theater. And viewed 50 years past the breakdown of the code, these films seem childishly naive, oppressive in their optimism and idealism, well-nigh fascist, or at least laughable in their squeaky-clean approach to life.

Moreover, it's not only students who see classic Hollywood this way. Many an educated adult has grilled me with the same questions my students do, only with a more jaundiced eye. They no longer suffer from any delusions about the authority of professors, and they have heard about the French lionizing Jerry Lewis. They're not going to stand for any nonsense, and they ask me to defend myself in taking these films seriously. Their suspicions, frustrations, and confusions are the same as the students. Yes, they concede, there is a charming simplicity to these films, and yes, they do bring back a certain lovely, hazy waft of optimism and elegance from the pleasant years gone by, but don't ask them to take these films seriously as works of art.

The attitude that these films are interesting as cultural by-products rather than artful in themselves is shared by academia itself, even the academic film world, if I am to judge from the number of papers and articles I've read that find their only interest in Hollywood to be an archeological one, in the way a film reflects this or that era or social trend. Whether it's a traditional study of screwball comedy as reflective of Depression-era poverty or a more contemporary piece by a queer theorist on the sublimated homoeroticism of Hitchcock's films, the idea remains the same: Hollywood films are more interesting as sociological artifacts than as works of art.

Theoretical trends change, but what has remained the same, over the years, is the large number of papers and publications that concern themselves with the Hollywood film only as a cultural stepping-stone to larger, more significant phenomena. Nearly 60 years after the French critics excoriated us for treating film like an inferior form of literature, many a professor is still drawn by the siren call of the literary adaptation film, even if these films have traditionally represented the worst of Hollywood and even if the professor's purpose in studying these films is, inevitably, to point out how far the film falls short of its original source. Apparently, many a professor shares the same puzzlement the students do when looking at the classic Hollywood film on its own, finding it a poor, denuded thing when shorn of its historical or sociological context. Many a film scholar seems to be able to look at a Hollywood film for itself, for its own virtues, for about the same amount of time that they can stare into the sun.

Even in the heart of the world of film aficionados there is evidence of a certain indifference toward the classic Hollywood film. The 2002 Sight and Sound poll of greatest films ever represents the opinions of a pretty impressive collection of film critics and filmmakers, but even there one is struck by the meager representation of classic Hollywood. Of the fifty top films chosen only eleven are from classic Hollywood. That may seem to some a fair representation. But there are a couple of things notable about the films that were chosen. First, ten of the eleven chosen films are postwar representations of Hollywood. Modern film audiences tend to warm up to later Hollywood more easily. Just a few years short of the breakdown of the code, these films have an edginess and cynicism that is compatible to modern tastes. And they tend to have a more baroque styling. Three directors are responsible for seven of the eleven choices—Ford, Hitchcock, Welles—all great visual stylists. Welles's films are so avant-garde that they probably more accurately represent the demise, rather than the fulfillment, of the Hollywood tradition. (F. Scott Fitzgerald recognized this when he wrote, "Orson Welles is the biggest menace to come to Hollywood in years.") The gravitation toward these high style films reflects the common conception, and one contrary to the basic ethos of the classic Hollywood, that the more obvious the art, the more serious or artful the film. I've noticed, for example, that while much of traditional Hollywood is a tough sell for students, they gobble up film noir with its existential bleakness and Expressionist angles and shadows. "OK," they seem to say, "this I can buy as art."

Those Hollywood filmmakers who are missing from the Sight and Sound list are the practitioners of the quiet art of the well-crafted film, filmmakers like George Cukor, William Wyler, William Wellman, and Mervyn LeRoy, whose films are well crafted but in such a way as to fly under the radar of modern audiences and their taste for visual élan. Other directors, like Sturges and Lubitsch, have more style (though not necessarily a striking visual style) but still go missing from contemporary favorites list because their charms are so quiet and subtle and because their light and elegant comic touch is read as superficial and frothy by modern audiences who seem wed to the social sciences and demand films with didactic lessons, messages, and portentous themes.

And of course film scholars and filmmakers seem curiously unimpressed with Hollywood before the war, despite the vaunted reputation 1939 has as the apex of the Hollywood studio era. Charlie Chaplin nearly stands alone as the representative of Hollywood's prewar heyday on this list. What's particularly curious in its omission is the period between the silents and the war, from 1929 to 1939, the period that has often been found to represent the core of the golden age of Hollywood.

Curiously, while critics like me might find the Hollywood studio underrepresented in a list like this, others find the list still too stodgy, too wed to the past. One critic, Ty Burr, has put some effort into polling filmmaking students as to their personal canon and reports in an essay, "Once Upon a Classic," that these students' cannon overlaps little with the Sight and Sound one. "*Casablanca* and *Citizen Kane* don't matter much anymore, even if you think they should," he concludes. Burr quotes David Fincher, director of *Fight Club* (one of the current films that, according to his polls, form for young filmmakers a new canon) as saying, "*Casablanca* now feels like a stage play. It's beautifully, classically made, but in terms of the language of cinema, it's almost irrelevant." In the same article, a professor of filmmaking at the University of Southern California notes that his students are "wired to take things much faster and more easily than older audiences, and they get impatient with very traditional storytelling. They want to break frames and skip around in time; they're used to doing that."[1]

The essay suggests an indifference to classical Hollywood within the world of burgeoning American filmmakers, a divestiture from a rich tradition one might think they would be building on rather than abandoning. And indeed a cursory look at the films referred to as "independents" reveals a cinema almost diametrically opposed to the Hollywood tradition. Where Hollywood studiously avoided the topical, these films search for political relevance. Where Hollywood sought to hide its technique, these films continue the French New Wave tradition of making technique apparent and often favor a jumpy, fragmented style. Whereas Hollywood worshipped the narrative arc and sought crisp, musical pacing, these films, again following the European art films they seem to prefer, favor languorous storylines and ponderous pacing. The essence of the classical aesthetic is to create films with technique so quiet and hidden that it easily goes unnoticed, a technique that does not call attention to itself or interfere with the drive and rhythm of the story. We are not, perhaps, in an era that celebrates this kind of quiet aesthetic or even understands it.

This book then, first and foremost, aims to address itself to those who sit somewhat outside of the world of film criticism and who are perplexed as to why the classical Hollywood film is treated with the high-mindedness with which it is, to those who want to clearly understand why we take these films, intended as light entertainments, as seriously as we do. But it is also addressed to those closer to the world of film studies, who tend to underrate this cinema either because it is not obvious in its style or because it steadfastly refuses to justify itself in terms of social relevance or didactic content. To defend classic Hollywood is, in many ways, to defend a cinema of pure form, the ideals of which are rhythm and structure, not literary ideas or social content. Hollywood is underrated in the same way a practitioner of naturalism like Guy de Maupassant is, because it keeps its meanings close to the vest and when it has something of significance to say builds it into the plastics of its story rather than spits it out like message on ticker tape.

I want to emphasize that my goal in this book is to synthesize certain essential aspects of the classic Hollywood film, not to delineate all the different features of the Hollywood system. Ever since the reaction against "auteurism" (the notion that the director is the overriding author of the film) in the 1960s, it has been de rigueur to bow to the collaborative nature of film and to emphasize that it is nearly impossible, as F. Scott Fitzgerald said, to gather together the "whole equation" of the Hollywood studio film. Consequently, there are a good many textbooks out there already on the multitudinous of the Hollywood film—the different studios, genres, the wide array of personnel that go into the collaborative effort of making a studio film, each one with their special claims of authorship. Perhaps film criticism has been so respectful of the multifariousness of the Hollywood film that it has lost sight a little that there is a core group of films by a core group of filmmakers that represent the cream of Hollywood's crop and that there are essential virtues in these films that represent the core of Hollywood's art. My goal in this book is to generalize, to isolate, and to gather those virtues that run throughout the very best classic Hollywood films, despite the time the films were made in or the studio they came from. Of course there are vast differences between Chaplin's *The Kid* (1921), coming out of the silent era, and Billy Wilder's *The Apartment* (1960), coming at the tail end of the Hollywood tradition, when the studios were more or less defunct and the code on the verge of being entirely broken down. And yet Wilder, in his interviews, often refers to Chaplin as one of his models of good filmmaking, and both *The Kid* and *The Apartment* represent excellent examples of the classical Hollywood aesthetic. What they have in common is the object of study in this book.

— 1 —

When Is Classic Hollywood?

Most critics agree that the studio era had reached a point of consolidation around 1917, both in terms of the machinery of production and the classical aesthetic that had been slowly hammered out during cinema's evolution as a form of storytelling and entertainment in America. David Bordwell points out that by 1917, Hollywood had more or less arrived at the essentials of the way it would tell a story, the way it defined time and space in a narrative film, and its laws of editing, lighting and storytelling. "By 1917," he asserts, "the system was complete in its basic narrative and stylistic premises."[1] The shock that the advent of sound, in the late 1920s, caused in Hollywood is sometimes overstated. Cumbersome sound equipment certainly led to a good number of static films with leaden acting, but there were bad movies before sound as well. The best directors, like King Vidor and Raoul Walsh, continued to innovate visually, and in the hands of pros like these, the classical Hollywood style continued to evolve. Robert Sklar notes that the turnover in Hollywood personnel was minimal during the transition from silent to sound film, which points to "an important but neglected fact—the visual aesthetics of Hollywood movies, the way shots were taken and assembled into a whole, changed little if at all from silents to sound."[2]

Hollywood scholars debate more on the causes and dates of Hollywood's demise but generally agree it began shortly after the war with the advent of television and the breakup of the studio monopoly by the forced divestiture of their theater holdings and finished somewhere in the early 1960s, where we see the last vestiges of a product that comes from the hands of studio-trained filmmakers and represents the principles of studio filmmaking.

POSTWAR HOLLYWOOD

World War II seemed to have changed things in Hollywood. There was a discernible change in worldview in many of the Hollywood films after the war. They seemed to insist on a darker understanding of the world and more realistic estimation of evil than Hollywood was willing to accord before the war. Perhaps this was most apparent with the advent of film noir, which, though building on the genre of the gangster film, offered a much bleaker and more menacing universe and a darker photographic technique to match that universe. Film noir was characterized by an Expressionist aesthetic that Hollywood had kept at bay for 20 years or so, an aesthetic at once gloomier and artier than Hollywood had previously advanced. It is a little ironic that so much of the nostalgia that modern audiences feel for old Hollywood focuses on this genre that is, in many ways, antithetical to the spirit of Hollywood and, in the long run, signaled its demise. Hollywood's prewar package of charm and innocence is far less in vogue and the subject of far fewer homages.

Hollywood felt the impact of the foreign films that had appeared in the wake of the war. The neorealist aesthetic of Rossellini and DeSica, which had grown organically out of the rubble of postwar Italy, put Hollywood's glossy charm in a bad light. In the early days of the Hollywood studios, Hollywood had proved its strength by absorbing European art technique. Montage became a preferred way of showing the passage of time in compressed form. Expressionism's oblique angles became a means of communicating psychological confusion. The classical aesthetic of Hollywood was a hardy creature, able to conquer more expressive, less classical styles by absorbing them, using them in a measured way, making them subordinate to its larger, more conservative system. But Hollywood did not seem to have that same resilience when it came to the new realism issuing out of postwar Europe. This aesthetic rode the reality of America's experience in World War II and seemed to spell the end of Hollywood insistence on a charming and stylized idealism.

Italian neo-realism found its parallel, in America, in the urban aesthetic of film noir and "New York" filmmaking, both of which thrived on gritty photography of actual urban locales. And the new emphasis on realism found expression in the 1950s in a new emphasis on realistic content in films as well as realistic photography. There was an appetite after the war for serious social drama, quite antithetical to Hollywood's prewar determination to avoid, at all costs, a cinema of messages. There was a vogue for the adult, realistic drama of the New York theater and social dramas by authors like Clifford Odets and Tennessee Williams. Films like those of Stanley Kramer and Elia Kazan abounded, films that were more topical and justified themselves, not by the old Hollywood criteria of charm and formal balance, but by their social heft. These "serious" works precipitated a war on the production code, which took place in a series of court battles from 1953 to 1968, when the code was replaced by a less oppressive rating system. And so the films became more explicit in their sexuality and violence as they became more ponderous in their themes. Even the Western grew up, bearing a new social weight that would have astounded the genre's forefathers. Westerns now might be political or social parables (*High Noon*, *Bad Day at Hanging Rock*), studies of darker cowboy heroes (Anthony Mann's Westerns), or exercises in baroque style and offbeat sexuality (Nicolas Ray's *Johnny Guitar*, Fritz Lang's *Rancho Notorious*), but they were no longer allowed to be simple oaters.

This more serious drama brought with it a more serious approach to acting. Films based on wrenching dramas encouraged the wrenching approach of method actors, extremely frustrating to many of the old Hollywood directors, like Hitchcock, Cukor, and Hawks, for whom acting was still an art that Gary Cooper epitomized, not a fierce expression but a calm letting go of technique, an easy presentation of one's self from film to film.

Put it all together, and you have much in the years just after the war that was contrary to the nature of Hollywood before the war: morbidity and pessimism instead of Hollywood's relentless buoyancy; gritty realism instead of Hollywood's carefully rendered ideal world; high seriousness instead of Hollywood's charming insouciance; messages, whereas Hollywood had prized above all showing rather than saying; mannered acting, where Hollywood had once favored the simple unforced presentation of the self; increasing "stylism," where Hollywood had favored invisible technique; an explicitness in depiction of sex and violence, where once filmmakers had sought, in the tradition of silent film, to express themselves suggestively or elliptically.

THE BREAKUP OF THE STUDIO; FREEDOM RUN AMOK

The causes most often cited for Hollywood's decline are the advent of television, which offered an alternative to Hollywood entertainment and precipitously drained Hollywood of much of its talent and clientele (particularly from the low-budget end of the Hollywood studios), and the suits, lodged by those in Hollywood who longed for more independent means of production and which brought about Hollywood's divestiture of its theater holdings, robbing the studios of a guaranteed venue for their releases.

The group of independent producers, directors, and actors who forced the studios to rid themselves of their theaters had as their goal a more independent cinema, not burdened by the capitalist machinery of the studio system. As Charlie Chaplin, one of these independents, famously said, "masterpieces cannot be mass-produced in the cinema like tractors in a factory."

Ironically, the move to a more independent cinema that was an immediate consequence of the breakup of the studios led, in many ways, to an exacerbation of rather than an escape from the squeeze of capitalism on film. When the studio controlled its theaters and could block book (sell packages of films that included not only A films but also B films, shorts, cartoons, and the like) they had the freedom to take a loss on a film here or there. After divestiture and the dismantling of the Hollywood studio, Hollywood had to make fewer films. Frank Capra decried the loss of the smaller film when Hollywood broke up its studio system. Eighty percent of MGM's product, Capra noted, was lower grade fare—medium-budget pictures with a single star or low-budget B pictures: "Into those very low-budget films they would put the beginners—the young starlets, writers, directors, producers—and turn them loose. Here was the trial, and it would be practically unsupervised. You could really experiment. They never threw a picture away." As Capra notes, this energy and experimentation were fostered by the very monster independent artists who were trying to do away with block booking: "They never could lose money, because no matter how bad a picture they made, MGM could always put it in as a second feature to one of their big pictures, because they owned the theaters."[3] Veteran B film director Budd Boetticher made the same point: "Directing is like any art form or any athletic form: the more you're allowed to do, the better you get. The studio let us make $100,000 pictures and make terrible mistakes because they knew these pictures would be the second feature on a double bill. So we had an opportunity that young film directors don't have today."[4] Without block booking and without B films the studios lost their source of energy and experimentation, the spirit of innovation and sense of fun that goes a long way toward explaining the allure of classic Hollywood. Most of the B film personnel were the first to flock to television. Many a second-tier director's filmography shifts dramatically to television in the 1950s.

As the studios dismantled, many directors and cinematographers came to the slow realization that life in the studios had been better than they realized at the time. Director George Sydney, speaking of MGM, said, "[T]here was great backing by the studio, more than we realized," adding, "[T]hey were putting all the ammunition in our hands."[5] Cinematographer George Folsey longed for the MGM photographic laboratory and cinematographer James Wong Howe for the rich variety of experience at MGM and Warner Bros.: "If I wasn't shooting a film, I had to go shoot second unit. I had to shoot inserts. But that was all wonderful because I learned a lot. I could afford to make mistakes on those inserts because it didn't cost much to make them over. I feel sorry for a lot of photographers today."[6] Howard Hawks felt that his 1965 film *Red Line 7000* had been a failure because he "didn't have the right technical equipment" to do the driving stunts: "It's difficult to make a picture like that today because you're not getting the same help you used to get from studio departments. They're all afraid that maybe they're spending too much money and the organization's gone."[7] George Cukor still found himself asking, "Oh God where is the stage department," when he'd begin a film in the 1970s. The studios, he emphasized, were far from the "big, horrible factories" they were reputed to be: "You got the best stories, the best scripts, the best actors, the best cameramen. They had all that, and I only realized it after it was gone."[8]

Over and over, veteran Hollywood directors paint the same portrait of studio bigwigs: they were certainly not intellectuals, but they had a nose for talent. Sam Goldwyn was "a great man, if only for the simple reason he always hired the best people he could possibly get," said Henry Koster. MGM musical producer Arthur Freed's "greatest talent," according to Charles Walters, "was to surround himself with talent." Darryl Zanuck at Twentieth Century-Fox "never hired bums," said Henry Hathaway. "He had great respect for talent and he always got top people." Harry Cohn at Columbia, according to George Sydney, "was really out for quality."[9] The old Hollywood moguls may have been "brutal and ignorant," writes Ethan Mordden, "but they did establish mediums of creativity and keep them operating. What more could you ask of a Capitalist?"[10]

After studio divestiture and the demise of block booking studios, Hollywood lost its safety net and became much warier of experimentation and the prospect of an unsuccessful film. Producers were more frightened about profit. Directors lost the feeling that producers were behind them providing them with ammunition. As one study on the subject put it, "without block booking the modern Hollywood distributors have had to count on each film carrying its own box office weight. Figuratively speaking, the new studios tried to score more home runs than ever before, even though they were at bat fewer times."[11] Looking for a home run every time they stepped up to the plate meant that Hollywood producers lost their interest in the small gem, the art project that leant their company a certain dignity. "What I used to do was try and make a big picture, a smash," John Ford told Peter Bogdanovich in the early 1960s, "and then I could palm off a little one on them. You can't do that anymore."[12] This new fear about profitability poisoned filmmaking for Billy Wilder. "Now," Wilder said in an interview in 1978, "they make you feel its life or death for a studio. 'If you don't hit with this picture we have to dismiss all the secretaries, all the policemen. Everything is going.'"[13] This kind of fearful atmosphere fosters homogenization, not variety or eccentricity.

Hollywood had long ago started screening its films before trial audiences, a practice that drove independent filmmakers like Chaplin and Orson Welles nuts, but now the desire to understand what an audience wanted, to consult the marketplace before making a film intensified even further. "When the studios broke up," said Vidor, "and the conglomerates took over there was nobody you could go to and say, 'This is an idea I have to make into a film.' They'll say, 'What stars have you got?' Immediately they start to think about bankability and financial insurance, and you'll have to say, 'This is a best-seller,' or 'Two stars have seen it and they're going to go for it.'"[14] The process was set in motion that would lead, first, to the cult of the hugely profitable blockbuster film and, then finally, to the phenomenon of green-lighting films for their "franchise" value alone, the absurdo ad reductum being a film, the idea of which generates, not with an artist, not even with a producer, but with a marketing department and a plan to sell subsidiary products through the film.

The independent filmmakers who forced divestiture aimed not only for a less commercial cinema in Hollywood but also for one of greater quality. Whether they got this is still a question. With the studios dissolved, independent producers found that they had to create the studio anew with each film. Independents had longed to escape the dictatorial head of the studio, but it was not long before they came to pine for that dictator, who, in hindsight, they realized had been fairly benevolent. It was not unusual to hear even the most rebellious directors longing, in the poststudio era, for the world where they simply went to one person to green-light a film. "In that period they didn't interfere," King Vidor said of the producers. "They were making too many pictures to interfere . . . I could tell the head guy an idea and he could say, 'Yes, go ahead,' that doesn't happen today."[15] Here again, Hollywood directors tend to be uniform in their admiration for the ability of Hollywood producers to make snap decisions and green-light a project just like that. Fritz Lang praised Richard Zanuck for the "free hand" he gave Lang.[16] Capra noted, "I would never have reached where I got to if I didn't have the liberty I had at Columbia to make the films I wanted to make."[17] Hawks praised "people like Jack Warner and Harry Cohn and Irving Thalberg and Zanuck" because they "started you out and let you go."[18] Journeyman director Michael Gordon said that "in Old Hollywood if somebody said, 'that's a deal', it was a deal. You didn't have to have the agreement on paper, you didn't have to have payment in advance."[19] All of these directors praising all of these producers exhale the same word nostalgically: freedom. "Joe Mankiewicz had a completely free hand, I had a free hand, Henry King had a free hand. Zanuck never bothered people he had faith in," said Henry Hathaway.[20] Howard Hawks concurs, "Back then, we had more freedom and I think the pictures showed it."[21]

Now, directors launching a film had to cobble the finances together for themselves.

The concern with finding money at the outset of production, coupled with the heightened worries about profit, meant independent directors spent a great deal more time thinking about money than in the past. Whereas earlier they spoke to one person about the financing of the film and then got to work, now, they complained, they were lining up dozens of financiers and spending much more time getting a project off the ground rather than actually working on the project. "You've got to go through a series of commands now," complained John Ford, "and you never know who the Hell reads the scripts any more. You can't get an O.K. here in Hollywood for a script—it's got to go back to New York, and through a president and a board of directors and bankers and everyone else."[22] Up till now Hollywood directors had always been notable for their humility when talking about film as art. They resisted the intellectualization of film by the new aficionados of the 1960s, and they were always more comfortable talking about film as craft than art. But they were not such anti-intellectuals that they were ready for their new roles as businessmen. "I stopped making pictures long before I wanted to," says Vidor. "The number one reason was that I didn't feel like being a promoter, a businessman."[23]

Moreover, as Gerald Mast has pointed out, as the studios declined "the large pool of expert studio craftsmen and technicians began to dry up—with fewer films to make and fewer challenges to their artisanry."[24] The voracious beast that was the Hollywood studio had the beneficent result of honing filmmakers' skills, and a great many film scholars have detected a decline in the fundamentals of the classical filmmaking style that Hollywood created since the end of the studio era.

In the later Hollywood films, then, the art of financing films was reaching new heights at the same time that the art of making films was dwindling.

One of the most obvious manifestations of this drying up of talent was the approach to scripts in Hollywood's films after studio divestiture. Both because they no longer had the immense stable of writers that they had in the heyday of Hollywood and because they no longer had the safety net of their own theaters in which to release their product, Hollywood studios increasingly turned to preexistent plays and novels for their films. It was easier for a producer to raise money for a film that had already been a literary or dramatic success. Gerald Mast described the period preceding World War II in Hollywood as "the age of the Original Scenario" and the years after the war "the age of the Adaptation."[25]

Of course Hollywood had always adapted preexistent literary works but never to this degree. And this was not a good thing for Hollywood because adaptations of literature, particularly serious literature, had never been Hollywood's forte. Hollywood had, and still has, a tendency to embarrass itself in proportion to how seriously it takes itself and shows itself particularly superficial when it tries to squeeze beloved novels into the 2 hours of sound and image that comprise a film or when it tries to translate the gravity of serious theater into the light rhythms of the classic Hollywood style. In these instances Hollywood has tended to create works that are antithetical to what it does well, films that are talky rather than visual, ham-handed in imparting their messages rather than suggestive or light in touch, films that are characterized by high seriousness rather than Hollywood's great ability to be wise and lighthearted at the same time.

This propensity for literary adaptation only deepened the propensity for more "serious" films in the era after the war. What had lessened was our opportunity to enjoy the kind of crackling dialogue that had evolved in Hollywood before the war, dialogue developed by the in-house scenarists. These scenarists were trained in a kind of language that had evolved with, and built itself around, film, a language that ceded ground to visual communication, that was spare and elusive rather than preachy, slangy and democratic rather than pronounced from a height.

The era that marks Hollywood's decline, from the late 1940s through the 1950s and into the early 1960s, then, was marked by a film system that produced fewer films. And those films were increasingly market-driven, which accounts for what Ethan Mordenn describes as "the bizarrely unambitious character of Hollywood in the 1950s." Boom times, Mordenn writes, "tolerate experimentation. The 1950s was a time of bust."[26] Those films that strived to be serious were often characterized by virtues that were antithetical to those Hollywood trumpeted before the war. They were sophomoric reflections of the European art cinema—lumbering, didactic self-serious works, as leaden in content as they were short in craft, misshapen offspring of the literary world, tailor-made to embarrass Hollywood and offering excellent fodder for anyone who wanted to argue that Hollywood and serious art should never be mentioned in the same breath.

The irony is that the independent artists who forced the dismantling of the studio system did so in the name of a cinema that would be less market-driven and of higher quality but might have created a cinema that was the opposite. The Hollywood studio, with its factory process and division of labor, had seemed like the essence of capitalistic repression of art. But it paled in comparison to the market-driven frenzy that succeeded it. It turns out that freedom is a tricky thing to define. The irony of Chaplin's assertion that "masterpieces cannot be mass-produced in a factory" is that his greatest films came from his, and Hollywood's, era of greatest mass production. Director Joseph Newman even used Chaplin's factory metaphor to describe the environment in Hollywood after the demise of block booking. Newman found that "picturemaking" had "become more of an assembly line operation instead of the individual effort that had gone into pictures by men such as Irving Thalberg, David Selznick and Hunt Stromberg. Picturemaking had developed into a committee process."[27] Newman turns Chaplin's logic on its head. It was filmmaking accomplished under the old studio system that had really been characterized by freedom and independence. Once Hollywood artists escaped from the repression of the studio into the freedom of the marketplace they found they were more constrained than ever. As Hawks said, referring to the actors who were behind the drive for greater independence from the studios, "Then came the day when the stars decided what they were going to do and, holy smoke, what a mess they made."[28] French critic and director Francois Truffaut came to the same realization after he and his fellow French intellectuals had tried to foster an environment in which their favorite American "auteur" heroes could film with greater freedom: "We said that the American cinema pleases us, and its filmmakers are slaves; what if they were freed? And from the moment they were freed, they made shitty films."[29]

LATE SUCCESSES

This is not to say that all of Hollywood suffered a decline in the years succeeding the war. Needless to say, Hollywood directors had struggled under a code that often made nonsensical demands upon them, and their work was invigorated, to a certain degree, by the new climate in Hollywood that ceded a little more territory to realism and pessimism and allowed a little more frankness in the discussion of sex. Ford, Hitchcock, and Wilder are all directors who saved much of their most memorable work for this period. Wilder in particular seems to have had the right personality for the era. He was a Hollywood pro who built a religion around story construction and cultivated a Lubitsch-like habit of expressing his ideas through physical business. He was too much of a Hollywood filmmaker to cave into morbid or self-serious realism. But he was also a cynic who seemed to welcome the opportunity to lace his films with a little more venom than he might have before the war. *The Apartment* is an example of a film that is classic Hollywood in its clever but conservative story construction, its charming detail, and its triumphant romance. At the same time it is very accessible to a modern audience because it is so adult in its tone and so frank in its depiction of a corrupt world.

Certain genres seemed to wake up a little in 1950s. The Western had enough moral rectitude in its nature to absorb a little realism and moral ambiguity nicely. Andrew Sarris has written that were he to have to choose between preserving every Western after *Duel in the Sun* (1946) or every Western before, he would reluctantly choose the latter. "The Western," Sarris writes, "is the one genre that has become richer in feeling and more profound in form as it rode ever closer to utter extinction."[30]

Similarly, film noir brought a stylistic quality to the gangster and police dramas that they did not have before the war. Film noir is a kind of mixed beast in Hollywood. On the one hand, in its deep pessimism and excesses in style, it seems antithetical to Hollywood and signals the end of an era; on the other hand, its elegant style seems to build on the rich atmospherics of Hollywood before the war. On the one hand, it brings in a vicious and gritty realism that seems to mark the end of Hollywood's idealized atmosphere; on the other hand, it is so elegantly stylish, both in its highly artificial script and its stylized images, that it seems to mark the greatest expression of Hollywood's dedication to style and atmosphere, to intensely realized artificial paradises.

Even certain actors seemed to find greater depth after the war. Critics have often commented on the changes in Jimmy Stewart's persona after the war. Stewart came back a decorated veteran, and both Alfred Hitchcock, in his suspense films starring Stewart, and Anthony Mann, in his Westerns with Stewart, seem to have spotted the difference. No longer a simple icon of American likeability, Stewart's persona in these films flirts more with emotional imbalance and moral ambiguity.

Some of the shadows that crossed Hollywood's vista after the war, then, gave it more depth and resonance. The fact that so many of Hollywood's greatest works came at this time, its period of decline, cautions us against thinking of Hollywood too much as a glorious linear arc, beginning in the silent era, cresting in the 1930s, and declining after the war. The greatest Hollywood films appear a little more arbitrarily along the line of Hollywood's history than we often acknowledge, because it is so tempting to contain Hollywood's history under the notion of a rise and fall. There are a good number of Hollywood classics that exist in its period of decline, many of them definitive statements on the Hollywood technique, summings-up that could hardly have existed but at the end of the long evolution of Hollywood. And there are scores of mediocre films resting cozily in the middle of its heyday. The fact that the Andy Hardy pictures exist in the "golden age" of Hollywood certainly does not make them better than Wilder's or Hitchcock's work in the 1950s. They have a certain studio burnish that makes them a part and parcel of the age, but that's about it. Great Hollywood films exist where talent found the right circumstances in which to assert itself.

Even these late masters, though, who seemed to thrive in the late era of Hollywood, found their creativity drying up by the early 1960s. There was a great flurry of accomplishment in the late 1950s and very early 1960s. Hitchcock made *Vertigo* (1958), *North by Northwest* (1959), and *Psycho* (1960). Ford made *The Searchers* (1956) and *The Man Who Shot Liberty Valance* (1962). Wilder made *Love in the Afternoon* in 1957 and *The Apartment* in 1960. Hawks made *Rio Bravo* in 1956. After this, despite the masters' touch in a few efforts (like Ford's *Cheyenne Autumn* and Hitchcock's *Frenzy*), there was a precipitous drop in quality, sometimes dramatic, as in Billy Wilder's descent from definitive Hollywood elegance (*The Apartment*) to bland television sitcom (*Irma la Douce*, 1963) in only 3 years and in the step-by-step descent of Hawks from *Rio Bravo* (for many, the culmination of the Western) to subsequent remakes of *Rio Bravo*: *El Dorado* (1966) and *Rio Lobo* (1970), each film a shell of the one that precedes it.

Thomas Schatz notes that Hitchcock, by the early 1960s, was no longer able to gather the production unit that had been so key to his success. Each Hitchcock film was from this point on "an utterly independent venture," and though Hitchcock had achieved a spot within the studio system as one of its most independent directors, this new kind of independence served him very poorly. Schatz notes the irony that just at the moment when Hitchcock was being feted as Hollywood's greatest auteur, his films were suffering the most from the loss of collaborative support: "Even a distinctive stylist and inveterate independent like Hitchcock required a base of filmmaking operations, a pool of resources and personnel, a consistent production unit, and a stable management setup. As Hitchcock and others were learning, creative freedom and control were of little value without the resources and the constraints that had been basic to the old system but were sorely lacking in the New Hollywood."[31]

The significant American films of the 1960s and 1970s are pretty much antithetical to the Hollywood tradition that preceded them. Their naturalistic settings, their wandering paces, their European art house camera work, their morbidity and explicitness of sex and violence seem antithetical to the classical Hollywood style. David Bordwell and Janet Staiger do a good job, in *The Classical Hollywood Cinema*, of showing that even these films avail themselves greatly of a certain Hollywood style of setting up and weaving together shots.[32] It is striking, some 30 years later, how certain films, like Roman Polanski's *Chinatown*, seem more a part of the classical Hollywood tradition than when they first were shown. Still, if some of the craft of these films represents a holdover, the spirit and purpose of these films nevertheless is very alien to old Hollywood.

Another way to chart the end of Hollywood is to look at when it begins to be celebrated. Once Hollywood had reached the point where it could be idealized, there was a pretty good possibility that its greatest power had been spent. By the time the French intellectuals were finished analyzing Hollywood, it was hard to do Hollywood with a straight face any longer. With celebration comes self-consciousness, and from the early 1960s on anyone doing a "Hollywood film" was, in many ways, participating in an intellectual exercise, doing it with a kind of irony that separated it from the genuine article, the hallmark of which was its utter sincerity.

From the 1960s to the present day there have been a great many films that imitate or pay homage to the classical Hollywood studio style. Certainly, the vogue of Hitchcockian suspense and film noir styling shows no signs of abating. The directors who are the more devout students of Hollywood, like the Coen brothers, Peter Bogdanovich, and Martin Scorsese, have at times taken on those genres in the Hollywood tradition, such as the musical, the melodrama, and the screwball comedy, that are more difficult to translate into modern sensibilities. The history of all of these homages to Hollywood is checkered, as they are often crippled by self-consciousness and characterized by a certain cutesy condescension toward, and nostalgia for, their genre. The celebration of Hollywood's craft was coincident with the diminution of that craft, certainly not the first time in the history of art that the consciousness of greatness came with the loss of greatness.

SHORT ANSWER

The short answer to the question "When was Hollywood?" is from the late teens, when the essentials of the Hollywood narrative tradition had been set in place, to the early or mid-1960s, when we see the last vestiges of the Hollywood studio tradition dying out and even Hollywood's greatest masters floundering.

Still, if we define Hollywood as being from the late teens to the early 1960s, we must be on guard against the tendency to see a logical or continuous arc of development within that span. Hollywood suffers ups and downs within its lifetimes. Certain eras are mixed bags. Many, for example, define the silent era as the purest tradition in American filmmaking, a time where filmmakers were forced to show rather than tell, where visual art and suggestiveness reigned supreme. On the other hand, that era is steeped in a good deal of melodramatic tripe as well. Others find Hollywood's high point in the precode films of the early 1930s. If these films were often stagy and static due to cumbersome sound equipment, they had a spiritual élan and freedom that was lost with the installation of the code. The films of the late 1930s have the greatest polish. To many, these seem like the definitive years. But these films can also seem stiff and propagandistic next to precode fare, most vulnerable to the criticism that Hollywood forced middle-American middle-class attitudes down the throat of its audience. The first half of the 1940s was boom time in Hollywood, a time of rich variety and a time when many of Hollywood's auteurs' talents were starting to ripen, but because it was boom time it was also a period where Hollywood produced its greatest amount of inferior work, as any consistent viewing of the television stations that feature old Hollywood will tell you. "No matter what crap is playing, all you have to do is open the doors and duck," Capra recalled one theater manager saying about the crowds that rushed to the theaters during the wars.[33] The 1950s and 1960s, as we have seen, represent Hollywood's decline into fewer, safer products but at the same time a moment of great efflorescence for many of its greatest filmmakers. Hollywood goes down then, but it does so, in the films of Ford, Hitchcock, and Douglas Sirk, in a blaze of technicolor glory. What decade represents Hollywood's greatest is a subject of infinite debate. About the best we can say is that this era, from the late teens to the early 1960s, represents the era of the classical Hollywood film.

2

Who Is the Artist?

One of the reasons Hollywood films are difficult to classify is that they do not conform as easily as other art forms, or even other epochs in film history, to that mode of classification that labels the work of art the product of a single guiding artistic progenitor. Hollywood's goal, since its birth, had been to carefully and painstakingly evolve a neutral narrative style that did not call attention itself and that allowed the viewer to enter the fictional world of its films with as little consciousness as possible of being in a made-up world. It was the goal of Hollywood to make its viewers so comfortable in their point of view and the way they were guided through the space of the film's world that they would forget they were watching a film altogether.

That they were successful in this aesthetic is evident in the confession of film scholar and philosopher Stanley Cavell, who, after his first reading of French film criticism in the 1950s, which singled out the director as a film's "auteur," felt "a clarifying shock to realize that films were directed, that some human being had undertaken to mean, or at any rate was responsible for all the angles of the film." Cavell further wrote, "[I felt] rebuked for my backwardness in having grown to fatherhood without really knowing where movies came from, ready to admit that I must have had an idea that they sprang full grown from iron-gated sun-glassed heads of studios."[1]

Cavell, of course, was not alone. "I used to think the actors made up their own lines," says Mildred Atkinson, the empty-headed hatcheck girl in Nicholas Ray's *In a Lonely Place*. "Audiences don't know somebody sits down and writes a picture," concurs writer Joe Gillis in Billy Wilder's *Sunset Boulevard*, "they think the actors make it up as they go along."

Both of these lines are from cynical films about spent, angry writers. Interestingly both of these films were made in the early fifties, at the time of the studios' decline and just before an era that would take a more academic look at Hollywood.

The films reflect a certain loss of innocence in Hollywood and acknowledge a time when we were just waking up from the dream of the Hollywood film. They seem to anticipate or express the need that is just starting to express itself more strongly in film studies, to take a good look at this thing called the Hollywood film and identify who creates it.

Ironically, both of these lines seek to wake the audience up to the underrated presence of the film writer. When the French critics of the fifties came along and awarded the title of "auteur," however, they gave it not to the writer—who they felt was an infiltrator from an alien art form and one responsible for much of the literary artificiality of films—but to the film director. In doing so they set off a reaction of outrage that has lasted for 50 years.

Defenders of writers have been particularly virulent in their attack on oversimplifications inherent in auteurism. Their rancor has, at times, been so intense as to render them vulnerable to their own oversimplifications and extreme opinions. Pauline Kael, in her famous essay "Circles and Squares," sought to wrest away the triumph of *Citizen Kane* from Orson Welles and give it to the film's screenwriter, Herman Mankiewicz. Richard Corliss, in his noted essay "The Hollywood Screenwriter," tried to establish a hierarchy of writers parallel to the elaborate hierarchy of directors that Andrew Sarris, translator and apologist for the French critics, had established in *The American Cinema*, assigning writers like Jules Furthman and Norma Krasna the status of "auteur." Capra biographer Joseph McBride suggested that it was Robert Riskin who was the real genius behind Frank Capra's works. He even managed to give the lion's share of credit to Riskin for those successful Capra films—*Mr. Smith Goes to Washington* and *It's a Wonderful Life*, for example—that Riskin *didn't* work on. Such is the ingenuity that critics have been moved to by their outrage over auteurism.[2]

Similar defenders have stepped forward to argue the crucial significance of almost every aspect of the filmmaking process, the point that links them all being, of course, that the film is too collaborative a process to be artistically "owned" by a single person. Thomas Schatz, for example, in *The Genius of the System*, wants us to consider how underrated the contributions of certain hands-on producers, like Irving Thalberg, David O. Selznick, and Darryl Zanuck, were.[3] Many critics have noted that Greg Toland's cinematography is so overpowering that it represents a kind of coauthorship in some of the films he made with directors Orson Welles, John Ford, and William Wyler—something Welles himself seemed to acknowledge when he gave Toland equal billing in the credits of *Citizen Kane*. MGM is famous for turning out many an enduring film while enforcing a system that did not give undue emphasis to the contributions of the director. "The auteur of some of Joan Crawford's early MGM talkies," Ethan Mordden points out, " may be Adrian, her costume designer; and the auteur of *Grand Hotel* is MGM's star system."[4] In the 50 years or so since the French made their pronouncements, it has been de rigueur in film criticism to always remind the reader that film is a collaborative process. To say otherwise amounts to a kind of political incorrectness, an insensitivity to the great pluralism of the film process. Auteurism, contemporary critics suggest, imports theories of authorship to film that don't apply and that don't do justice to the vitality of Hollywood's collaborative system.

Mordden identifies what has actually always been the biggest challenge to the auteur theory: the star system. Academics can babble till the cows come home on different theories of authorship, but for the majority of filmgoers today, just as for earlier generations of filmgoers, a Hollywood studio is defined by its star. It took me awhile to find recent DVD releases of Joseph von Sternberg's films because they are packaged within a product titled *Marlene Dietrich: The Glamour Collection*. If one wants to find the most recent releases of Hawks's *Ball of Fire* or King Vidor's *The Wedding Night*, one would have to first look for "Gary Cooper: MGM Movie Legends Collection" (a collection of independent and Sam Goldwyn productions whose rights have fallen to MGM), where the two films are jammed together with less stalwart entries in the Cooper cannon, like *The Cowboy and the Lady* and *The Adventures of Marco Polo*. Stars sell now, as they did when these films came out, and apparently DVD marketers have decided that a substantial segment of their market does not care who the director, cinematographer, or producers of the film were. When I search for a film in my local library network I have success finding the film more often when I punch in the name of the star than I do when I use the director's name. And, in fact, when one picks up the film from the library, one finds that the library, using antiquated filing stickers, has listed the film's star under the category of "author." There is something humorous about the spectacle of academics and film critics furiously debating the nature of film authorship while the world of general film consumption goes pottering along blithely, assured in its assumption that a film's real auteur is its star.

ORGANIZING BY DIRECTORS ANYWAY

In short, there is much in the way Hollywood films were manufactured and in the way they have been studied that resists the categorizations inherent in auteurism. Even Hollywood directors felt, at times, that they got too much credit. Wilder felt that writers were "vastly underrated and underpaid. It's totally impossible to make a great picture out of a lousy script. It's impossible, though, for a mediocre director to completely screw up a great script."[5] Welles said that he didn't "understand what a picture is if there is bad acting," adding, "I don't understand how movies exist independently of the actor. . . . As I've said, the director is the most overrated job in the world."[6]

And yet the briefest sweep through film criticism in the last 50 years tells us that there *is* a core canon to Hollywood, though one hotly contested as all canons are. And that core collection of great films, despite the collaborative nature of the art, despite 50 years of protest to auteurism, and despite Wilder's and Welles's becoming modesty, is inextricably linked to the great directors of Hollywood. Despite the half-century of critical outrage aimed at them, the auteurists gained ground they never lost. We still tend to find it easiest, despite the most creative efforts of auteurism's detractors, to categorize Hollywood films by directors. Corliss was not able to establish an oeuvre for writers as stable as that of directors. And no other member of the collaborative process has stepped forward to rival the director's claim to authorship. Producers are even less likely nominees than writers. Almost everyone who participated in the making of films in Hollywood felt that the greatest quality in a Hollywood producer was his or her willingness to green-light risky productions, provide excellent resources, and then get the hell out of the way. MGM's decision to package Gary Cooper's films according to his star voltage alone only reinforces the argument of auteurists. The best films in the collection (*Wedding Night, Ball of Fire*) are by great directors, the worst (*Cowboy and the Lady*, for example) are not.

Jimmy Cagney is such a powerful presence on film that we are likely to give him precedence in referring to any film he is in. We call it a Jimmy Cagney film. In fact the principal collaborators in a Cagney film would seem to be the actor, Cagney, and the studio, Warner Brothers. Warner Brothers' gritty textures were a perfect match for Cagney's streetwise, tough personality. And yet the four gangster films that represent Cagney at his best and which are probably most responsible for his cult (*Public Enemy, Angels with Dirty Faces, Roaring Twenties*, and *White Heat*) were all helmed by Warner Brothers' best directors, William Wellman, Michael Curtiz, and Raoul Walsh—all esteemed auteurs. Cagney was always great, but his greatest films were with good directors. The Cagney gangster film represents a fortuitous conjunction of director, star, and studio.

Organizing Hollywood by directors seems the best, if not the perfect, way, to get a handle on which films were the cream of the crop. And, of course, the preeminence of the director in Hollywood predates French theories of auteurism. That Paramount is responsible for so many of Hollywood's greatest works is due to the deference it paid, and freedom it accorded, its large stable of first-rate directors: Lubitsch, Mamoulian, von Sternberg, Sturges, and Billy Wilder, just to name a few. Harry Cohn built Columbia studios by respecting Capra's talent and need for independence.

In fact, the coincidence of good filmmaking and directorial freedom in Hollywood calls into question the notion that Hollywood magically created its great films through the team effort of the studio system. A good number, if not the majority, of Hollywood's greatest films came from directors who prized their independence and fiercely defended it: the Paramount directors; rovers from studio to studio, like Hitchcock and Hawks; the directors Fred Zinneman described as "the handful of nonconformists, Ford, Stevens, Wyler, Capra," who "found it possible to defend their own ideas and beat the factory approach."[7] Far fewer are the directors, like George Cukor and Michael Curtiz, who managed to work up a sizeable oeuvre as career, in-house directors, working for lengthy periods in studios like MGM and Warner Brothers, where the role of the director was sublimated to a much greater extent into the factory process of creating a film. The rate of success due to directors who prized their independence represents one of the greatest challenges to the notion that Hollywood's greatest films were the results of the "genius of the system." Even in the heyday of Hollywood, directors operating in conditions that were as close to independence as the studio allowed were the surest bet to create films of lasting quality. As Frank Capra said, "When we had more control over our pictures, even though we were still working in studios, our films got better."[8]

Henry Koster showed signs of being, potentially, a top-notch director in such movies as *The Bishop's Wife*. But his explanation for why his career didn't amount to more, in the end, is very telling. It wasn't because he didn't work well with the system. It was, he felt, because he didn't fight it enough: "I do not blame anybody but my own personality, of not being able to be really tough. The truly great directors are very strong in mind and fist. . . . I believed in security of production and security of my job. I was under contract to studios. It would have been better if I had been independent and just done the pictures I wanted to."[9] Koster's assessment of how to be a great director is born out by the career of Hollywood's most successful filmmakers. The genius, here, is not "of the system" but in stubbornly bucking the system.

Hollywood directors exhibited an admirable modesty for the most part and were uncomfortable considering their films as art or themselves as artists. When Peter Bogdanovich asked Allan Dwan if he thought the director was the closest thing to a god on the set, Dwan said, "No, I'd go back further than that. I think the story is the number one thing."[10] But few directors, like Capra, King Vidor, and Rouben Mamoulian, always spoke straightforwardly about their belief in what Capra liked to call the "one man, one film" system. Vidor emphasized that the director being in control was as important to the crew as it was to the director: "The strength of filmmaking has got to be the viewpoint of one person. If the writer doesn't want to accept that his story is going to go through the hands of the director, then he should write a book. You simply have to take that stance, and I think when you do, everybody working on the film feels a hell of a lot better."[11]

Vidor's point of view is born out in the comments of the more analytical and successful technicians in Hollywood who repeatedly express respect for the leadership role of the director but at the same time emphasize that the good directors always sought their opinion. Cameraman George Folsey's comment is typical: "I would say that it's certainly the director's prerogative to decide, and if he says, 'I want the camera here,' you put it there, because it's his baby and not yours. I would say most directors are cooperative, and if you have a better idea, they'll listen to it and use it if they like it."[12] It is striking how important it was to the best directors to express a creed in which they consulted everybody on the set, right down to the lowliest technician. And it is equally striking how their devotion to that creed is supported by the technicians themselves, who, time and time again, report being consulted for their opinion. Being a successful director represented a balancing act in which one strove for as much independence as possible from the studio while, at the same time, taking advantage of the enormous resources the studio offered.

DIRECTOR PLUS COLLABORATION

Since part of a director's job, in Hollywood, was to create the atmosphere of a family on the set and to consult the expertise of the crew, it is difficult to say that the director was the sole progenitor of the film's art. Hence, the organization of Hollywood by directors is never secure, always vulnerable to attack. If it is true that we rarely find a truly great film without also finding a great director behind it, it is equally true that we rarely find a great film that is due solely to a director. There is always, *and this is an infallible rule*, some fortunate combination that explains why a film has lasting value—the way the director clicks with a certain writer or actor, for example, and the fortuitous circumstances provided by the studio at which a director works. The greater number of these combinations, the more pistons the work is firing on, the greater the work.

Stagecoach, for example, is a film firing on all of its pistons, blessed as it was by, not one, but two of Ford's most fruitful collaborations—his work with screenwriter Dudley Nichols and the beginning of his long shared opus with John Wayne. One might offer up as a third collaboration Ford's relationship with certain excellent character actors in *Stagecoach* (Andy Devine, Thomas Mitchell, John Qualen, Donald Meek), all of whom clicked so well with Ford that he used them over and over again in his films. There are a lot of spokes to the wheel, but they all find Ford at their hub.

Autuerism, the notion that the director is the most significant agent of creation in Hollywood, then seems to me as much of an unassailable truth today as it was 50 years ago. But the collaborative nature of film makes a simplistic application of the auteurist principle suspect. There is one way to group films that is better than by director, and that is to group them by director and his greatest collaborations. A director's total output can be a varied thing, particularly those directors who were unable to achieve as much independence as a Hawks or a Hitchcock and had to toil within the compromises of the studio system. Even Hawks's and Hitchcock's oeuvres are filled with compromised projects. Are we to take a film like Howard Hawks's *Redline 7000* as seriously as a great Hawks work like *Rio Bravo* just because his name is above both titles? That makes as much sense as saying *The Cowboy and the Lady* is as good as *Ball of Fire* just because Gary Cooper is in it. But if we look for those directors' films that are charged by their most fortuitous collaborations, then we arrive at a dense core of their best work and a core of Hollywood's best films in general.

There is probably a strong argument to be made that the most important collaboration in Hollywood is between director and screenwriter, if we are to judge by the enormity of great films that seem to be due to felicitous examples of this collaboration; the works of Ernst Lubitsch and Samson Raphaelson, von Sternberg and Jules Furthman, Frank Capra and Robert Riskin, Billy Wilder and Charles Brackett, John Ford and Dudley Nichols, Howard Hawks and Ben Hecht or Charles MacArthur are just a few examples that come to mind. We can't help but notice that Hitchcock struck upon a lighter, more humorous, and charming style when he enlisted the services of John Michael Hayes in the fifties. Take the works from these collaborations and you really have zeroed in on a core sampling of the very best of Hollywood. Certain writers like Furthman and Hecht pop up so often in the creation of Hollywood's best films that we understand Corliss's desire to award them with the mantle of auteur, were it not for the fact that even these great writers' best scripts end up bearing the unmistakable stamp of the director's personality in the end.

But an equally strong argument can be made for the most important collaboration being that between director and star. Certain actors (like Cary Grant, Jimmy Stewart, Gary Cooper, John Wayne, Barbara Stanwyck, Marlene Dietrich, and Jean Arthur) had such a great ability to find, or be found by, the great directors, that the assemblage of their films represents a core of Hollywood's greatest work, acting. What would Hitchcock's oeuvre be like if we removed the pictures involving Grant and Stewart or Frank Capra's if we removed the films with Stewart, Cooper, or Stanwyck? Both directors were adept at using the star system to full advantage, but both were also dependent on it for their greatest successes in Hollywood. More than once Hitchcock explained the failure of his films on poor casting. Hawks's creative juices seemed to really be stirred if Cary Grant or Walter Brennan were in the vicinity. Von Sternberg along with Marlene Dietrich and John Ford along with John Wayne are cocreators of a large body of work, the accomplishments of one not possible without the other.

Many of classic Hollywood's best films came about when the director found the right fit in a studio. Lubitsch's European charm found a home at the more sophisticated Paramount Studios, as did the subtle comedy of his heirs, Wilder and Sturges. Cukor's quiet style, theater experience, and feeling for women were the right fit at MGM with its great women stars, its stagy material, and its impatience with directorial excess. Cukor's humility in technique allowed him to take advantage of MGM's wealth, to steer it to his advantage. Sam Goldwyn created one of Hollywood's great triumvirates when he joined forces with director William Wyler and cinematographer Greg Toland to create the polished composition and in-depth style his studio is famous for. It's a style which, despite not appealing to the French auteurists, with their cult of energy and nonchalance, sometimes seems today to represent the acme of classic Hollywood technique, an example of the most substantial craftsmanship Hollywood has to offer. Capra seemed to have found the perfect studio for his talents when he wandered into the impoverished Columbia studio, where he developed a style of filmmaking characterized by crackling energy, with little interest in luxurious sets.

The collaboration between director and cinematographer has been potent as well. Much of Welles's and Wyler's essential style seems to issue from cinematographer Greg Toland's principles. Ford's *Long Voyage Home* is another film that fires on all its pistons. Here again are the collaborations with screenwriter Nichols, star John Wayne, and a host of favored character actors (including, again, Thomas Mitchell and John Qualen), and here too there is a collaboration between Ford and Toland, two of the great visual stylists of the studio era. How much of the berserk noir charm of *Night of the Hunter* is due to Charles Laughton, in his one-time effort as director, and how much due to veteran cinematographer Stanley Cortez? Gabriel Figueroa's photographic work on Ford's *The Fugitive* is so distinct that the film seems to stand apart from the rest of Ford's work, as close to Luis Bunuel's Mexican films as it is to Ford's Hollywood work.

Composer Bernard Herrman is another example of someone whose contributions to certain films are so strong that he threatens to rise to the level of cocreator. He certainly seemed to have felt that when he said, "Hitchcock only finishes a film sixty percent. I have to finish it for him."[13] And indeed our response to the films he worked on with Hitchcock and other directors are so keyed into his rapturous music, particularly in the case of *North by Northwest* and Mankiewicz's *The Ghost and Mrs. Muir*, that it is impossible to think of the essential quality of the film surviving the loss of the music, which strikes the keynote for the entire film and progressively, in its use, deepens the film's themes and ideas.

COLLABORATIONS THAT TRUMP THE DIRECTOR

The director, then, is pivotal in the creation of the Hollywood film, but so are the director's collaborations. And, it has to be admitted, there are certain films so rich in these collaborations that the significance of the director is dwarfed. There aren't as many of these films as the "genius of the system" advocates would like us to believe, and they tend to be found in the lower echelon of Hollywood's greatest films. (The directors' influence is more manifest as we climb higher in the hierarchy of Hollywood's great films.) But there are films that are limited by bland or inept direction and yet have too much going for them for us to write them off. In fact, we might even find, from time to time, that we are tempted to return to them more often than the well-directed films we know we should be watching.

Here we inevitably find ourselves turning to MGM, the studio that showed the least respect for the director and hardly encouraged the director in the development of his individual craft. MGM has, as time has passed, been duly reprimanded by the critics for its indifference to those filmmakers who might have been able to accord their films an artistic integrity. MGM has the worst batting average in terms of creating films that have earned lasting critical repute. "It was pure size and money," Capra said of MGM, "and whatever they made had that same look about it. Furniture with Grand Rapids polish was what it was to me. They didn't make many pictures that were of lasting importance because they were a mixture of minds."

But if MGM created the fewest "pictures of importance," it probably broke records in providing guilty pleasures. I bow to no one in my appreciation of Ford's *The Fugitive*, but I must confess that, late at night, reclining on the couch, given the choice between that film and some silky smooth precode Norma Shearer vehicle, I might very well choose the latter. MGM is the studio that, through pure elegance, charm, and star power, makes us not give a hoot about auteurism, at least for a while.

The MGM Garbo vehicle *Inspiration*, for example, should not be underestimated. The film does not bloat with sentiment as badly as other MGM melodramas, maybe because of the contributions of Gene Markey, a writer a shade more cosmopolitan than others at MGM. Few cases have been made for the film's director,

Clarence Brown, being an auteur, but the film has some memorable touches, for example, in the scene in which the camera tracks Lewis Stone as he descends a long, winding staircase after he has just broken off his relationship with a courtesan who lives on the third floor of the building. Stone does not seem particularly affected by the end of the relationship until, upon exiting the building, he comes across the woman's dead body on the pavement, where she threw herself from above.

But, it has to be admitted, this was a little staging conceit MGM pulled out several times, and in the end, the success of the film has little do with Brown, who had, for the most part, a leaden touch. How does one explain the susceptibility of even the most inveterate auteurist to the charms of this film, knowing, as they do, that the direction is not very acute? The explanation is, of course, Garbo, and Garbo coupled with the same triumvirate that is the glory of many of MGM's films: Cedric Gibbons (sets), Adrian (gowns), William Daniels (lighting). In other words, *Inspiration* is a fortuitous collection of actress, set design, costume design, and cinematography, with the director's greatest accomplishment being that of staying out of the way.

Inspiration, of course, represents high quality MGM stock. It had all of the studio's vast resources at its disposal. But we find surprisingly good work even at MGM's lower levels. A more minor work from MGM that might be described as anywhere from perfectly serviceable to quite charming is the Frank Morgan vehicle *Paradise for Three*. (And here I'm pulling a film from a hat; any number of small MGM films would fit this bill.) Certainly director George Buzzell's reputation would not lead us to this film, and, indeed, there is no particular stylish élan to make us take special note of him, though, as always in these cases, we have to acknowledge the art in turning out a competent film. There are even a few awful scenes, such as one with a dishwasher running out of control, the kind of broad comedy that anticipates television situation comedy.

But the film has several merits. First, it is filled with great character actors. Frank Morgan is at its helm, playing a wealthy industrialist masquerading as a poor man at an exclusive hotel. And he is surrounded by a coterie of Hollywood's best imports: Sig Ruman, Herman Bing, and Henry Hull, as well as the incomparable Dame Edna Mae Oliver, trotting out the more prudish side of her personae. (I like her better when she plays worldly, cynical old ladies, spurring young lovers on to commit indiscretions in the name of love.) Other actors play to form. Mary Astor does her gold digger; Robert Young and Florence Rice play the predictably bland MGM lovebirds, though they act with enough intelligence and have enough chemistry to manage a couple of effective love scenes together.

The film really rises above itself for two reasons: First (yet again), because of Gibbons's sets. This time he had fashioned a moonlit skating scene so striking that it could never be paralleled in real life. It is everything a winter skating scene should be, as though one had walked into a snow globe, and would serve very nicely as an emblematic example of MGM's ability to remove us to artificial paradises. And the set is used nicely as a framing device for the young lover's most essential romantic scene. Second, again, the script is a cut above, somehow surviving MGM's script by consensus of thousands, perhaps due to the uncredited work of Dalton Trumbo. The script rarely falls prey to the treacle that swarms up so many MGM vehicles and is particularly elegant and efficient in the heartfelt scenes between the two lovers and between Morgan and his daughter, so that if the Morgan persona has a great influence on you, as it does on me, the film becomes, at times, quite moving.

Hollywood abounds in small pleasures like this film, little films that come together fortuitously despite the absence of a strong directorial vision. And though you won't find many of them among the A listers (where directors really do dominate), you find a good many in the second tier of Hollywood. There the director loses some sway, and we discover the surprising effects of Hollywood's collaborative system. And there we are reminded that though the director is of immense importance in Hollywood, he doesn't deserve all the credit.

CONCLUSION

We must be careful not to spend so much time rooting the marginalia of Hollywood, fascinating as that is to the Hollywood aficionado, that we lose sight of who really made the greatest Hollywood films. That distinction belongs to the greatest Hollywood directors. There *is* authorship in Hollywood, and despite its vast, labyrinthine collaborative system, it can, to a great degree, be organized as the other arts are—by great artists and their works. It is even apparent that despite "the genius of the system"—Hollywood's ability to create works of art out of a collection of talents that, in many ways, dilute the idea of single authorship—a good many of Hollywood's greatest films were made by directors who prized their independence, who found ways to rise above the collaborative system and to create a set where they were able, to a great degree, to call their own shots. The greater works by Hollywood's more independent directors represents the lion's share of Hollywood's best films.

That said, the collaborative nature of film has to be given its due. When we look at the filmography of directors we see that their greatest films cluster around their greatest collaborations. In these films, writers, actors, cinematographers, producers, composers become coauthors to varying degrees, though the director most often is the pivot around which these talents circulate.

And even the most dyed in the wool auteurist has to concede the occasional film that has so many of these successful collaborations operating, that is firing on so many pistons, that its lack of significant direction seems less important—though it must be emphasized these films exist more in the lower echelon of Hollywood's successful product and not in the top where the directors hold sway.

That said, our final thought in watching one of these directorless wonders—say a lovely little MGM film with Cedric Gibbons's snow globe sets, Adrian's clinging silk gowns, William Daniel's milky light, maybe even some snazzy sophisticated dialogue by the likes of Dorothy Parker and Anita Loos—our final thought as the credits roll may still be "That film was not bad at all, too bad Cukor didn't direct it."

3

What Is a Great Hollywood Film? The Difficulty in Establishing a Hierarchy

INTERTEXUALITY

Hollywood presents singular challenges to critics who would like to cleanly separate its great work from its weakest efforts. First, the Hollywood film system operated at several levels. Generally we say Hollywood studios made B films as well as A films. But, as Ethan Mordden notes, Universal Studios alone "had so many gradations of expenditures that it could market Red Feathers, Bluebirds, Butterflies, Jewels, and—as Carl Laemmle worried and grouched—Super-Jewels."[1] This kind of variety in project and ambition makes it difficult to define success in Hollywood. Is Hollywood's success in the polish of the super jewel or in the ingenuity and efficiency of its lower-end product?

Another reason it is often difficult to separate the great films from the weak in Hollywood is that there is a kind of intertextuality in Hollywood, a rich and complex system of repeated motifs and cross-references between films that makes separating one film from another akin to separating plants that have grown close together in a garden.

For example, a director's weaker efforts are often made interesting by their close relationship to his greater ones. Once you get to know some of Hitchcock's tricks, it's hard not to enjoy even his lesser works. *Young and Innocent* lacks the star power to be one of his greatest works, but it's an efficient little film with hardly a frame that is not captivating in some way. And if it doesn't seem to have the resonance of *Notorious*, it does have a tracking shot (of the drummer's twitching face in the film's climax) that is just as impressive as Hitchcock's famous tracking shot of the key in Alyssa's hand during the party in *Notorious*.

Howard Hawks would often use very similar verbal motifs in his films, particularly in the scenes between his romantic protagonists, and it is interesting to see the various permutations of this dialogue from film to film, even in his weaker films.

The same pitter-patter that is electrifying when it comes out of Lauren Bacall's mouth in *To Have and Have Not* is still pretty good when translated by Angie Dickinson in *Rio Bravo* but (as even Hawks admitted) falls flat when JoAnne Dru tries it in *Red River*. Frank Capra used the exact same shtick in *Platinum Blonde* that he does in *Mr. Deeds Goes to Town* of a newly minted millionaire with regular guy roots enlisting his stuffy butlers in a game in which they hoot and holler and compare the various timbers of their echoes in the cavernous palace he now inhabits. It's great business in *Platinum Blonde* and even better in *Mr. Deeds*.

Actors' performances are interconnected from film to film as well, whether they are good or bad. Once we have grown to love Gary Cooper for his work at Paramount or with Capra we find it difficult not to seek out, and enjoy to a degree, his more anonymous *One Sunday Afternoon*, despite James Stephen's flat direction and Cooper's turn as a thin-skinned murderous dentist, a role that doesn't draw enough on Cooper's charm or moral breadth. Once we have grown accustomed to the persona of Jimmy Stewart through his work with Lubitsch, Capra, or Cukor, we find that this persona, which we have become so expert at reading that we notice its slightest nuance, engages us even in second-rate efforts like H.C. Potter's *Shop Worn Angel*, where he and Margaret Sullivan offer pale versions of themselves in Lubitsch's *Shop Around the Corner* and *Vivacious Lady*, where George Stevens falls short, as so many directors have, in the quest for successful screwball comedy. Once we know Greg Toland's greatest work in *Citizen Kane* and *The Long Voyage Home*, his cinematography makes even a weepy melodrama like Goldwyn's *Dark Angel* of interest to us, despite Sidney Franklin's uninspired direction and the film's susceptibility to those two great viruses in Hollywood screenwriting: melodrama and martyrdom. Each of these contributors to a Hollywood film is at the same time toiling away at, and adding a little more scrimshaw to, their own work, a body of work that exists outside the boundaries of the film itself.

Sometime the cross-textuality with which we watch a film has to do, not with the actor, but with the kind of role he plays. It's fun, for example, to compare Edward Everett Horton's repeated turns as an unsuccessful suitor in Lubitsch films from the early 1930s to Ralph Bellamy's repeated playing of the same role in screwball comedies of the late 1930s and early 1940s. Horton's elegance and resonant comic voice seem to preserve his dignity even while he suffers the cruelest indignities at the hands of women who just can't love him and wits who tease him for being such a stuffed shirt. Bellamy comes charging into Manhattan from the West or Middle West with a wealth of good will and comic innocence that serve as significant ballast for the cynicism inherent in screwball comedy. Montgomery Clift, Humphrey Bogart, and Frank Sinatra often seemed to find their ways separately to the same role: the romantic interest who is as vulnerable in his physical slightness as he is in mental precariousness, the man who hates himself and, somehow, in his self hatred, draws the love of women and excites their desire to save and protect him. Hollywood churned out so many films during the studio era, and these films were so densely packed with repeated roles and motifs, that their very structural equations make them hard to analyze separately.

It is this interrelatedness of Hollywood films that leads Ethan Mordden to compare them to the serial publications of Dickens or Thackeray, where "the fascination of the whole redeems the weakness of an entry here and there,"[2] and Andrew Sarris to note, "If Hollywood yields a bit at the very summit, it completely dominates the middle ranges, particularly in the realm of 'good–bad' movies."[3] Even a mediocre film has something to recommend it, especially to the addicted aficionado. Hollywood filmmakers were a studiously unintellectual breed. (At least that is how they often presented themselves.) They were loath to make great artistic claims for their films. But a repeated phrase that runs throughout their interviews is "There were a lot of good things in that film." They were always more comfortable talking about the ingenuity of their films' parts than they were about the meaning of the film as a whole.

Of course, we can make the same kind of case for the significance of lesser works of writers, composers, or artists. If we have grown to love Thomas Hardy for *Far from the Madding Crowd* and *Tess of the d'Urbervilles* then we are also able to take a good deal of pleasure from his lesser works, like *A Pair of Blue Eyes* and *A Laodecian*—and for many of the same reasons. Hardy's early novels in particular are characterized by repetitive patterns. He got a lot of use out of those memories of courting his wife along the cliffs of southern England. The difference is that a Hardy book is attributable to Hardy alone. A film is a compilation of a variety of talents, some of whom may be operating at their best, while others are not doing anything special. We might watch a Hollywood film because it is the lesser work of a great director and at the same time because it includes a prime example of a certain character actor's work. At the same time, perhaps a top grade cinematographer was assigned to the film, or perhaps the film transcends typical Hollywood melodrama due to the contributions of a notable screenwriter. A Hollywood film is a puzzle of interlocking parts, and many of these parts have their own interesting case history. They represent a highly detailed and densely codified work of their own.

Even the best Hollywood films tend to be an amalgam of contributions that vary in their effectiveness. Andrew Sarris, for example, noted, in *The American Cinema*, that "Greta Garbo is "genuinely good" in *Camille*, and Robert Taylor is "genuinely bad," and "George Cukor's direction of Garbo is extraordinary, but his direction of Laura Hope Crews is much too broad."[4] I would concur with all these judgments and offer a few more. Henry Daniell, one of Hollywood's great character actors, is even better than usual in this film at doing what he does best: playing snaky villains for whom we feel strangely sympathetic. Daniell's aristocrats are oily, stuffy, unctuous, and pretentious, but we always feel that they got that way because they just weren't good at making friends. Lionel Barrymore, on the other hand, gives one of his weaker performances in *Camille*, representing the mouthpiece for the brand of middle-class moralism that prevailed at MGM and lapsing into melodramatic cadences as he lectures Greta Garbo on the beauty of sacrificing love for the sake of a young man's career. Barrymore was often an effective ingredient in a film but often a deadly one as well. He sets some kind of standard for the most scenery eaten up in the least amount of time on the screen. And Cukor's direction of Garbo is not only extraordinary, it is one of the great cross-fertilizations in Hollywood's history, representing one of those rare times we get to see Garbo work with a grade A director and one of the few times the picture she was in gave breathing room to the intensity of her performance.

In short, *Camille* is one of Hollywood's greatest films, but even it is not without its glitches. Conversely, the weakest Hollywood films are rarely without their points of interest. Such are the difficulties in weighing the merits of the Hollywood film, which is, in the end, a creation of many diverse talents: composers, cinematographers, actors, directors, and writers, for whom this film is only one installment in an ongoing artistic creation.

THE FRENCH AND THE CULT OF THE GOOD BAD FILM

The attitude of those who first took Hollywood seriously, the French critics of the 1950s, has also contributed to our difficulty in separating the wheat from the chaff in Hollywood. The tendency to take the Hollywood film seriously probably can be dated to the film critics of the French film journals (most notably *Positif* and *Cahiers du Cinema*) of the 1950s and 1960s, many of whom later went on to be directors themselves and to create the cinema of the French New Wave, a cinema inspired by the charm and verve of Hollywood but in itself wholly different than Hollywood.

These critics, reacting against what they saw as a certain stuffiness in French cinema, a tendency toward period pieces and "tradition of quality" filmmaking, vaunted the Hollywood cinema for its vigorous rhythms and its lack of artistic pretension. They argued that there was more life in Hollywood films, despite their commercial aims, than in "tradition of quality" French films that aimed for a more artistic flair but, in the end, only made film look like second-rate literature. French film criticism of the fifties represents one of the most fertile periods in Hollywood criticism, because it appreciated Hollywood not for its sociological relevance or for its pale reflection of the other arts but for its own aesthetics, its own rhythms and structures. The French were the first to praise Hollywood rather than fault it for its lack of intellectual ambition.

Moreover, the *Cahiers du Cinema* writers particularly sought Hollywood directors who had a striking visual style, who were so expressive visually that they could speak to the audience outside the constraints of the Hollywood system, and who could subvert the conventional and commercial constraints of the studio system through their own personal visual language. The *Cahiers* critics had such a sympathy toward visual expressiveness and, at the same time, so little respect for the written word (because they celebrated film for itself, not as an adjunct to literature) that they ended up glorifying certain visually expressive directors, like Nicholas Ray and Samuel Fuller who worked in low budget, B films, often neglecting certain A film directors who, they felt, were too wed to the written word. Billy Wilder and Frank Capra, for example, whose work, today, seems to represent some of the best Hollywood offers, are not *Cahiers* favorites.

It is in the writing of these critics that the gap between what the intellectual sees in Hollywood and what the average filmgoer sees starts to really widen. Whereas the French critics might see a filmmaker exercising great craft within the restraints of a small budget, speaking to his audience through the true language of cinema—sounds and images, ignoring that lesser aspect of cinematic art, the written word—the average filmgoer might simply see a cheaply made film with a weak script.

The most famous example of this gap between the French intellectual and the average American filmgoer is the case of Jerry Lewis. The French appreciation of Jerry Lewis has been so often remarked upon that it has become one of the reference points for a certain lazy tendency that has developed in American culture in the last 20 years or so to denigrate the French character in general. The French, particularly the critics at *Positif*, saw in Lewis's first five or six directorial efforts a wonderful send-up of the materialism and worship of technology in American culture in the early 1960s. He was to them, as David Thomson summarizes him in a brief biography of Lewis, the "adman's man, a robot degenerate over-programmed by the conflicting gods of Americana, made schizoid by the clash of material luxuries and abstract ideals."[5] This is the kind of vaunted description of Lewis that makes many Americans, whose chief image of Lewis is as a kind of maudlin Las Vegas shuckster for muscular dystrophy, drop their jaws in astonishment.

Lewis's persona was shaped most meaningfully in the films he made for Frank Tashlin, another French favorite. Tashlin was a cartoonist turned filmmaker and his films (*Artists and Models, Will Success Spoil Rock Hunter, Hollywood or Bust*) have the large scale and Technicolor brilliance of cartoons. Along with Hitchcock, Douglas Sirk, and Stanley Donen, he contributed to that blaze of Technicolor glory with which Hollywood went out in the late 1950s and early 1960s. And he too had a sharp eye for the absurdity of corporate America. Moreover, the mechanization of man in America and Americanized Europe was a popular theme in Europe in the late 1950s and early 1960s. (Witness the infinitely quieter cinema of Jacques Tati at the time.) So there is some context for the favor Lewis finds with the French. If the French overinterpret him, Americans tend to oversimplify him, bundling his directorial efforts of the early 1960s with the earlier juvenile comedies he made with Dean Martin and with his later years as a smarmy, ubiquitous presence on American television.

But Lewis is only the most extreme case of the French intellectualizing of what might seem to us to be low culture. The debate over Lewis is the most polarized, but the same argument goes on over scores of other filmmakers who had seemed decidedly second-tier in talent until the French got through with them. There is no doubt that many of the directors heralded by the French critics—like Frank Tashlin, Budd Boetticher, Nicholas Ray, and Sam Fuller—have made some great films and films that provide particularly savorous pleasure, coming, as they often did, from the nether regions of the studio system. The successful B film seems to prove the power of Hollywood to survive, even thrive, in the worst circumstances, its unique ability to create silk purses out of sow's ears. And these films underline one of the most important things to keep in mind about Hollywood, that it follows an art of form, not content; said differently, an absence of enunciated ideas does not mean an absence of beauty as well. In that vein, I would nominate Fuller's *Pickup on South Street* and Ray's *In a Lonely Place* as two films worthy of any Hollywood canon. Boetticher's *Seven Men from Now* is a kind of small, perfect Western, beautifully shot, lean in its narrative, and nicely unified in its structure. It makes an art out of austerity.

At the same time, these filmmakers, toiling in the B film industry as they did, had to often work under rushed circumstances, with weak scripts and lifeless actors, and their general oeuvre reflects those conditions. The French critics and their followers tended to inflate the value of these filmmakers because the aesthetic of the B film suited them. These critics became the directors of the French New Wave, and they were already evolving the aesthetic of the New Wave style in their mind as they reflected on these filmmakers. French New Wave cinema recoiled against an excessive, lifeless craft and aimed for a sloppy, studiously unpolished aesthetic, with an eye toward catching something real. And so these critics were not put off by the necessary sloppiness of the B directors they heralded. In these critics' minds, the messiness of these films was part of their success. Their films had some éclat. They were not muffled by a tradition of quality, which is all well and good until you have read your umpteenth frighteningly serious article on Ray's *Johnny Guitar* or Fritz Lang's *Rancho Notorious*, films that have obvious visual appeal but which are also marred by significant flaws and to which the term "kitschy" does not seem indiscriminately applied.

It becomes confusing for the average filmgoer, trying to get the hang of Hollywood, when flawed but striking films like the above are placed on an equal footing with the best representatives of Hollywood's seamless classical style, films like Billy Wilder's *Apartment*, for example, and Capra's *Mr. Deeds Goes to Town*. The French critics were aficionados, so well-versed in Hollywood that they took its greatest products for granted, preferring to root out its hidden glories. Their critical acumen is unquestioned, but, at the same time, 50 years later, a good many of their judgments about directors who they saw as too enmeshed in a tradition of quality filmmaking style, or too governed by the written word, have been proven very questionable.

We can only shake our heads in disbelief that Andrew Sarris, the American translator and apologist for the French critics at the time, listed Billy Wilder, William Wyler, and Carol Reed in his fifth tier of directors in *The American Cinema*, the tier he titled "Less Than Meets the Eye." Sarris, himself, some years later, professed surprise at his earlier judgments and, it should be noted, even when he wrote *The American Cinema*, recognized there was much in the French attitude toward Hollywood that suggested "the classical highbrow gambit of elevating lowbrow art at the expense of middle brow art." Auteur critics, he also noted, were "vulnerable to the charge of preferring trash to art because they seek out movies in the limbo of cultural disrepute."[6] In short, even the most avid fan of the French film critics of the 1950s had to allow for a certain snobbish tendency, on the part of those critics, to set themselves up as the blessed few who had the sensitivity to find art where others callously ignored it.

There has been, in the film criticism that has followed French criticism of the 1950s, a certain tendency toward cultism. The intertextuality of Hollywood films, of course, contributes to cultism in film criticism too. The fact that there are so many flawed but interesting films feeds the appetite for film scholars to bring the small, underappreciated films to light. Omnivorous aficionados and professors, anxious to stake claim to new ground on their way to publication and tenure, race each other to the most remote regions of the Hollywood landscape. Studies of the "so bad they're good" films of Ed Wood or the political implications of cheap 1950s sci-fi proliferate. Since these films are too thin to warrant much attention in themselves, scholars turn to the social sciences to prop up their studies. Film studies become an adjunct to sociology, and we are back where we started, with a criticism that really doesn't have any faith that these films are worth looking at in themselves, with a criticism that says these films are interesting "for their time." Much has changed in film criticism from decade to decade, but one tendency has remained stubbornly intractable, whether its in the criticism of the stodgiest old-timer or that of the trendiest modern theorist: a fear of celebrating classic Hollywood for the merits of its own aesthetic accomplishment and a susceptibility to justifying the significance of the Hollywood film by reference to other, more serious sciences.

An adverse effect of this kind of criticism is that it leads to a sense of Hollywood as a medium to be valued for its kitschy pleasures, as a subbranch of pop culture, on a par with television and other detritus of the media age. If we ask students to believe that Sam Fuller's *Shock Corridor* (a film with truly lyrical passages, I agree) stands up to Carol Reed's *Third Man* or Alfred Hitchcock's *North by Northwest* or that explosions of vitality in B films are equal, even superior, to the best classical craft Hollywood has to offer, should we be surprised if they start to question our judgment or accuse us of overintellectualizing Hollywood? There is much in modern film criticism that suggests the emperor's new clothes.

Again, it is important not to be prudish or reactionary in approaching Hollywood. Hollywood's depth and variety is also its glory. The "good bad" film is an essential paradox in Hollywood, a legitimate subject of study. But at the same time there is something easy and puerile in the cult of the Hollywood ne'er-do-well. If I want to impress students with Hollywood in a quick and immediate way, the easiest way to do so is to show them something surprising, something outside of the Hollywood tradition, a precode film that surprises them with its sexual explicitness or general perversity, maybe Todd Browning's *Freaks*, or a B film from the 1950s with brutal noir violence, lighting, and angles. All these impress the modern sensibility but, in a way, by cheating. They all reach modern audiences because they are a little weird, because they aren't typical of Hollywood. And in that sense, they are not fully instructive of what made Hollywood great; in fact, they only confirm the modern audience's suspicion of Hollywood as repressive and warping real creativity. Just think of the films Samuel Fuller could have made, this attitude teaches, had he not been chained in the prison of Hollywood.

It is far more difficult, but a great deal more rewarding, to convey the quiet art of classical Hollywood, the extraordinary attention to framing and continuity, the careful story structure, and equilibrium in pathos and comedy—what Scott Eyman has described, in describing Ernst Lubitsch's art, as the "grave, methodical intent supporting a blithe, carefree, beautifully, textured surface structure."[7] There is a Romantic tendency in much of film criticism to show the passionate personality trapped under the repressive regime of Hollywood. And perhaps there is a corresponding lack of careful analysis of the meticulous art that lies beneath a surface that seems light and unstudied.

Hollywood's most persuasive argument for its worth rests in its greatest product. Because of Hollywood's great variety—and because that variety is one of its great distinctions in the art world—critics tend to throw up their hands in a kind of orgy of open-mindedness. No one has, or ever will, they all agree, find the "whole equation" of the studio industry. Who's to say what a good film is?

But although there is a lovely fluidity to the artistic process in Hollywood, things aren't quite that mystical or ephemeral. Lubitsch's *Trouble in Paradise,* Sturges's *Lady Eve*, Hitchcock's *Rear Window*, Ford's *Stagecoach*, Wilder's *Love in the Afternoon,* Capra's *Meet John Doe* are all great films, textbook examples of Hollywood's craft. These films represent an important first object of study for anyone trying to understand why Hollywood should be taken seriously as an art form. We can reserve for later the savorous pleasure of the B films, as rich in vitality as they are in flaws.

4

Taking Classic Hollywood Seriously

The seriousness with which French intellectuals in the 1950s took American film soon found its way to American campuses, where film criticism was further informed by all sorts of esoteric schools of interpretation—structuralism, post-structuralism, deconstruction, Marxist, and psychoanalytic schools, gender studies. This of course led to the ironic spectacle of books and articles written in an impenetrable jargon, a kind of code language for doctorates, about films that had been, by their nature, designed to be transparent in meaning and accessible to the most ordinary filmgoer. If the seriousness with which the 1950s French intellectuals took Hitchcock is a bit much for some, what are they to make of works by academics such as *Hitchcock's Bi-Textuality: Lacan, Feminisms, and Queer Theory* or "The Metafictional Hitchcock: The Experience of Viewing and the Viewing of Experience in *Rear Window* and *Psycho*?" Here we have the absurdo ad reductum of an excessively intellectual approach to classic Hollywood: works designed as light, frothy entertainments suffering dissection at the hands of critics armed with the most arcane of interpretive language and theory. Without denying the potential worth of these critical works, we can understand why someone who was actually around when *Rear Window* came out and experienced it as a light entertainment created by an industry intent on making a tidy profit might snort with derision.

That said, it is just as important not to cede too much ground to those who scoff at the intellectualization of the classic Hollywood film. The generation, for example, that lived during the classic Hollywood years, and which finds the seriousness with which we take these films ludicrous, is not to be completely trusted. If they were, we would still think that only films of high seriousness and topical relevance, such as *Best Years of Our Lives* and *The Grapes of Wrath*, deserved serious attention and that Alfred Hitchcock and Howard Hawks were little more than good storytellers.

Few people look to Bosley Crowther any longer for elucidation on the Hollywood film.

There is much to be grateful to the French for their combat against middlebrow art and in their salvaging of films from the tyranny of a criticism that appreciated those films only for their content. The French tapped into the most fruitful vein in Hollywood film criticism, one that appreciated Hollywood, not for its pseudoliterary content or topical value, but for its form, rhythm and energy. As John Hess noted, the French critics sought, in their analysis of Hollywood, to "remove film from the realm of social and political concern, in which the progressive forces of the Resistance had placed all the arts in the years immediately after the war."[1] They celebrated an art that did not aim to serve a "higher cause," but instead was satisfied with the significance inherent in superb formal structure. "In Hitchcock's work," Eric Rohmer and Claude Chabrol wrote, "form does not embellish content, it creates it."[2]

And in many ways the job the French critics started still needs to be finished. The events of the 1960s quickly transformed *Cahiers du Cinema* into a highly politicized journal that came to prize politically engaged cinema. Forty years later the tendency to weigh films for their political heft, to value them for their high seriousness, still persists. The lax habit of studying the Hollywood film for what it has to say (something in direct contradiction to the Hollywood aesthetic of showing what you have to say, not saying it) seems to be a difficult one to break. The old Hollywood and the new don't have much in common but the habit of handing awards to the most self-serious topical fare and snubbing comedies, no matter how ingenious. The habit of valuing content over form persists.

Hollywood does deserve to be taken seriously but not in the ways it often is—not for the depth of its ideas, its literary content, its topical relevance. These are the things Hollywood seeks when it wants to tart itself up and impress. In those instances, then, as now, Hollywood tends to embarrass itself, coming off as sophomoric and pseudointellectual. There is a striking correspondence between the tendency of a Hollywood film to vaunt its seriousness and its literary qualities and the tendency for that film to age badly.

And Hollywood's seriousness or relevance does not lie in its usefulness to academics as a means of buttressing their sociological studies. When an academic studies *Rear Window* for what it has to say about "queer theory" or McCarthyism, he or she is conceding a point that cynics about Hollywood have long held: these films are not to be taken seriously in themselves but only as stepping stones to the more serious sciences, particularly sociology which, unlike Hollywood, has something significant to say about the world. A quick glance at the most recent issue of a prestigious film journal to which I subscribe features five articles on, respectively, the porn industry, lesbianism in television shows, colonialist themes in Australian Westerns, ethnographic narratives of education in *The Blackboard Jungle*, and the relation of South Korean cinema to the International Monetary

Fund. It's a collection of articles that testifies to that powerful twin tendency in academic film criticism: first, the academic's tendency to explore the marginalia of his or her field of study, to stake new ground, no matter how incidental the subject matter; and second, the tendency to see film as worthy of study only when the film reflects something about more serious sciences. In this issue, film takes a backseat to psychology, anthropology, history, and political science. You don't have to be utterly against putting film into political context to suspect that the light, airy art of classical Hollywood suffers in a critical climate like this. In fact, it's probably noteworthy that the one "Hollywood" film being considered here, Richard Brooks's *Blackboard Jungle* is from the later period in Hollywood when, competing with Europe's more adult fare, Hollywood sought to make more "serious, socially relevant" films. Here's a film that has "ideas" you can study.

Hollywood deserves to be taken quite seriously but not, above all, for its explicit ideas or its relation to the social sciences. The Hollywood film deserves to be studied for itself, for the complexity of its form, its structure, the elaborate and concise art it arrived at to tell its story, its tight sense of unity, consistent story structure, rich and varied characterization, its emphasis on visual rather than verbal communication, its musical rhythm, its stylistic flair, its classical sense of equilibrium, its subtle balance of pathos and comedy. It's when we consider these elements that Hollywood's art asserts itself most powerfully, not when we talk about its literary content or topical relevance.

THE NAY-SAYING DIRECTORS

The best guides to the beauty and complexity of the Hollywood film are often not the film critics and scholars but the practitioners themselves, the Hollywood directors and technicians who loved to speak to the art of the Hollywood film. But these filmmakers can be curious guides to the significance or seriousness of the Hollywood film, because they, themselves, at times seem not to take these films seriously as works of art. Though some, like Frank Capra, King Vidor, and Rouben Mamoulian, were not shy about referring to themselves as artists, the majority of Hollywood filmmakers seemed to share Robert Frost's notion that "art" is a praise term one doesn't use about oneself or one's work. It was an ingrained habit, almost a point of pride on the part of the greatest directors, to avoid thinking of their films as "high art" and rather to see themselves as sturdy craftsmen turning out good product. Whether it was Ford talking about the construction of a shot or Wilder talking about the logic of a storyline, these filmmakers tended to talk about what they were doing as if they were putting together a solid chair and not aiming for a transcendent experience. They shared a repugnance toward the notion of themselves as great "artistes" and saw boasting about the artfulness of their work as bad form. Howard Hawks tended to prefer the word "professional" to "artist." He compared himself to an athlete or flier, for whom "the primary thing is to do a really good job" and to "forget everything else in order to do it right." When Peter Bogdanovich asked him if he ever thought of moviemaking as an art, Hawks answered no. When Bogdanovich pressed him as to what he did think of it as, Hawks responded with two words, "Business. Fun."[3]

Hawks loved to take potshots at the French intellectuals who celebrated his work. "I just aim the camera at the actors and they make up all these things about me," he would repeatedly say.[4] Similarly, some of the most amusing moments in Peter Bogdanovich's famous filmed interviews with John Ford are those in which Ford, with a kind of humorous disgust, gruffly dismisses Bogdanovich's earnest inquiries into the significance of Ford's films. When Bogdanovich, comparing Ford's later film *The Man Who Shot Liberty Valence* to his earlier *Wagon Master*, asks Ford if he is aware of an increasingly sad and melancholic attitude to the West in his films, Ford answers curtly, "No." Bogdanovich perseveres. "Now that I've pointed it out, is there anything you'd like to say about it," he asks Ford. "I don't know what you're talking about," says Ford. When Bogdanovich later asks if Ford would agree that the principal idea of *Fort Apache* is that the tradition of the Army is more important than one individual, Ford does not even take time to reflect. "Cut," he says.

Bogdanovich engages in similar repartee with Hawks. Bogdanovich, for example, in one interview praises Hawks for having included a reading of Edgar Allan Poe's "El Dorado" in Hawks's Western *El Dorado*. The poem, Bogdanovich opines, "expresses the theme of the movie—and of so many of your movies: that it's not whether a man achieves his goal that counts, but how he searches for it." This would seem to be an obvious and legitimate observation, especially considering the film takes its name from the poem, but Hawks resists the idea nonetheless. "Wait a minute—you're going to get awful complicated with that. [Screenwriter Leigh] Brackett and I simply liked it, so I asked her to put it in."[5]

Hitchcock was more politely evasive than Ford or Hawks in his interviews, embarking on long stories that tended to make interviewers feel like they were really getting somewhere until those interviewers read other interviews with Hitchcock in which he dutifully hauled out the same tired arsenal of bon mots and shaggy-dog stories. Ford was a man of few words (at least in his interviews), Hitchcock quite voluble, but neither really revealed that much about their personal feelings toward their films. For example, Norman Bates's and Marion Crane's lengthy discussion on human loneliness, in *Psycho*, in which Norman expresses his view of humans as caged birds clawing at one another, represents one of Hitchcock's most personal and lucid statements on the human condition and one that is movingly reflected in the mise-en-scène of countless of his other films, and yet Hitchcock would always persist in interviews in talking about *Psycho* as a kind of purely formal stunt, an experiment in technical expertise.

This gap between what a film is and how the Hollywood director represents that film reaches epic proportion in the case of Ford   (Photo 1). When you put his rich compositions, as overtly artistic or mannered as any in Hollywood, and his taste for lush, weeping sentimentality next to his frighteningly gruff, antiartistic demeanor,

Photo 1. John Ford, an artsy director who hated the word "art." Courtesy of Photofest.

you get what amounts to a case of artistic schizophrenia. But most directors had this schizophrenia to some degree. George Cukor, who was more overtly intellectual than some of the other Hollywood directors and whose films are characterized by an elegant mise-en-scène, nevertheless took pride in the overall quietness of his technique and recoiled in irritation at the stylish excess of the 1960s art film and, indeed, at any film that called attention to itself as "art." Billy Wilder's book-length interview with Cameron Crowe is striking in how unswervingly Wilder portrays himself as a craftsman, someone who understood the logic of the Hollywood story, and how uninterested he was in arguing for artistic merit or creative genius. When Crowe praises him for creating great films without overly complicated shots (high praise indeed for the Hollywood director), Wilder responds, "If it does not follow the story, why? It's phoniness. The phoniness of the director."[6] And yet Wilder's oeuvre, as much as any single directors, represents a test case for the auteur system, a body of work that represents Hollywood at its most artful and which bears the mark of distinct artistic personality.

But Wilder's remarks are typical of Hollywood directors. They are reverent about certain things—story, character, craftsmanship, professionalism—but gravely suspicious of the word "art." "I'm still not sure if movies are an art form," Minnelli said, "And if they're not then let them inscribe on my tombstone what they could about any craftsman who loves his job: 'here lies Vincente Minnelli. He died of hard work.'"[7] Like Hawks, Minnelli is more comfortable thinking of himself as someone who did a good job than he is thinking of himself as an artist. And yet several of the works on Minnelli's high end, like *The Clock*, *Some Came Running*, and *The Bad and The Beautiful*, represent top-notch Hollywood fare. If he's not sure these films are art, it puts those who think they are in a funny position.

The anti-intellectual streak in the Hollywood director is, for the most part, one of his more endearing features. It represents a refreshing antidote to the stereotype of the self-absorbed, self-serious, and self-proclaimed modern artist. And it is an attitude that seems consistent with a certain hard-boiled and common sense tradition in American art, in which respect for craft is proportional to a distaste for pretense and effete nonsense. "I've found," said Warner Brothers director Vincent Sherman, "that most of the time real artists are tough, hard-boiled, hard-working, practical people with their feet on the ground. Their artistic opinions come out of honest and real relationship to life and people. There's none of the preciousness of people who live in a rarefied atmosphere."[8] This is a distinctly American notion of the artist. It is diametrically opposed, for example, to that of an aesthete like Baudelaire who conceived of the artist as an albatross, majestic in flight, ridiculous when forced back down to ground. But Sherman's description of the artist sums up pretty tidily how the Hollywood director liked to think of himself: tough, lacking pretense, as determined to make a good film as he was not to take that film too seriously.

As charming as Hollywood directors could be in their lack of pretension, however, their attitude toward film as art represents something of a challenge to those who would take these films seriously. If their progenitors don't take these films seriously, why should we? If these directors thought of their films only in terms of craft, entertainment, and financial success, aren't we finding art where there is none?

TAKING THEM SERIOUSLY ANYWAY

But, just because the Hollywood directors don't want to talk about their films' meanings doesn't mean the meaning is not there. The Hollywood director's repugnance toward preaching was so strong that he felt that if he was reduced to explaining his film he had failed. All of his craft went into making his ideas tangible in the structure of his story, the plastics of his style. He had a horror of explaining himself to anyone. Truffaut was tickled by Hitchcock's tendency to say to actors who quarreled with him on the set, "It's only a movie." When an acquaintance of Truffaut's held that comment out as proof that Hitchcock didn't take his films as seriously as his admirers did, Truffaut explained that what Hitchcock really meant was, "It's only a movie to you."

Hitchcock is the prime example of the director who, to his own generation, seemed only to be about entertainment, a good storyteller, the author of a cinema devoid of content, but who has, in the years following the studio era, assumed the mantle of one of film's great artists. Hitchcock scorned explicit, didactic ideas religiously ("I am not interested in content at all. I don't give a damn what the film is about"),[9] but critics have not found his films wanting in ideas anyway. These ideas grow organically out of his story structure. By the time Hitchcock has finished with his love story involving a photographer in *Rear Window*, he has said quite a bit about, men, women, love, marriage, human loneliness, photography, filmmaking, voyeurism, and television—and all without any overt speeches. His ideas are built into and grow out of the story and the way that story is shot.

"The Americans," wrote Jean-Luc Godard, "who are much more stupid [*sic*] when it comes to analysis, instinctively bring off very complex scripts. They also have a gift for the kind of simplicity which brings depth."[10] Hollywood filmmakers are not particularly analytical, themselves, but they are awfully good at creating films that engender analysis. And that analysis is not initiated by ideas within the film but by the film itself, its story and structure. Hollywood directors speak to us through the construction of their film. The director's thought "appears," Fereydoun Hoveyda writes, "through his *mise-en-scène*. What matters in a film is the desire for order, composition, harmony, the placing of actors and objects, the movements within the frame, the capturing of a movement or a look."[11] The director speaks to us, not in words but in his arrangement of the shot or scene. His art is one of concretes, not abstractions. It represents its own kind of highly interpretable language, but it doesn't speak directly to us in words. "The evidence of personal expression" in a Hollywood film, according to Thomas Elsaesser, is "in the *mise-en-scène*, the visual orchestration of the story, the rhythm of the action, the plasticity and dynamism of the image, the pace and causality introduced through editing."[12]

Many of Hollywood's greatest films succeed not because of, but despite, their ideas. Capra's films are somewhat justly criticized for veering into populist preaching. And these are often the weakest moments in the film. But these momentary weaknesses of didacticism are dwarfed by the monumental way Capra puts his populism, his idealized notion of community, into plastic form. His films pop with energy. His crowd scenes spill out of the frame with dramatic power. His careful attention to the smallest character actor gives his film a warm, teeming sense of humanity. Capra's humanity best expresses itself in the care of his craft. The speeches, while often fine, are also often precariously close to *Reader's Digest* fare.

In short, the best way to get at Hollywood's seriousness is to look to the craft; the art and ideas will follow. The directors didn't care to explain themselves, but in this respect they are acting no differently than scores of modern artists who invest themselves wholly in the creative process of filmmaking and scorn offering interpretations. As acutely different as the Hollywood director is from the modern abstract artist, they both share a reluctance to talk about, explain, or interpret their art. They both are content to leave that grunt work to critics.

In the best Hollywood films we will find ideas, but we will find them sublimated into the story, growing out naturally from the film's story. They are not obvious;

they don't stick out like handles, but they are there, in the clever construction of the story, in the way someone is lit or framed, in a clever bit of comic business meant to explain pictorially something about a character. And on this subject—the subject of their craft, the way they tell their stories, the way they translate ideas into concrete matter, the way they shape this matter into interesting patterns and rhythms—the Hollywood filmmaker could be as voluble as he was silent about "what the film meant." He didn't like to talk about "art" or "meaning," but he loved to talk about the "business" he put in his film.

THE UNCONSCIOUS DIRECTOR; THE DIRECTOR'S UNCONSCIOUSNESS

If it's kind of fun to watch tough old birds like Ford and Hawks swat down the sophomoric interpretations of those who would intellectualize Hollywood, there is also some pleasure in watching the film directors, on the lecture circuits late in life, being awakened by new students of their films to meanings they had not realized were there in their films. To be sure, a few directors like Hawks were tough to convince. When, for example, he was asked how he felt about his celebrity with French intellectuals, Hawks's response was flat, "You know, I don't go in for analysis. Every time I go to France, I meet with thirty French directors who know most of the dialogue of my pictures and ask me questions. They are very interested in how you make pictures. They go into it and analyze it and read things into it that I had no idea of when I made the picture."[13]

But Hawks here cynically refers to something other directors were more open to: the possibility that their films might mean more than they realized at the time. Not all directors were quite as crusty as Ford and Hawks. The more gracious John Huston, for example, admitted that he was not conscious of any themes linking his films, but he was curious about those who were. "French and Italian critics have described my philosophy to me," Huston said, "but as I say, it's never conscious. It was very interesting what they told me—that I believe in the pursuit rather than the achievement, that it's the game and not the gain. Things like that."[14] There's something gently comical in Huston's patience here as European intellectuals explain him to him. His comments also reveal how little it mattered to him, when he made a film, what that film "meant."

William Wellman, characterized by a more boyish bravado, seemed quite tickled when somebody pointed out the importance of rain in his films to him at a retrospective of his films sponsored by the British Film Institute. "Did you notice, there's a lot of rain in them," he said to Richard Schickel. "It was always raining every picture. I don't know why." Wellman noted that in Ford's films "it's all wind," adding, "You know, when you see people come out, wind is blowing the hair. He's wind crazy and I was rain crazy. It's an odd thing, yet I don't remember doing it. But they brought my attention to it in London."[15] Again, the almost shocking indifference on the part of the director to something that, in hindsight, seems so obviously significant. Again, the master is revealed to himself by the student, the American artist by the European intellectual.

King Vidor spoke of visiting the house he was raised in and realizing as he ascended the staircase that he was "in the exact scene from *The Crowd*" with the boy walking up a stairway. "Over the years," Vidor said, "I have learned that things will be dug out of your unconscious. This is particularly true of silent films, where we didn't have all those words to explain things and we thought in terms of symbols and graphic arrangements or possibilities."

Here Vidor ties the interpretability of Hollywood films to their very refusal to explain themselves, to their tendency to stick to the plastics of cinema to convey their points, hence the even greater depth of mystery and interpretative possibility to silent film. "We were trained in those terms. When you had to explain something, you didn't think the way you do when you're writing. You thought, 'What's the picture, the symbol I'm looking for, to explain what I am trying to say?' I think with that scene in *The Crowd* I was trying to suggest a painful moment in my youth that I felt without being entirely aware of it."[16] Paradoxically, it's the silence of Hollywood films that makes it so rich in meanings. The best Hollywood films traffic mostly in visual and concrete information that the viewer *has* to interpret.

Once the Hollywood director had hit on the right visual idea, the bit of concrete business that he felt best got across his idea, he saw his work as done and, for the most part, was strangely mute about the "meaning" of his films from that point on. Devoutly anti-intellectual craftsmen that they were, the Hollywood directors rival the most arrogant of modern "artistes" in their unwillingness to explain their works. They saw it as their function to translate ideas into images, not vice versa. The film, they seem to feel, should speak for itself. Some, like Ford and Hawks, recoiled at the interpretive fervor their films set off (though it is not difficult to discern pleasure even in their hardened responses), while others seem genuinely touched. But none were comfortable in expounding about their films in that way.

But their reticence in analyzing their own films should not be taken as evidence of their films' lack of depth. In fact, it is their very unwillingness to expound didactically that led to such densely visual, concrete, and symbolic films, films that in their lack of explicitness and visual complexity beg for interpretive response. The glory of the Hollywood film is reflected in the quiet and solidity of the artisan's craft and also in the excited, interpretive response of the viewer to that craft.

5

Hollywood's Classicism

CLASSICAL BALANCE

One of the best ways to understand the significance of the Hollywood film is to reflect some on why it is referred to as "classic" filmmaking. For many the word "classical" is simply a synonym for "old." But Hollywood films are referred to as classic because they adhere to the same aesthetic principles that artists did in classical Greece and Rome. Classic Hollywood aims for an art of balance, proportion, and symmetry. It respects unity, a seamless technique and an artfulness that hides itself. Like classical art, it values a simple structure that is touched with an understated elegance. And it aims for a mimetic effect, a realistic imitation of reality but one that also streamlines and elevates that reality.

Of course, Hollywood arrived at its classical technique, not out of a careful study of classical culture, but because of its desire to create a clean product that was highly marketable and good for mass consumption. The industrial nature of the Hollywood system led to practiced labor and a polished product. Its desire to reach a wide audience led to a film where art sublimates itself to the story.

David Bordwell notes that the French were the first to be comfortable referring to Hollywood cinema as "classical." As early as 1922, Jean Renoir referred to Chaplin's and Lubitsch's films as examples of a "classical cinema," and Andre Bazin felt that Hollywood, by 1939, had acquired "all the traits of a classical art." We are likely to agree with Bordwell when he writes that "it seems proper to retain the term in English, since the principles which Hollywood claims as its own rely on notions of decorum, proportion, formal harmony, respect for tradition, mimesis, self-effacing craftsmanship, and cool control of the perceiver's response—canons which critics of any medium usually call 'classical.' "[1]

Of all the classical ingredients that comprise the Hollywood film, perhaps the most important is balance, whether it be in its balanced shot arrangement, its care in graceful editing and continuity, or the "roundedness" it values in story construction. "I never overestimate the audience, nor do I underestimate them," said Billy Wilder, "I just have a very rational idea as to who we're dealing with."[2] "Rationalism" is not a word we often associate with Hollywood, but, in the end, it is a rational art, an art of temperance, balance, and equanimity. Bazin prized Hitchcock above all for his "equilibrium," and that is a trait that unites the greatest of Hollywood filmmakers.

The visual hallmark of Hollywood's classical sense of balance is, perhaps, the classically composed shot, often built around a group of three, framed carefully, with attention to balance, symmetry, proportion, and recessive depth. When we think of Hollywood's great shots, we first think of stills from the films of its masters: John Ford's groups of cowboys, for example, spilling through doorways and arranging themselves around the door in lush Renaissance formations; George Cukor's elegant double images in boudoir mirrors, nicely appointed with all the sparkling debris of MGM's lavish sets; William Wyler's and Greg Toland's highly balanced compositions, characterized by baroque depth and chiaroscuro; Frank Capra's energetic compositions, framed by teeming crowds that threaten to burst the boundaries of the image; Hitchcock's clever games matching the microscopic with the macrocosmic, as in the famous shot in *North by Northwest* that includes both a close-up of Cary Grant and the image of an airplane over his shoulder and the famous tracking shot from *Notorious* that moves from a far shot of a large party and finishes in such a tight close-up of the key in Alyssa's hand that we can read the script on the key.

But these are just the characteristics of Hollywood's greatest visual stylists. You can examine just about any scene in any Hollywood film and find yourself looking at a carefully arranged shot. This is one of classic Hollywood's great strengths and one of the ways in which it compares quite favorably to filmmaking that came after it. It sought balance in the most incidental shot. Even weak classic Hollywood films have a solid construction to them, a sturdy handsomeness in the shot arrangement. Hollywood films may have been put together by directors and technicians who were less intellectual, less self-consciously artistic than the film artists who would follow in their wake, but they operated in an atmosphere, or within an ethic, that would not allow them to treat a shot indifferently. This professionalism or craft ethic is one of the many reasons it is not always easy to draw a clear line between the best and the weakest classic Hollywood films. Even the weak Hollywood film often has an arresting attractiveness, a solid craft that seems worthy of study.

The same meticulous care and construction is apparent in Hollywood editing and its devotion to smooth continuity. Even the strongest visual stylists in Hollywood, Hitchcock, for example, were careful to use their effects in moderation and to slowly and surely build their shots and their films, so that any shock of style they chose finally to indulge in could be sustained by a solid structure. Hitchcock's *Rear Window*, for example, has its Expressionist moments; one thinks of the famous sequence in which Jeff defends himself with camera flashes that fill the screen with explosions of orange color. But even in a stylish film like *Rear Window*, careful classical construction is the foundation. Hitchcock's editing is careful and patient. Jeff picks up his camera to watch a neighbor. Cut to subject in far shot. Cut back to reaction shot of Jeff, indicating what he is thinking. Cut back to subject now in medium range. Cut back to Jeff's reaction shot. Cut back to subject in close-up. Hitchcock edits in such a way to slowly build a shot that we are sure of our space, move gradually to it, and never lose sight of our viewer and the mental context in which the shot is held. Careful, deliberative filmmaking.

Bordwell notes that by the late teens, Hollywood had made such advances in smooth continuity from scene to scene that its filmmakers were no longer concerned with basics like making sure a person occupied the same place from one scene to the next but with aesthetic issues like how to minimize "eye fatigue" for viewers. If a viewer's eyes have been drawn to the left in one scene, then the next should pick up on the left. If a scene finishes with bright light, don't begin the next in the dark, advised the film manuals of the time: "Pictorial rhythms must seem to sway from scene to scene, must pick up naturally from one to another, and must vary enough to avoid monotony."[3] Howard Hawks had pictorial rhythms in mind, and also the self-effacing nature of the Hollywood aesthetic, when he advised filmmakers to "always cut on movement and the audience won't notice the cut."[4]

One fine example of Hollywood's graceful editorial continuity is the scene in John Ford's *Stagecoach* in which actress Louise Platt, playing a Southern belle named Lucy Mallory and John Carradine's Southern gambler eye each other flirtatiously, she through her departing stagecoach window, he through the window of the saloon where he is playing poker. It's a small sequence, comprising only 20 seconds or so, which only makes us marvel all the more at how carefully it is crafted.

The sequence begins with a lovely shot of Carradine playing poker near a window in a saloon. The shot is from above, with light from the window flooding Carradine's portion of the frame on the left and illuminating the smoke that billows above him from his cigarette. He looks out the window to the lower left of the frame and, in a moment of typically competent continuity, Ford cuts to Lucy framed by her carriage window, casting her glance to the upper right. The angles of their glance match, thus satisfying the demands of spatial continuity, but the images match nicely also because the slant of the saloon window and the slant of the carriage window, both parallelograms leaning to the left, match perfectly. This design element is not to accomplish spatial continuity but that ease of vision, that "pictorial continuity" that the film manuals of classic Hollywood encouraged.

Ford cuts back to Carradine, this time, from outside the saloon, through the saloon window. He too now is framed by a window, and here is where Ford's match cuts are particularly poetic. Whereas Clementine is framed by the black of the carriage, the gambler is framed by the white frame of the saloon window. Whereas her face emerges from the dark shadows of the carriage, his is bleached by the sun coming through the window. And now the windows are not parallel but oppose each other nicely; both are leaning rectangles or parallelograms, but hers leans down to the left, his to the right. Here Ford's shots are not only picking up naturally from one another, as the manual suggests, but also "varying enough to avoid monotony." However, "avoiding monotony" does not seem a sufficient summary of the poetic effect of this sequence, which Ford edits in such a way that the two environments, and not just the man and the woman, seem to square off amorously.

Hollywood constructs its stories as deliberately as it does its shot and its arrangement of shots. The word Billy Wilder most venerated, when it came to film writing and directing, was "construction." One of the wittiest of screenwriters, Wilder nevertheless emphasized that good screenwriting was more than a question of being funny. Wilder, for example, praised Raymond Chandler for his dialogue and his original descriptions and observations, such as "out of his ears grew hair long enough to catch a moth" and "nothing is as empty as an empty swimming pool." But, Wilder emphasized, Chandler "could not construct." For Wilder, great lines and jokes did not add up to a great film. "I do the joke if the joke is germane to the whole story, to the picture," Wilder said.[5] The whole is more important than the particular. In his reticence to use a big joke, Wilder, as a screenwriter, parallels the director who is reticent to use an excessively stylish shot. The Hollywood aesthetic is one that finds protuberances disturbing. Everything must be streamlined for the efficiency of the product.

Hollywood was not a didactic art or a stylishly extravagant one. It kept too close an eye on its audience to allow itself such extravagances. Its goal, ultimately, was not to impress but to entertain. When it analyzed itself, it tended toward musical, not literary, terms, taking care about its pacing and rhythm, its success as a whole from beginning to end. Wilder, for example, spoke of the "roundedness we had at the time," of the gag that you would plan, "and then you come back with again, and then you pay it off." Hollywood filmmakers tended to speak of their art in this manner, in terms of construction and execution more than in terms of expression. "If you find a good prop . . . then you use it," Wilder said.[6]

The cracked mirror owned by Shirley MacLaine's character, Fran Kubelik, in *The Apartment* illustrates what Wilder means by good construction. In this film, Jack Lemmon's nebbishy character finds a cracked lady's mirror in his apartment, which he has been loaning to his boss for his boss's extramarital trysts. He returns the mirror to his boss. Later, he buys a new hat, and his love interest, Shirley MacLaine, pulls the same cracked mirror out of her purse so that he can see how his new hat looks. In this manner, Wilder conveys to us that the woman he loves is sleeping with his boss. This is what Wilder means by solid construction: first setting up a gag and then paying it off. A Hollywood script "needs that kind of architectural structure which is completely forgotten once you see the movie," said Wilder. "We have to put those pillars in or that beautiful ceiling is going to come crashing down."[7] Here, Wilder is echoing the advice of the earliest manuals on Hollywood screenwriting. "The art of the theater is the art of preparations," wrote one advisor to Hollywood dramatists. He advised dramatists to "place the requisite finger posts on the road he (the dramatist) would have us follow." Bordwell similarly writes of "the classical cinema's tendency for direct audience attention forward by frequent 'priming' of future events in the plot."[8] All of these references to Hollywood writing emphasize that it is an art of careful construction. The Hollywood writer primes the pump, places finger posts, introduces a gag, revisits it, and finally pays it off. In sum, the writer aims for the same balance and rhythm in story construction that the director does in shot arrangement or in continuity editing.

CRAFT THAT "MEANS" SOMETHING

The fact that classic Hollywood filmmakers liked to see themselves as craftsmen who aimed, above all, to turn out a well-crafted, nicely balanced product might lead to the supposition that their films, then, were intellectually ambitionless and that Hollywood directors were just what they said they were, solid craftsmen turning out sleek works of entertainment.

The directors themselves certainly often did little to mitigate this supposition in their interviews. Sometime they were mocking of their interlocutor's pretensions in trying to find deeper significance in their films than they intended. And yet these filmmakers, despite their unwillingness to grandstand as artists, to show off stylistically or to speechify, nevertheless held it dear to their aesthetics that every element that went into the making of the film should have a purpose, should contribute significantly to the whole of the film. Ironically, these filmmakers who so often balked at discussing the "meaning" of their film insisted over and over in their interviews that their sets and camera angles, their shot arrangements and plot elements should "mean" something, should exist for the greater good of the film and not just in themselves. This leads to a cinema where almost everything we see, even the ways in which we are led to see, "means" something. Ironically, one of the things that makes these films most artful is their repugnance toward show-offy artiness. Because they would not interrupt their stories with arty design or didactic speeches, because they insisted on speaking to us through the mechanics of the film, all of those mechanics become more meaningful. Instead of being paraded, meaning goes underground, threatening to erupt subterraneously all throughout the film.

For example, it is part of the Hollywood ethic that the shot composition should be attractive, but to a person these directors were unimpressed with shots that were simply pictorially attractive. They abhorred the strictly handsome postcard shot. Camera and shot arrangement should, William Wyler said, "make the scene more interesting." If "it doesn't help the scene it means nothing."[9] The majority of shots in a classic Hollywood film were decided, not simply for how attractive they were or for their artistic flourish, but for how much they meant, what the shots themselves said about the scene that was taking place. Hollywood shot construction, particularly in the best hands, is not only solidly handsome but significant as well. Jean Cocteau said of Orson Welles that his camera was "always placed just where destiny itself would observe its victims."[10] But he might have made the same point about many of the great Hollywood directors, whose point of view seems to so often unerringly match the mood and tenor of the scene, even if their camera angles were not quite as loud as that of Welles.

For example, if we look again at that scene from *Stagecoach*, mentioned earlier, in which John Carradine's Southern gambler eyes Lucy through the window of the saloon, we notice that Ford does several interesting things when he shoots Carradine at the gambling table within the saloon. First, we note that the shot is attractive in the way shots typically are in Ford's film. We see Carradine playing cards at the table from a slightly elevated angle that frames the image tightly. The light above the table shines on Carradine and consigns the other players to a dark frame on the outskirts of the image. The lighting is crisp, and we note Ford's attention to costume in the quality and texture of Carradine's southern gentleman garb. Simply in terms of its photographic properties, the shot is striking. The window beside him pours down sun that illuminates his part of the frame, highlighting his white hat. The light also catches the smoke that billows from his cigarette. It's typical of Ford's originality that I can't think of another scene in any Western in which a cowboy or gambler is sitting by a window, soaked in the glory of the midday sun.

But Ford seems interested in something more than just a lovely photographic shot here. Ford seems to want to say something about the character of the gambler in the way he sets up the shot of the poker table and the cuts that follow. Lucy is something of a haughty and proud woman, too good, she feels, for the ruffians with whom she shares the stagecoach. And yet she is filmed in much darker shadows than the gambler who is flooded with light normally accorded angels. This lighting is in keeping with this film's reverse moralism. In *Stagecoach* the heroes are the outcasts (the gambler, the outlaw, the prostitute, the drunk) and the villains are the upstanding citizens (the banker, the women's league of decency, Lucy herself, for most of the film).

And the smoke that rises above the gambling table seems a tangible manifestation of the gambler's misty romanticism, as he turns from seeing the lady in the window, sighs and mutters to himself, "Like a lady in the jungle." The gambler's character is rich in romanticism even before the lady arrives on the scene. He is a Southern gentleman, an aristocrat, who, soured by the war, has ditched his good name in gambling and gunplay. At this point he is simply looking for an elegant means of dying. None of this is said explicitly, but it's the beauty of Ford's cinema that it is all there in the light, in the meticulous layout of the scene, in the emphasis on the smoke. And it doesn't really matter if Ford cops to such "highfalutin" intentions in interviews or whether he was fully conscious of the significance of his scene or had fully articulated it to himself. Probably, he had not. If a director has a specific idea he is trying to get across it usually comes off as forced and didactic. More likely, Ford, with his exquisite pictorial sense, was feeling his way through a scene, trying to make it mean *something*, not mean *one* thing. That's certainly how screenwriter Edward Chodorov felt the great Hollywood directors operated. Frank Capra, he said, "couldn't explain why he shot certain sequences the way he did, no way, he just did it. Intuitive. That goes for all the great ones. John Ford? Take the scene in *The Grapes of Wrath*, where the little Okie guy has his outburst, and he says, 'you can't take this land away from us!' And he gets down and holds some of the soil in his hand, and you don't see his face. Ford can't tell you why he told his actor "keep you head down, I don't want to see your face.' Another director would have shown the face. Not Ford. And he didn't know why, he just did it."[11] Ford's unwillingness to analyze his films doesn't point to their lack of meaning but rather to his uninterest in doing anything with those scenes aside from realizing them as fully as possible. He had a great gift for intuitive mise-en-scène. Analysis bored him to death.

Under the duress of an interview with Peter Bogdanovich, Orson Welles admitted that he filmed the confrontation in *Citizen Kane* between Kane and his best friend Jed from such a low angle (floor level) because he wanted it like a "big mythical encounter between the two," but before that he says, "Oh, I don't know—I think if it doesn't explain itself, I can't explain it." Here is the ethic of the Hollywood director. The meaning of the shot is built into the shot itself, subterraneously. Welles and company put a lot of work into burying those meanings, and they were reluctant to dig them up. "I don't think a moviemaker should explain what he means. About anything," said Welles, sounding as much like a Fellini and a Bergman as the humble Hollywood craftsmen.[12] Of course Welles was Hollywood's resident artsy director, but any studio henchman tended to say the same thing when probed with questions about the meaning of his films. For all their anti-intellectualism, classic Hollywood directors shared, with more overtly artistic directors, a reluctance to pick at their movies, a satisfaction with the work they accomplished in the creative process, an unwillingness to pursue things beyond that point. The difference is, of course, that the arty director's films provoke analysis by their overt mysteries, whereas classic Hollywood films provoke our curiousness by burying their mysteries so cleverly within the confines of what seems to be a perfectly understandable film—in short by making us wonder if there is not more here than meets the eye.

UNITY

The fundamental law of Hollywood, that every element in the film should contribute in some way, should mean something, is closely linked to a second fundamental law, that every element that goes into the film should contribute in the same direction, enrich, or deepen the central story and idea of the film. Hollywood favored a brief story, in the manner of a short story, which was clearly articulated and tightly organized and had a strong, classical sense of unity. Everything that went into the film should contribute to the story or advance the film's principal theme. There should be no pointless frills. "Do not put into your story a single word or action, or bit of description, or character, or anything that does not in some direct or indirect way help or produce the effect you desire," says one scenario guide. "All the incidents of the story must be made to cluster about a single central animating idea," says another. It is this attention to the relationship between the details of the film and its purpose in general, to the film's unity, that to Jean Renoir marked Hollywood as a "classical cinema," one where "nothing is left to chance, where the smallest detail takes its place of importance in the overall psychological scheme of the film."[13]

John Huston thought of the film script as being "like an engine. Ideally everything contributes—nothing is in excess and everything works," further saying, "I feel as though I've cheated in a script unless everything has a function." He professed admiration for modern stylists like Godard, but not nearly as convincingly as he expressed his reverence for "the well-constructed screenplay, done from the inside out, from an idea, and where every line echoes that idea."[14]

Over and over again the greatest Hollywood directors and screenwriters emphasize the importance of every shot, joke, plot element contributing to the film as a whole. No shot should be so extravagant, no comic sequence so extended that they interfere with the logic and wholeness of the story. There is a cult of the rounded whole in Hollywood and a natural antipathy toward the messy and ostentatiously expressive.

Hollywood's cult of unity obviously lends itself to an art form of great symmetry. But a strong sense of unity often deepens a film's content as well. There is a curious process that occurs when these filmmakers stay as closely as they do to their subject. Often, the more they stick to a theme, the more they work a subject or motif and the more meaning they draw from it. A good sense of unity is intimately tied to a film's interpretive richness.

Hitchcock was singular in his mania for unity. If you have Mt. Rushmore in the background of one scene, he would repeatedly joke, make sure your hero is dangling from Abraham Lincoln's nose by the end of the film. Everything should be used. Nothing should be there simply as scenic backdrop. He was fond of quoting Chekov's theatrical dictum that if a rifle is hanging over the fireplace in Act I, make sure it goes off by Act III. Hitchcock would work and rework his motifs until they seemed to bubble over with meanings, perhaps even beyond those he had consciously intended.

For example, Hitchcock's film *Notorious* is about a woman with a drinking problem that has left her with a "notorious" reputation. Taking that as his keynote, Hitchcock stocks his film with references to drinking. The husband she has married in her capacity as a spy will attempt to poison her by drink. The plutonium that everyone seeks in the film is stored in wine bottles in Nazi Claude Rains's wine cellar. The film's greatest suspense sequence is built around drinking. Cary Grant needs time to investigate Claude Rains's wine cellar, where he suspects plutonium to be hidden, but the liquor is running out at the party that is taking place on the floor above him, and Ingrid Bergman's character, Alyssa, fears that the steward will soon descend to the wine cellar and discover Grant there. Alyssa starts to notice and fear every swig of champagne at her party, each sip a tiny ironic punishment for her past indiscretions. Hitchcock even builds his cameo around drinking. Once it becomes clear that the rapidly diminishing stock of champagne could represent Alyssa's doom, Hitchcock impishly bellies up to the bar and downs a glass himself, as if to merrily send her on her way to destruction.

By the time he has finished, then, Hitchcock has had great fun in playing with his drinking theme. And he has created a film with a strong sense of unity, one that is tightly knotted in its ideas—in short, a more symmetrical film than another directors would have come up with.

But these references to drinking that multiply and reflect upon themselves are there as more than markers in a well-ordered exercise. As we watch the film we can't help feeling that these references to drinking that are multiplying and reflecting upon each other add up to something. We note that although Alyssa has poisoned her life through liquor and men like Dev judge her severely for her drinking, it is through the civilized practices of morning coffee and afternoon tea that Sebastian is poisoning her. Is Hitchcock suggesting that the oppressive rituals of domestic life are more poisonous than the Bacchic liberation of drinking to excess? Dev has more or less forced Alyssa to take this spy job because he thinks she is a lost cause, a hopeless alcoholic who could never commit to a real relationship. Does her step by-step poisoning through coffee represent a kind of vicious sobering up at Dev's hands? Interpretations spring naturally from Hitchcock's films. By stockpiling references to a theme, by intensifying the unity of his film, Hitchcock also contributes to its interpretive richness. Hitchcock stuck to a few motifs or symbols, but worked them tirelessly. By keeping a tight lid on the elements of his film, he was able to draw more meaning from them, to deepen and enrich their significance.

Hitchcock's *Rear Window* is another film in which all sorts of curious themes and questions arise due to the way Hitchcock relentlessly works over his symbols and motifs. The film tells the story of an action photographer laid up with a cast from the waist down, the result of a broken leg he sustained while on assignment. With that in mind, Hitchcock set his mind to using the camera, the symbol of the man's (not to mention Hitchcock's) profession, as often as he could. Jeff, for example, uses the camera (with its telephoto lens screwed on) to spy on his neighbors, making it a symbol of his voyeurism as well as his job. Hitchcock centers his climactic action sequence around the camera with Jeff trying to ward off a nighttime intruder with his camera which he loads with flashbulbs that blind his attacker. Throughout the film, Hitchcock, famous for his lascivious jokes, places the camera, with its enormous lens, on Jeff's lap, giving it the look of a substitute phallus.

Now, with images like that it does not take long for critics to get heated up. Jeff has a prurient habit of watching scantily clad women in the windows across the way, and yet he is quite cruel and indifferent to the woman who really loves him (Grace Kelly's Lisa Fremont). These tendencies, coupled with his paralyzed state from the waist down, have led critics to see the camera as a symbol of his impotence, his tendency (like a film artist) to prize fantasy women over real ones—hence the shots of the camera in his lap. The use of his camera as a shield from an attacker provides an ironic comment on Jeff's tendency to shield himself from life with a camera and the uselessness of the camera now that real life has come knocking at his door.

Hitchcock is not on record authorizing any of these interpretations, though they have been made so recurrently as to represent standard analysis of the film. We know that Hitchcock was a complex and clever man who meticulously planned his films, so it strains credulity to argue these jokes and images just "happened" in his film. We know he had a famously lascivious sense of humor, so the camera on Jeff's lap with its telephoto lens hardly seems accidental. We know he was a keen student of the psychology of the filmgoer, so it is hard to buy that he was entirely unconscious of the ideas on voyeurism and cinema implied in his images.

On the other hand, Hitchcock did not spell out in interviews an explicit consciousness of any of these themes. He may have, to a great degree, simply followed the Hollywood doctrine of unifying the film, making disparate elements tie into its central idea. He may simply have stockpiled his motifs, complicated them and bound them together, leaving it for the critics to trace the interesting trajectories they have.

The kind of playfulness that Hitchcock exhibits in *Rear Window* has earned Hitchcock comparisons to Shakespeare, who also had an endless appetite for working and reworking the substance of his plays. Since "Julius Caesar" is by necessity a play about civil strife, the cause of Brutus's sullenness at one point in the play must be that "poor Brutus, with himself at war, forgets the shows of love to other men." The wild storm in Act II that unnerves Casca so much must be due to "civil strife in Heaven." In Hitchcock you find the same cascading of themes that you do in Shakespeare, the same mania for working and reworking motifs and seeing, in the process, what comes of them. Much of the richness of classic Hollywood film comes from this tightness of structure, this working and reworking and strengthening of themes and plot elements.

We see the same tendency in Billy Wilder to stick with his props, to return to them, work with them, make them more meaningful as the film goes along. In Billy Wilder's *The Apartment*, for example, when Jack Lemmon's character wants to coax Shirley MacLaine's character out of her suicidal funk, he does not turn to grand speeches. His character (a kind of mindless company drone, ripe for a small awakening) would not be up to that; it would be out of character. Instead, he pulls out a deck of cards. There is something rather touching and pathetic in this choice of suicide counseling. It is exactly what we would expect from this lonely bachelor whom we have already witnessed wiling away many lonely hours at night alone.

Later, when MacLaine's character arrives at Lemmon's apartment at midnight on New Year's Eve to announce that she loves him, she chooses to express her love, not in words, but by pulling out a pack of cards and starting to play gin, just as Lemmon had during her darkest hour. When Lemmon tries to speak she tells him to shut up and deal. Here too the emotions seem to be too powerful for words. When Lemmon first pulled out the cards, MacLaine had been bored and confused, as though she had no conception of how someone could find pleasure in such a bland pastime. By dealing the cards now she is telling Lemmon that she has been won over to his quieter life. She is telling him what he told her that day he dealt the cards to her: that she has plenty of time at her disposal for him, that she is not going anywhere, that she is in it for the long haul.

This is another example of what Wilder describes as good "construction." He has found a means for connecting the beginning of their relationship to its culmination. And he has linked the two moments not in words but in a concrete action, something that plays out in images, the quality material of cinema. Moreover, by avoiding words, Wilder has managed to say more. If his characters speak their love they tell us what they think, tell us what *to* think. The card game motif gives us room to observe them, interpret their actions, to chuckle over Lemmon's nebbishy but touching approach to love and later over MacLaine's slightly irritated unwillingness to admit in words that a nebbish like Lemmon has won her over.

This is what Wilder refers to when he talks of aiming for a "roundedness" in his films.

But this emphasis on sticking with, and returning to, gags or props has a greater effect than just giving the films a more solid structure. In Hollywood good construction, attention to unity engenders meaning. The more one returns to the motifs, the more they accrue meaning. The card game, through its repeated use, takes on depth and resonance, becomes a central symbol of the most important aspects of Hollywood. The good Hollywood film is like a good essay; it sticks to its thesis and makes something of it. It's not half-baked; it doesn't go wandering off, introducing things it cannot finish off. It is careful not to introduce an element unless it means something to the film in its entirety, and then, once introduced, the film returns to that element, drawing more and more meaning from it with each use, till, by the end of the film, that motif has become like an old friend to the audience.

INVISIBLE STYLE

The classical virtue that seems closest to the heart of the Hollywood film is its cult of an invisible technique, "the art," as Ovid said, "that does its art conceal." Hollywood developed its aesthetic around the ease of the viewer. Its aim was to create a technique that allowed the viewer to navigate the space of its films, to look around, with as little sense as possible that he or she was visiting an artificial world. It was as if the viewer had been fitted with an exceptionally responsive set of eyewear, one that would duplicate actual viewing with the least encumbrance possible.

Brought up in this milieu, directors were trained to value a technique that did not call attention to itself. The one consistent trait that runs throughout interviews with Hollywood filmmakers is their almost universal tendency to see themselves as craftsmen; another is their pride in a quiet, nearly invisible technique and their corresponding chagrin at extravagant technique. "Don't worry about camera angles, don't shoot up somebody's nose," Mervyn Leroy said, "or through their ears or under their arms because it doesn't mean a thing."[15] William Wyler concurred: "A lot of directors use the camera as a toy. They think it's something to play around with. You see a lamp or post sailing across the foreground for no damn reason. It doesn't help the scene; it means nothing."[16] This disdain for directors who use the camera as a toy was common among Hollywood's experienced directors. An excessively stylish cinema was, to them, a childish one. "Young people," said journeyman director Arthur Lubin, "have a tendency to shoot straight through chairs or from imposing angles."[17] John Ford complained of "kids from New York" who forget all the essentials of storytelling and instead "concentrate on this new, wonderful toy, the camera."[18]

Other directors, like Cukor and Wilder, tend to disparage excessive camera movement as a kind of provincialism or bad taste. "I never set up the camera to astonish," says Wilder. "In France they call it *epater le bourgeoisie*, to astonish the middle classes. 'Boy, do I have a setup going to shoot through the fireplace with the flames in the foreground.' I don't do that because I think this is from the point of view of Santa Claus."[19] Still others saw, in excesses of style, the mark of ambition, not art. "To be a show-off may be an enormous accelerating factor in one's career," said director Michael Gordon, "but I have serious doubts that it contributes to an artistic achievement."[20]

Over and over again, the most successful Hollywood directors and its journey-men alike stress that a shot has to "mean' something, that it has to have a "reason," that it has to be tied into a point of view, to be anchored within the narrative. It was part of these filmmakers' notion of professionalism that their shot should serve the purposes of the film, contribute to its overall energy and movement. Neither shots nor directors should call attention to themselves. "I despise doing fancy-shmancy shots," Wilder said. "I cannot stand it. If anybody in the middle of a picture suddenly grabs his partner's knees and say, 'Ooooooh, look at that setup!' then the picture is dead to me because he knows that there was a setup."[21] Artistic shots result in a level of consciousness, on the viewer's part, that is horrifying to the Hollywood filmmaker, aiming as he is that the viewer be totally immersed in the story and its characters. Arty shots result in a less moving experience, a less memorable film.

And arty or expressive shots lose their power in proportion to how much they are used. Wilder felt that inserts were "a tremendous thing unless you blow it right from the beginning and you just waste it—like playing a trump card too early."[22] Hawks detested an excessive use of close-ups and advised using them "only for absolute punctuation . . . you save it—not like TV where they do everything in close-up."[23] Classic Hollywood is an art of reserve. What makes it boring to some is the same thing that makes it appealing to others. On the one hand, it seems rather static and inexpressive compared to the art fare that came in its wake. On the other hand, it attracts us by keeping its most stunning tricks in reserve. One of the most graceful aspects of the Hollywood craft is the way it holds its fire.

Wilder chose where his camera would go according to how "economical it was for the telling of the story." But not monkeying around with the camera too much was economical for production reasons as well, like Wilder said: "Every time you move the camera, you lose time. If you move lights it's half an hour or forty-five minutes, sometimes longer if it's a complex shot. So, I try to accomplish as much as possible with one shot."[24] Clever technique often leads to waste, waste in narrative economy, waste in audience involvement, waste of production time. John Ford took great pride that he didn't shoot more film than he needed. ("Film is very expensive and I hate to waste it—I was brought up that way.")[25] The hurried process of the Hollywood studios could be inhuman, inhospitable to creativity, and productive of some pretty mediocre films, but the efficiency of the process is also linked to the efficiency, the classical simplicity of its best product. There was an ethos in Hollywood that avoided waste at all costs. Efficiency of production led to a light, airy product. Technique got out of the way, and much of Hollywood's disarming charm is due to its simple directness, the way its stories unfold with ease and without pretension.

It's striking how many of the really great Hollywood filmmakers had the film shot, edited, and planned in their head. It was a point of pride for many of them to note how few meters of film were left over after production, partly so that editors wouldn't be able to monkey around with the film when they got it but partly also out of the Hollywood craftsman's pride in his light touch. William Wellman disparaged four-walled sets and shooting for a lot of coverage. He felt that a simplicity in production led to a simple elegance in the film. He tells one story that has the air of being apocryphal, but is telling nonetheless, of John Ford calling him up one day and running down both Wellman's last films and his own (Ford's) for being too artsy. "We're beginning to get too tricky. Moving the camera too much. You're doing it more than I am. So let's stop it," Ford supposedly said to Wellman. Ford, Wellman said, went on to invoke their old days working together at Fox on Tom Mix and Buck Jones Westerns: "Let's do what we used to do. Make the picture the simplest, easiest, nicest, most quietest [sic], most natural way, you can make it and stop all this stuff. Do you agree with me?' I said, 'One hundred percent.' And I've never been on a dolly since."[26]

The Hollywood director takes pride in simplicity, in quiet technique, and in not succumbing to the lure of the dolly, to the temptation of moving the camera too much. The less the camera moved, the greater the story communicated itself. "When people stand still, the camera should stand still," said Warner Brothers director Irving Rapper. "I let the actors come to the camera if possible, " said another Warner Brothers veteran, Vincent Sherman.[27] Hollywood is a calculating art. Most often the camera doesn't track the action. It isn't so spontaneous. The Hollywood camera knows what's going to happen. The mise-en-scène is set up according to it, not vice versa. It doesn't like to have to go chasing after things. The Hollywood camera records with the quiet dignity of a power that refuses to exert itself unceremoniously. As Welles said, the camera regards the action it records from the point of view of destiny.

George Cukor also tried to avoid the kind of waste that comes from excess of technique. He liked to get as much out of one shot as possible. Cukor cited as among his favorite scenes the long telephone scene in George Stevens's *Place in the Sun*, "where the camera never moved and there was no cut," as well as a scene in his own *The Marrying Kind*, where he "did almost a whole reel where there was no movement at all for the camera, and none of the characters moved. But the scene was good—and it had two fascinating actresses—so then you don't have to do all kinds of tricks." Cukor was expert at imprinting an actor's presence on the screen and arrived at a kind of minimalist technique that interfered least with gaining that imprint. For him, cinema's powers were to be coaxed out of moments of stillness and were chased away by frantic technique. Like Wilder, Cukor felt that "the director and his camera work should not intrude on the story," but whereas Wilder, the strict constructionist, emphasized the virtues of economical storytelling, Cukor emphasized the emotional payoff when the technique stays quiet: "One can do very dazzling tricks—dazzling beauty and pyrotechnics—but unless the human heart is there I don't think it goes very deep."[28]

A good story, with characters who you are worried about, a film that engages the viewers' feelings—these were the goals that Cukor, Capra, and Wilder pursued and which they felt were a great deal more difficult to arrive at, if less obvious in their effect, than showy technique. Showy technique, they felt, was the quickest way to get oohs and aahs from people who didn't know much about real filmmaking but was, in the end, detrimental in creating a film that left a lasting impression or offered a rich experience.

—— 6 ——

Hollywood: An Art of Silence and Ellipses

A central aspect of Hollywood's classicism is its quiet elegance and gift for under-statement. This understatement is a consequence, in many ways, of Hollywood's respect, even in the sound era, for the principles of silent filmmaking.

It has become a truism to say that the silent era represents the era of purest filmmaking in Hollywood. And yet there are still a good many people who are puzzled by the idea of taking silent filmmaking seriously. Silent film seems to them laughably primitive, replete with wildly melodramatic plots and imbecilic overacting. But silent film does need to be understood, not only in itself, as representing a golden age of Hollywood, but also for the influence it exercises on Hollywood in the sound era as well. The filmic principles of the silent era represented an ideal that Hollywood continued to emulate long after sound had arrived on the scene.

Hollywood's cult of understatement and suggestiveness dates back to the silent era, during which the goal was to communicate to an audience as much as possible without recourse to words and explanations, to make the audience actively read the visuals. Contrary to the notion of silent filmmaking as childish and primitive in technique, silent film actually made greater demands on the audience. The audience had to pay more careful attention to the screen, read the visuals more actively. "You couldn't turn away from the screen as much," said King Vidor, "When sound first came in, that's when popcorn and all the drinks started, and necking in the theater, because you could turn away and do all sorts of things and still hear. You wouldn't miss anything."[1] Words allowed filmmakers to spell out their ideas more tediously. Silent film audiences were attentive, forced to rake the screen for visual clues. Sound film audiences' eyes were free to wander from the screen. The films became a smaller part of the filmgoing experience.

At the same time, as I've mentioned earlier, the drama of the transition from silent to sound can be overstated. For the most part, the personnel and the narrative strategy of the Hollywood film industry remained constant during the transition from silents to sound, and even within the first couple of years of sound film the greatest filmmakers were continuing to innovate visually and, now, aurally as well. And the silent film tradition continued to exert great influence on Hollywood technique, even after the advent of sound. Most of the great filmmakers aimed to live up to the visual standards of the silent era. What made silents great is at the heart of what made Hollywood sound films great as well. Showing rather than telling, making the audience active viewers, making them figure things out for themselves rather than explaining those things to them didactically—these are the great virtues of silent cinema, and they remain the great virtues of Hollywood, even after the arrival of sound.

Hitchcock's greatest sound films, for example, are characterized by huge swaths of silence. He favored scenarios such as a man peeping on his neighbors (*Rear Window*) and a man following a woman all day (*Vertigo*) that negated the possibility of speech and forced, or allowed, him to speak to his audience through his camera rather than through his characters' dialogue. Truffaut described *Psycho* as "a half-silent movie; there are at least two reels with no dialogue at all."[2] *Rear Window*, with its peeping on neighbors from a great distance, even allowed Hitchcock, in a sense, to return to silent filmmaking. We can only watch—we can't really hear—the stories unfold in the apartments that Jeff watches across the back courtyard of his building. And because the actors are so far away they tend to use the clear, deliberate gestures of the silent film actor in order to make themselves understood. Arranging shots through the medium of Jeff's telephoto lens also allowed Hitchcock to pay homage to the iris effect of silent films, in which the image is viewed through a circle surrounded by darkness. In *Rear Window*, Hitchcock had arrived, through the story of a man peeping on neighbors from afar, at a means of shooting a variety of small silent films within his film.

And many of Hitchcock's greatest sequences are set pieces of silent filmmaking: the murder and cleanup of the murder in *Psycho*, the cornfield scene in *North by Northwest*, and the climax at Royal Albert Hall in the second *The Man Who Knew Too Much*, just to name a few of the more well-known. Sometimes the principal purpose of Hitchcock's films seems simply to arrive at those points of climax where he can return to the purity of silent cinema. And when Hitchcock's cinema does go silent we know we have arrived at an important moment in the film.

But it was not just set pieces that were silent in Hitchcock's films. He tried whenever he could to communicate to viewers through images, to reduce his films to the simple and fundamental communication of silent film. The goal, for example, of the early sequence in *Rear Window* in which Hitchcock's camera pans over a sleeping Jeff's apartment is purely expository. Its goal is to introduce Jeff's profession and the accident that led to his being bedridden. But rather than reduce this exposition to a static dialogue, Hitchcock takes us on a visual tour of Jeff's apartment, letting the apartment speak for itself. Time and again, Hitchcock seeks to translate even the most fundamental aspects of his stories into visual images that need to be actively read by the viewer.

By speaking to his audience visually, rather than verbally, Hitchcock cultivated a more alert audience and a cinema that was more charged in physical detail. Sequences like this represent a kind of pleasureful puzzle or game. Since they are silent and all information is communicated visually, the audience has to work a little: it has to pay attention to, and assemble, the information Hitchcock provides it. "That's the great trick in any enterprise that looks for public acceptance—make the public work," said Allan Dwan, veteran director of many silent films. "If you do all the work for them they sit there bored to death."[3]

At the same time, Hitchcock's sequences of silent exposition are carefully calibrated challenges. Hitchcock knew how far to go with his audience. Early on in his career he had learned how easily visual puns that had seemed apparent in production slipped by unnoticed in the rapid experience of viewing a film. Hitchcock's silent sequences are laid out very carefully, with large, clearly delineated units of information. "Just aim slightly above their head and they're going to get it," Billy Wilder said of the audience. "Make it clear to them, but don't spell it out like they're a bunch of idiots."[4] This is a fairly good summary of what Hitchcock does in his films, which represent that classical balance between clarity and understatement. In Hitchcock's films, the audience plays a game that, due to its great emphasis on images rather than words, is always challenging but, because of its great visual clarity, is always a pleasureful challenge.

CONVEYING THOUGHT

A nice by-product of a cinema that tries, whenever possible, to be silent is that it makes the audience curious about what its actors are thinking, rather than spelling out those thoughts explicitly. An audience watching a silence sequence, like those we find in Hitchcock, is not just sorting through the clues that the director has left them as to the meaning of the scene but also scrutinizing the actors' faces, trying to fathom their thoughts, figuring out what they are up to. "When you can make an actor sit dead still and think of something and have the audience know what he's thinking, you've got a hit," said Dwan. "If an actor can do that, he's a great actor, and that's what [director D.W.] Griffith's girls learned to do. These little movements they made and the silences that followed—you knew what they were thinking, what their problem was, and your heart went out to them."[5] According to Dwan, we feel most deeply for the Gish sisters in Griffith's films, not when they are acting or when they are talking, but when they are thinking, in those "little silences" after the action, after the gesture. There is something very intimate about reading someone's thoughts. It is in those moments that we are most actively engaged in the text of the film, penetrating most deeply into the feelings of the person and the film.

This is why my students hush up the most when I show them the purely silent sequence in *Rear Window* in which Miss Lonelyhearts entertains an imaginary suitor. They are struggling to puzzle things out, figure out what she is up to. "Is this all in her mind," they ask themselves. "Oh, she can't hold on the illusion any more," they say to themselves as she slumps to the table in despair at the end of the sequence. "Give them some person they can worry about and you've got them," said Capra.[6] The more we try to puzzle out a character's thoughts in a film, the more invested we are in the character and in the film. The quieter and more visual a director is with the audience, the more deeply involved the audience becomes in the psychology and drama of the film.

It is interesting to observe an audience watching people think on the screen. The audience tends even to instinctively mimic the emotions they are witnessing in their own faces, so wholly do they enter into those emotions. Hitchcock understood this. As famous as he is for his subjective, point-of-view shots, where we look through the eyes of a character at an object, these shots work so well because they are carefully edited with reaction shots. We may look through Scottie's eyes while he watches Madeleine doing something mysterious and confusing in *Vertigo*, but it is not until Hitchcock cuts back to Scottie's reaction shot that we know what to do with that subjective information. If, in the reaction shot, Scottie looks confused we think to ourselves "what's up"; if he narrows his eyes in understanding we start racing our minds, trying to figure out what he has figured out. Often these emotions that we are mimicking will be traced in our face. These are the silences after the action that Dwan refers to as being so important, the moments where we are most psychically engaged with the film. And whereas Dwan emphasizes the importance of good actors, actors who can convey their thoughts, in making these moments occur, Hitchcock reminds us of the importance of the director's part in making these moments register. His careful and intelligent use of reaction shots makes his films particularly rich in thoughts we can read and emotions we can infer.

Hitchcock was tickled by the power of the reaction shot and enjoyed immensely how he could use it to make his audience identify with his villains—thereby advancing one of his most clearly articulated themes: the relativity of evil. In *Psycho*, for example, Hitchcock shoots the sinking of Marion Crane's car (with her body in the trunk) from Norman Bates's point of view. For a moment, the car appears to stop sinking into the bog. Hitchcock cuts to Norman for a reaction shot that conveys alarm. Hitchcock well understood that for a moment we identify with Norman's concern so wholly that we are rooting for him to get away with murder. We throw our morals out the window when we enter as intimately into someone's consciousness as we do in movies. We are too much who they are at that point to judge them.

Similarly, in Hitchcock's *Notorious* we viscerally experience the grief of Claude Raines' character, the Nazi Sebastian, the morning he slowly realizes that his wife is a spy, because Hitchcock charts this progress through a carefully laid out sequence of point of view shots. After entering into so many of Sebastian's thoughts, seeing so many things through his eyes, as he discovers his wife's deceit, we would have to be heartless not to feel sympathy for the man. We lose sight of the fact that he is a Nazi. We are too caught up in his thoughts, his humiliations. We are too much "him" to have a moral distance from him. Such is the power of film to make us read characters' thoughts and, in reading those thoughts, identify deeply with that character. And that identification with a character is fostered in a silent cinema, where the characters do not speak to us but, rather, simply look and think, thus inviting us into their consciousness and into a much more intimate relationship with them.

GOING SILENT AT KEY MOMENTS

Hollywood's veneration of silent filmmaking is evident in its habit of turning to silence at the moments of greatest intensity in its films. Ironically, when classic Hollywood wants to be most eloquent it clams up. This tendency flies in the face of the more common tendency in art to underline or grandly announce drama, as, for example, the loud musical flourish that scores a moment of great passion or violence. Hollywood was certainly often capable of this kind of overstatement. The history of Hollywood musical soundtracks is not a subtle story; check out, for example, what Stanley Cavell referred to as the "nonstop Wagnerama" of *King Kong*.[7] But the greatest filmmakers knew that the best way to treat their film's moments of greatest intensity was through a quiet counterpoint.

The sequence in John Ford's *My Darling Clementine*, for example, in which Doc Holliday (played by Victor Mature) operates on his dance hall girlfriend (Linda Darnell) is one of the most evocative scenes in the film, and it is so, in great measure, because of its silence. The shot is classic Ford. The operation is an impromptu affair in the back of a saloon. Ford floods the makeshift operation table with light, surrounded by several lanterns meant to help the doctor. But Ford buries the action of the operation deep in the saloon and shoots if from afar. The light of the operation represents a small chiaroscuro affair amid the great darkness of the shut down tavern. A line of cowboys darkly silhouetted in the midrange of the shot seals off the operating table from the rest of the saloon.

The quiet and discretion of the image is matched by the quiet of the soundtrack. No one talks; the scene is presided over by a silence punctuated now and then with pained murmurs of the girl and the barely audible consolations of the old woman who is nursing her. There is no soundtrack music. The sounds that really register with us are the distant whoops and hollers from another saloon some distance away. The quiet reminder of life going on quite indifferently in proximity to the operation is a much more effective means of making us feel the drama of the event than any dramatic dialogue or music meant to underscore the scene's drama would be. One of Ford's most recurrent complaints about the studio system was the large orchestral music they slapped on his films. He tended to prefer tucking in a folk song here and there. "Generally," he said, "I hate music in pictures—a little bit now and then, at the end or the start. . . . I don't like to see a man alone in the desert, dying of thirst, with the Philadelphia Orchestra behind him."[8]

George Stevens also had a tendency to let us know which parts of his film were most important by treating them with a kind of hushed reverence. He is unique among Hollywood directors in his ability, and willingness, to slow down the pace of his films, to create scenes that are as quiet as they are deliberate, so quiet that they waken our senses to all sorts of tiny, charming detail.

For example, the sequence of scenes in which the nervous young couple in *Penny Serenade* (played by Cary Grant and Irene Dunne) brings their new baby home from the orphanage stretches nearly 20 minutes, and in the course of this sequence there is almost no dialogue. A highlight in this sequence is the scene in which Dunne's inexperienced mother tries to give her baby its first bath, while her husband and several of his employees watch. The scene is a marvel of patience, as Dunne struggles with the elaborate bathing contraption she has brought home with the baby, while the inert men about her watch with the impassivity of cattle, slowly reducing her to a nervous wreck. The only sound is the periodic cracking of walnut shells that one of the men is eating. Each time this sharp sound cracks, Dunne's tension ratchets up one notch. As in the scene from *My Darling Clementine*, Stevens uses sound here, not for dialogue, but as an adjunct to silence, almost as a way to make the silence more tangible.

Directors often turn to silent filmmaking at the end of their films in an effort to finish with the greatest resonance. In *The Long Voyage Home*, for example, Ford finishes the film with a scene in which a sailor reads a newspaper, then sadly lets its drop into the harbor where his boat is docked. The camera tracks the newspaper in the water, where we read the paper's headline. The headline informs us of the sinking of a ship that we had seen depart from the docks the previous evening and which we know carried with it one of the film's central characters, Driscoll, played by Thomas Mitchell. We read the headline as the paper lands in the water. Ford then cuts to a close-up of the newspaper trapped under a boat, submerged under water. The headline is just barely visible through the thickness of the water, suggesting the drowning it describes. The final image of the film is a silhouette of the sailor who has just dropped the paper. He is the only one of Driscoll's friends (who are humming about the deck) to know of Driscoll's fate. He bows his head in sadness and Ford finishes the film with a technique right out of silents, a slowly diminishing iris effect on the sailor that closes to darkness. Here, as in *My Darling Clementine*, Ford chooses silence to convey his moment of greatest sentiment. At his most dramatic moments he doesn't trust words to get his point across. There is a hushed reverence in the silent film tradition that accords better to the depth of emotion he's trying to convey.

The end to Ford's *Searchers* is one of his greatest endings, in no small part because of its silence. A film that has been characterized by a great deal of vicious emotion concludes with a lyrical sequence that is all image and music, something right out of the silent film era. The film's final dialogue is in the penultimate scene of the film, a comic one in which Ward Bond's character, Reverend Captain Samuel Johnston Clayton, has to submit to the indignity of getting the wound in his buttocks treated. The comic sequence sets up the quiet dignity of the film's final sequence nicely. The final sequence takes about 2 minutes and has no dialogue. Its second half is scored to the gentle folk song, "Song of the Searchers." Here Ford manages to escape the Philadelphia Orchestra. The scene describes the conclusion of the quest of Ethan Edwards (played by John Wayne) to return a girl stolen by Indians to her family. The final shot of the film is a long take shot, from within a cabin through a backlit doorway that opens up to a Western landscape dominated by blue sky. This kind of shot, from within a dark cabin out into an expansive landscape, is a trademark Ford shot and never more so than in this film that stresses the vulnerability of the family to the violence of the West. The shot is lovely in its composition, with the doorway framing two porch columns, one on the left and one on the right, which, in turn, frame the old couple who will care for the girl waiting for her in the doorway. The old couple, in turn, frame John Wayne, one on either side of him as he carries the girl to them. The scene, despite Ford's dusty cowboys and naturalistic lighting, is ritualistic and idealized. Nothing in real life happens quite this elegantly and with such exquisite balance.

The old man and woman take the daughter in their arms and scurry her into the darkness of the cabin, leaving Wayne framed by the doorway. He has to move aside though to let Laurie Jorgensen, played by Vera Miles, pass. She has run out to collect her boyfriend, Martin, played by Jeffrey Hunter. Martin had accompanied Ethan on his search for the girl. Martin comes up from behind Ethan, and the young couple whisk by Ethan, with eyes only for each other; Ethan is now left completely alone again and still silhouetted in the doorway. The sequence has a melancholy feel as Ethan watches these two reunions, while everyone seems to forget his presence. Wayne, then, tiredly rubs his left arm with his right, as though the aches of the voyage were just starting to be felt. Wayne has often commented on how he picked up this gesture from Harry Carey, who used it to humanize the cowboy heroes of his silent oaters. Wayne, still framed by the doorway, turns and walks away deep into the frame and deep into that vast, expansive Fordian Western landscape.

The doorway frame, which removes a third of the screen on each side, creates a kind of iris effect reminiscent of silent movies, reinforced by Ford's reference to his silent films with Harry Carey. These last two silent minutes of the film represent a kind of homage to silent film. Like so many other great directors, Ford turned to silence when he really had something to say.

SILENCE AND SEX SCENES

Scenes depicting sex often elicited some of Hollywood's loveliest silent and suggestive technique, because, in these instances, filmmakers were not allowed to show certain things and had to suggest them instead. This has led some to emphasize the beneficent influence of the code on Hollywood technique. However, even before the code Hollywood was in the habit of expressing its most intense moments with its quietest and most elliptical technique. The code, however, did, in many ways, play to Hollywood's strength—a tendency toward the elliptical and suggestive rather than the explicit. Sex scenes brought out an expressiveness and ingenuity in the best Hollywood filmmakers.

In George Stevens's *Penny Serenade*, for example, Cary Grant and Irene Dunne get married in a rush, in the middle of the night on New Year's Eve, because Grant has been called to Japan for his work as a journalist. They hurry to his train, where they will have 3 minutes to say goodbye. Their wedding night will have to be postponed. Dunne sees him to his stateroom, and we watch them embracing through a door half-closed to hide them from the nosy attention of the train conductors. Dunne's friends wait for her outside the train, but as Dunne and Grant embrace, the train starts to move and the door, swinging under the volition of the moving train, slowly closes.

Stevens cuts to a close-up, from outside, of the snow-encrusted, fogged-up window of the couple's stateroom, then to a shot of the window from the inside. The train is now in motion. The window is slightly open, and through the opening we can see a road sign with an arrow pointing in the direction opposite to the train and reading, "New York, 113 miles," giving us a fairly precise idea of how long they have traveled since the train left New York and, hence, how long their honeymoon has lasted. The train comes to a halt at a station where Grant and Dunne have finally allowed themselves to part. The couple emerges from the train and falls into one last embrace in the snowfall of the night. Stevens shows a certain reverence for the couple's lovemaking by keeping the scene silent. As they embrace we only hear the bells of the train clanging and then the surge of the engine. Grant climbs back on the train, and they exchange words, but they are so distant as to be almost inaudible—as was true of their exchange in the stateroom before they made love. The scene, characterized by a reverence for silence and an indifference to dialogue, represents a lovely example of the elliptical way in which Hollywood was forced to convey sex and also how that requirement converged so well with Hollywood's artistic principles anyway.

A lighter example of how Hollywood would often go silent when dealing with sex comes from Gregory LaCava's *Fifth Avenue Girl*. In this film, character great Walter Connelly plays one of screwball comedy's stock characters, the weary scion of a wealthy Manhattan family, tired of his wife and children's spoiled excesses. He hires Ginger Rogers to pose as his mistress in order to provoke concern on his family's part. The plan is that his society-addicted wife (prone to her own romantic dalliances) will reawaken to her role as a wife and that his ne'er-do-well son will step up to his responsibilities in the family business when he sees his father neglecting that business for a young floozy. The plan works marvelously, and the film culminates in a touching scene where Connelly's character, Mr. Borden, and his wife (played by Vera Teasdale) reunite over a beef stew in the servants' kitchen. The stew had been referred to throughout the film as a kind of symbol for the plain satisfaction of their domesticity before they were wealthy. They had, in the early years of their marriage, often eaten alone, like this, in the kitchen. Everything about the evening suggests that the middle-aged couple has regained the romance of their youth and that the evening will culminate in a sexual rapprochement as well. But, that night, Ginger Rogers's character, Mary Grey, cracks under the pressure of the role she has been playing and reveals the ruse to the whole family.

His wife in particular is furious at the deception. Mr. Borden's plans, and his hopes for that evening, seem to be dashed.

Rogers's confession takes place in the foyer of the Borden mansion. And after she has let the cat out of the bag, Connelly begins to mechanically climb the long winding staircase of his mansion up to his bedroom, mumbling pathetically to himself all the way. He seems in one fell swoop to have been consigned again to his role of the subservient husband, the mule of the household. The wife follows him upstairs, a picture of imperious disdain. When they reach the top of the staircase they part ways, the shell-shocked husband to his bedroom, the indignant wife to hers. The camera follows the husband. But as Mr. Borden, still mumbling dejectedly, opens his bedroom door, he hears his wife call his name. He walks toward her bedroom. Her door is open but she is no longer on screen. LaCava shoots Connelly, from some distance, standing before the open door of his wife's bedroom. Connelly is a small figure in a large grand hallway, staring confusedly at an open door. But as he looks in the doorway, Connelly's posture changes. He looks away sheepishly, with a shy smile. His body language, despite the bulk of Connelly's fifty-some years at the time, becomes that of a shy schoolboy who has just been embarrassed by praise, who is tickled pink but can't make eye contact. He slowly shuffles into the room, quietly shutting the door behind him. The beef stew has done the trick after all.

It has become something of a cliché to praise scenes like this as examples of Hollywood's great discretion in sexual matters. Hollywood films didn't have to show sex, as, the cliché goes, they were subtle enough to suggest it and leave the rest to our imagination. It's a refrain constantly heard from contemporary moralists, shocked at the explicitness of films today and nostalgic for a more tasteful cinema. And there is a great deal of truth to this attitude. Scenes like the ones just described point to a certain tastefulness as being one of the qualities Hollywood can chalk up on the assets column.

But these scenes also have more going for them than just good taste. There is, for example, a hushed reverence in the way Stevens plays the love scene in *Penny Serenade*. The loveliness and solemnity of the event are, paradoxically, amplified by the quiet way in which the couple's lovemaking is alluded to. It's the opposite of the approach that tries to make us experience the high drama of a love scene through dramatic music, gestures, or words. It's a technique that quiets itself as things get more serious, that recognizes the almost mathematical rule that the more powerful a subject, the less should be said. The filmmaker's job here is not to intensify but to quiet the drama, to let the gentle solemnity of the event speak for itself. The best Hollywood films avoid a base explicitness in matters of sex, but even more importantly they steer clear of the puffed-up drama and tired clichés that sex scenes engender.

The example from *Fifth Avenue Girl* speaks to another aspect of Hollywood's attitude toward sex—one of humor. The teasing, elliptical way in which Hollywood alludes to sex is the result of a cinema that tends toward a humorous, lighthearted attitude toward sex in general. One of the original aspects of Hollywood treatment of sex scenes is that it incorporates humor into its sexuality, that it acknowledges humor might be a vital aspect of sexuality. For all of it childlike innocence, Hollywood often strikes a breezy, sophisticated attitude toward sex that can only be described as adult.

Lauren Bacall's scenes with Humphrey Bogart in *To Have and Have Not*, for example, are often thought of as the epitome of a certain bygone Hollywood sexiness. We know the reasons why scenes between Bacall and Bogart work. Partly it's Bacall's natural star quality, a quality that leapt from the screen in her first picture. Part of it is the chemistry between her and Bogart, who were falling in love in reality at the same time as they were on the screen. Part of it is the glamor of the Hollywood film: Casey Roberts's exotic sets and Sid Hickox's rich noir lighting, among others. Another reason is the opaque dialogue Hawks specialized in. Steve and Slim engage in an unusually lengthy romantic repartee the night they meet, but good luck finding any explicit reference to their ostensible subject matter: her sexual experience and their desire to sleep together.

But a principal reason why these scenes are so sexually charged is the humor with which these two banter. They never let themselves get moony, never stoop to romantic cliché. It's a matter of pride among Hawks's characters, even when their ardor is plain as day, to never let themselves act the fool. In fact, the less they cop to the ardor, the more it tends to pronounce itself and the more their partner tends to appreciate it. Hollywood, at its best, avoids heavy-handedness in sex; it refuses to take itself too seriously. It doesn't strain to make us experience the monumental gravity of romance and sex. It avoids dramatic tone. It has a light touch.

Moreover, we are struck by the cleverness of the way Hollywood dealt with sex. When directors like Stevens and LaCava approached their sex scenes, they seemed to realize that they were at one of those points where the clichés might run as thick as mud. Sex scenes seemed to ignite the inventiveness of the best Hollywood directors, to challenge them to do it in a way that hadn't been done before. Tough guys that so many of these directors were, they were determined to avoid treacle, and so sex scenes led to some of their deftest and cleverest structure. For Hawks, the sex scene elicited the indirect, or "three cushioned," dialogue for which he's famous, but in Stevens's and LaCava's films it leads to three-cushioned mise-en-scène. We smile in appreciation when Walter Connelly trails his wife off to the bedroom, not just because LaCava was discreet, but because he found a clever, quiet way of making his point and of dealing with the oldest subject in the book. He got by the whole thing nicely. We often chuckle to ourselves when watching a scene like that in a Hollywood film, saying to ourselves, "Nicely done." We appreciate the discretion but also the ingenuity. It requires inventiveness to take all the heavy baggage that accompanies sex and transform it into something light, nimble, and charming. It's often emphasized how discreet Hollywood was, how it delicately managed to avoid the explicit. It is sometimes underestimated how many of these scenes are technically clever or ingenious. Whereas so many pedestrian films see romantic scenes as an opportunity to be monumentally serious and dramatic, to inject great turbo blasts of intense emotion, Hollywood often saw them as an opportunity for structural cleverness.

SILENT FILM AND ELLIPSIS: CHAPLIN, LUBITSCH, AND HITCHCOCK

Silent film ingrained in its practitioners a tendency to show what they meant rather than say it, no small part of what made films visually clever in the sound era as well as the silent era. But there is another tendency, developed in silent film, that is a big part of what makes Hollywood great, in both the silent and the sound eras, and that is a tendency toward the elliptical in exposition. Silent filmmakers, constrained always to a kind of pantomime, developed an efficient communication, one that aimed to convey the maximum of information with the minimum number of signs and images. The best filmmakers became adept at suggesting as much as they were at showing, of indicating things that were occurring in the gaps or interstices of their narrative.

If there is a key progenitor of this style of Hollywood filmmaking in which a little information is left out, an ellipses left for the audience to fill, it has to be Charlie Chaplin. Chaplin sometimes suffers by comparison to silent film's great stylists. He certainly did not have the lush visual style of Murnau or Von Stroheim. There was a period in the 1960s and 1970s when cinephiles took great pride in preferring the much more innovative technique of Buster Keaton to that of Chaplin, which they felt was static and too closely linked to stage performance. Chaplin can't compete with Keaton's wildly large-scale shots or the extravagant visual conceits Keaton came up with that stretched the nature of the medium. On the other hand, few can compare with Chaplin in the quietly deft use to which he put the medium. Chaplin's art is one of charming ellipticalness.

In the beginning of *The Kid*, for example, Charlie first appears promenading in an anonymous city's back alleys, strutting in his best lord of the manor mode, dodging from time to time garbage dumped from windows above. When he comes upon an abandoned baby in the alley, he looks perplexed and then casts a glance up at an upper floor window of the building before which the child lies. The audience is left to read his thoughts. Charlie, a simpleminded fellow at times, and prone to literal interpretations, is thinking, we realize, that someone has discarded the child with the garbage. In this moment Charlie does what Hollywood does best. He creates an ellipsis and asks the audience to fill it. He makes a joke that requires the audience to finish it off.

When Charlie comes home with the baby, several of the poverty-stricken house-wives who inhabit his part of the city gather around him and ask the baby's name. Charlie looks at the camera with a brief expression of confusion. He quickly enters a building nearby and then returns with a confident answer, "John." I find that my students (who can be excellent and attentive in reading this film) have often not reflected on or processed this gag; it's so small and goes by so quickly. Obviously, Charlie hadn't given a moment's thought to the child's name—or even its sex up to this point. (The tramp is not prone to a great deal of forethought.) Once the question arises, he discreetly steps into the building's foyer to check the baby's sex and, with admirable decisiveness, names the baby in a matter of seconds. No baby name books for Charlie. In this manner, Chaplin manages to bury, offscreen, both an off-color moment (checking the baby's sex) and the point of his gag (his charming insouciance). The gag is built around an ellipsis that the audience has to fill. *The Kid* is chock-full of these moments, big and small; it's Chaplin's preferred mode of communication. He loved scatological humor and off-color references to the workings of the body, but he tended to avoid coarseness by framing his humor in these discrete, elliptical ways that were as charming as they were bawdy.

Hitchcock often referred to one sequence from Chaplin's *The Pilgrim* as an archetype for what he, Hitchcock, saw as the best kind of filmmaking, one that was creative and efficient. "The opening shot," as Hitchcock describes it, "was the outside of a prison gate. A guard came out and posted a Wanted notice. Next cut: a very tall, thin man coming out of a river, having had a swim. He finds that his clothes are missing and have been replaced with a convict's uniform. Next cut: a railroad station, and coming toward the camera, dressed as a parson with the pants too long, is Chaplin. Now there are three pieces of film, and look at the amount of story they are told."[9] This is efficient filmmaking. Chaplin only gives us the information that we need. The rest he leaves for us to fill in. The result is a cinema that is spare and light but rich in suggestiveness. Chaplin has calculated how much he can get us to fill in the blanks, how much he can use our deductive skills to fill in his gaps rather than waste time filling in the gaps himself. And it's the deductive work involved that makes the scene funny. We don't laugh just because Charlie looks funny in his outfit; we also laugh because we have figured out how he came to get those clothes. We've put together the coordinates of information Chaplin has provided us and figured out his joke. One of the pleasures of Chaplin's cinema is this steady stream of little delights the film provides, tiny little comic riddles that we have the pleasure of solving. The laughter of a crowd at a Chaplin film has its own distinct sound. It has a note of self-discovery to it, a sense of arriving at an understanding. It seems, constantly, to express the happy thought, "Oh, I get it."

The heir to Chaplin's charming ellipticalness is Ernst Lubitsch (Photo 2), who was famously stunned by his viewing of Chaplin's *A Woman in Paris* and who also became a kind of touchstone for Hollywood filmmakers on how to construct a sequence. Billy Wilder had the sentence, "How would Lubitsch do it," embroidered and framed on his office wall at Paramount. He thought of Lubitsch as always having a "solution" for narrative tangles, as always being able to express himself both efficiently and cleverly. It is remarkable how often directors, when struggling to explain or sum up the Hollywood craft in interviews, would turn to a sequence from a Lubitsch film to explain what they meant. It seemed easier to cite a Lubitsch sequence than to struggle to convey the ineffability of the art. Lubitsch was an iconic figure in Hollywood, the director's director, whose art was, for many, the definition of the art of Hollywood.

Photo 2. Ernst Lubitsch, the director's director and master of the elliptical. Courtesy of Photofest.

Billy Wilder, for example, liked to cite the scene in Lubitsch's *The Merry Widow*, which opens up in the bedroom of the king of Marshovia (George Barbier), with the king snuggling with his young, pretty wife (Una Merkel). The king dresses for the day and leaves the bedroom. On the way out he salutes the young guard, Count Danilo (Maurice Chevalier), who protects the bedroom. Danilo clicks his heels in response. The king safely out of sight, Chevalier casually enters the bedroom. The camera does not; it respectfully remains outside the bedroom doors. But the king has forgotten his sword and soon returns to the bedroom. Lubitsch shoots him entering the bedroom but still does not cut into the bedroom. This is a key aspect of Lubitsch's art. He likes to capitalize on our imagination, to suggest what's going on rather than show it, to tickle our fancy rather than dully reveal things. The door opens again, and the King sails out happily, much to our confusion. We had expected him to surprise the queen and Danilo. The queen, we deduce (and deduction is what we do when we watch Lubitsch) must have quickly hidden her young lover. She seems to have gotten away with her tryst. But as the king descends the palace staircase he finds that his sword belt is much too small for his waist (an insult as well as a clue). Only now does the king piece together what we did when we first saw Danilo slip in the queen's door.

Rouben Mamoulian liked to tell the story in which Lubitsch asked his writer to communicate that a man was tired of his wife and had developed a roving eye. The writer, says Mamoulian, brought Lubitsch four pages of "introductory exposition of the character," which Lubitsch immediately rejected: "Just put down this—the man walks into the elevator with his wife, and he keeps his hat on. On the seventh floor a pretty blond walks in, and the man takes his hat off."[10] This sequence has the same virtues the Chaplin sequence Hitchcock refers to does: it's quick and efficient; it's comic; and its comic success in part rests on the pleasure we take in getting the joke.

This is the technique that has always been referred to as "the Lubitsch touch," this ability to play with an audience, to appeal to its imagination, and, in doing so, to tell his story more deftly and with greater charm. We can, for example, only gauge the intensity and decadence of the Russian ambassador's party in *Ninotchka* by the vast number of excited cigarette girls and harried waiters bearing various liqueurs and savories that pass in and out of the ambassador's suite and by the noise (steadily intensifying) that escapes from the suite each time one of the waiting staff comes or goes. Like all who wish they were at a party to which they were not invited our imaginations run wild as to the pleasures there within.

Lubitsch was at his most imaginative when he lingered outside doorways, particularly when something promiscuous was going on behind the door, a habit his pupil Billy Wilder picked up. In Wilder's most Lubitsch-like film, *Love in the Afternoon*, we know when Gary Cooper's rich playboy has bedded another conquest when we see the group of gypsy musicians (that travels with Cooper to aid in his wooing) tiptoe out of the hotel room, shoes in hand.

One of my favorite Lubitsch moments, and again it involves sex and doorways, is in *Design for Living*. Miriam Hopkins has forsaken the two men she really loves (competitive suitors played by Gary Cooper and Fredric March) for a safer, more practical marriage to wealthy prig Edward Everett Horton. The night of the wedding, as her conjugal responsibilities approach, she finds herself examining all the flowers that have been sent to the couple, as a means of forestalling her doom. The flowers have been gathered in the waiting room just outside the newlyweds' bedroom. She finds that one plant, a simple two-headed tulip that stands out among the rich floral displays in its simplicity, has been sent by her twin beaus. The flowers, in their simple beauty, remind her of the awful compromise she has made, and she kicks them over on her way to the bedroom (Horton deliriously happy behind her). But moments later the door opens, and she rushes out to right the plant. It seems her affection for her old suitors has not flagged. She then bravely squares her shoulders and returns to the bedroom, ready to confront her conjugal duties. Some time passes as Lubitsch leaves us to stare awhile at the flowers. Now the groom, Horton, exits the bedroom only to head directly to the tulip plant and give it a swift kick. Apparently things have not gone as he hoped on his wedding night, and apparently the two lovers and their two-headed proxy have something to do with it. But, of course, what exactly happened behind the closed doors of the couple's wedding night bedroom we will never know.

If Lubitsch liked to linger lasciviously, but discreetly, outside bedroom doors, Hitchcock's camera tended to hover around windows. A significant number of his films begin with an opening shot of a window, expressing a dominant idea in his films—that humans, like the buildings in which they live, wear a facade of normality but are actually teeming with hidden abnormalities, strange sexual and violent tendencies. But like Lubitsch, with his doors, Hitchcock is wary of opening his windows to show us explicitly what is going on. In *Rear Window*, for example, the camera pans by Mrs. Thorvald's apartment the night of her murder. Her shades are closed and just as the camera has passed her apartment, we hear a brief, distant scream and a tinkling of glass. The murder is conveyed purely by sound from offscreen. There are no visuals of the murder or even the apartment in which it takes place.

The murder of Babs in *Frenzy* is an archetypal example of Hitchcock's ability to delicately convey violence, to achieve the utmost in effect by the minimum of means. It's ironic that you would find one of Hitchcock's best suggestive or elliptical sequences in this film because by the time of *Frenzy* (1972), Hitchcock was free of the code, and many other scenes in the film are so explicit (particularly the rape/murder of Barbara) as to dispel the myth that Hitchcock was irrevocably wed to good taste in his depiction of violence. (The shower scene in *Psycho* might have alerted you to that reality as well.) But it is worth noting that Hitchcock's filming of Babs' murder, in the classic Hollywood mode, seems to sum up the best of his technique, while the explicitly rendered rape and murder of Barbara strikes many as a sordid lapse in Hitchcock's otherwise elegant oeuvre.

The scene begins with a murderer known as "the necktie strangler" escorting Babs up the winding staircase to his apartment. We know he is a murderer; Babs does not. "I don't know if you know it Babs, but you're my kind of girl," the necktie strangler says as he ushers her into his room. We recognize his comment here as the same tagline that preceded an earlier murder. As the door to the murderer's apartment shuts on our faces, Hitchcock's camera, in a single long take, slowly retreats back down the winding staircase we have just ascended, simulating the feeling of a cowering voyeur backing away from something he does not want to get involved in. After a neat bridge cut at the front door threshold of the building, Hitchcock continues the camera's backward retreat through the foyer of the building, out the front door, and across the busy Covent Garden street, till we are positioned to gaze at the murderer's second floor window (decorated in typical Hitchcock irony with flower boxes before the windows). Hitchcock holds this shot for a good while, making sure that we have had sufficient time to consider what exactly is occurring behind the window.

This scene reminds us of the Zen-like simplicity certain artists discover toward the end of their career. Hitchcock here had found a means to get more out of his audience by giving them less, to harness the power of their imagination. It's a style that effortlessly uses the audience's energy rather than one that exhausts itself in trying to get the audience's attention through louder and more obvious means. And it's this scene that a critic is moved to review over and over again, not the explicit rape/murder earlier in the film that only makes us grateful that the code was not lifted too early in Hitchcock's career.

In his documentary on great cinematographers, *Vison of Light*, the cinematographer William Fraker tells a story of setting up a shot for Roman Polanski, one of the real heirs to Hitchcock's style, during the filming of *Rosemary's Baby*. Polanski had asked Fraker to frame a shot in which the villainous Minnie Castevet (played by Ruth Gordon), during a visit to Rosemary's apartment, makes a mysterious call on Rosemary's bedroom phone. Polanksi asked Fraker to film Gordon from outside the bedroom and to frame her within the bedroom's doorway. Fraker set up a shot where Gordon was framed centrally by the doorway. To his surprise, Polanski, when he saw the setup, moved the camera to one side, so that Gordon was barely visible, only a strip of her back showing through the doorway. But, Fraker said, he came to understood Polanski's motives when, during a screening of the film he watched the audience en masse tilt their head to look through the doorway at the barely glimpsed image of Gordon on the phone.

Polanski understood what both Hitchcock and Lubitsch did, that often the less you show the audience, the more they are engaged; the more you hold back, the more they lean forward. In this way, the Hollywood director operates in almost the same vein as a Symbolist poet, like Claudel, who spoke of building his descriptions around an ellipsis, a hole that would draw the reader in like smoke through a chimney. In this aesthetic, the most important thing in the shot is what is left out. The goal, as French filmmaker Robert Bresson put it, is "to trace the invisible wind by the water it sculpts in passing."[11]

ELLIPTICISM AND VIOLENCE: WELLMAN'S *THE PUBLIC ENEMY*

In a sense there was bound to be a good amount of elliptical technique in Hitchcock's films because they had a good deal of violence in them, and violence, of course, had to be handled carefully in Hollywood. During the code years, for example, you were not allowed to show a shooter and a victim in the same frame, to show the actual act of violence. But this prohibition led to some of Hollywood's more stylish shots, as directors were forced to convey acts of violence without showing them. A close-up of a gun might be followed by the shadow of a body falling or the close-up of a grimacing face. The result is a more expressive, purely visual cinema and one that is defter and more suggestive. In these sequences, the action itself is not filmed but is rather conveyed by its effects.

Again, the question arises: did the code have a beneficent effect on the Hollywood films? And again, it needs to be emphasized that it was part of the Hollywood ethos to handle violence carefully, aside from the dictates of the code. The murder scene described above in *Frenzy* comes from a time when the code had broken down. The motive of elliptical technique there was that Hitchcock felt it was a way to better give us an internal sense of the queasiness of the crime. He wanted us to use our imaginations. And a precode film like William Wellman's *The Public Enemy* is characterized by subtle, elliptical depictions of violence, born, not just from moral delicacy, but from the director's desire to find a more creative way of depicting violence, a way of making it register poetically and psychologically.

In fact, three of the most effective and memorable sequences from *The Public Enemy* are murder sequences, where Wellman found a clever way to make his audience feel the violence of the crime without actually showing it. Tommy's final battle with the gang that has betrayed him, for example, is carried on completely offscreen. Tommy enters a building which the camera holds on (as Hitchcock does in *Frenzy*), while Wellman conveys the shootout through a distant barrage of shots and muffled, but startlingly realistic, moans of pain. One of the happy side effects of turning to silence to convey drama is that silence, in turn, invites an innovative use of sound. Paradoxically, the quieter a scene, the more conscious we are of the resonance and significance of sound. We are struck, in this sequence, as we are in the operation scene in Ford's *My Darling Clementine*, by the poignancy of distant sounds, here the distant but disturbingly painful moans of a dying man, in Ford's film the distant hoops and hollers that are so incongruous with the mortal seriousness of the operation.

Another effective scene depicting violence in the film is the one in which Tommy and his best friend Matt slay the horse that had, days earlier, reared up and killed their gang leader, Nails Nathan. Tommy and Matt enter a stable and ask the stable keeper within where they can find Rajda, the horse that killed Nails. Behind them is a wide corridor that recedes back into the screen, boarded by stalls on each side. Horses hang their heads over most of the stall doors. Tommy and Matt pay the stable keeper the $1000 he tells them the horse is worth and advance into the stable, though the camera stays where it is, the stable keeper still in the foreground of the scene. Tommy and Matt are still wearing the tuxedos and tails that they wore to Nails's funeral, which adds a bit of decadence to the scene, not to mention providing an interesting contrast to the rusticity of the stables. Cagney just begins to reach into his vest pocket as they turn left in the stable and disappear offscreen. A pause follows, as the stable keeper cranes his neck back in curiosity. The pause is followed by a series of gunshots and the sound of a heavy, slumping body hitting the ground. Wellman smartly decided to register the reports of the gun on the scene rather than overlaying them into the soundtrack later, because what really brings home the violence of the killing is the way the many horses in the stalls all startle sharply at the sound of the gunshots. It's a clever way of registering the violence of the action without showing it. Matt and Tommy emerge from the stable with a trophy, a blanket bearing the name of Rajda.

But the loveliest murder sequence in the film has to be the one in which Matt and Tommy bump off Putty Nose, the man who had once been their mentor and helped them break into the crime business when they were just kids. Putty Nose desperately begs for his life but Cagney's character, Tommy, is deaf to his pleas. Tommy's gentler sidekick, Matt, however, is troubled by what they have to do. In an effort to remind Matt and Tommy of the good old times, Putty leaps to his piano and plays a bawdy saloon tune that he had once taught the boys. Cagney's Tommy stands behind Putty as he plays the piano and, though merciless up till now, he flashes a smile at Putty when Putty looks back to see if the song is having any effect. Putty is reassured by Tommy's smile and turns back to the piano, playing with renewed vigor. He hopes in this manner to save his life. But Tommy's smile is just a taunt because as soon as Putty turns back to the piano, Tommy pulls out his gun.

At this point the camera pans away from Tommy, holding his gun and smiling vindictively, and towards Matt who is moving slowly to the door that exits from the room. Matt is hunched and troubled. And through his body language we read what is going to happen and why he knows it is time to leave. Offscreen we hear Putty's song, "Lazy Jones, big and fat, slipped on the ice, and broke her . . . ." The shot rings out just at the moment we expect the final word of the verse, accenting the sadism of the act and leaving us wondering just what it was that Lazy Jones broke.

The moment of Putty's death is registered in the sound of the gunshot, in the ellipsis in the song lyrics, in the image of Matt's guilty flinch at that sound, and in the frenzied sound the piano keys make when Putty falls on them in his death throes. Again, Wellman finds concrete means to drive home the violence of the murder without actually showing it, as he did with the mournful cries in the film's final shootout and the startled horses in the stable killing. This kind of filmmaking is what Bresson refers to when he writes of tracing the wind by the water it sculpts in passing. Classic Hollywood was expert in the art of omission, an art that, at once, intensifies the audience's attention and conveys action with a haunting suggestiveness.

7

Hollywood, Style, and Decoration

Hollywood film of the studio era, then, represents first and foremost a classical approach to film. It aimed for a conservative aesthetic that subordinated itself to the story and produced a sleek, marketable commodity.

But of course novelty is important too in marketing, and Hollywood was founded by showmen who were vitally interested in packing people into the theater by promising their audience something new. Hence there existed in Hollywood a tension between a conservative aesthetic that was determined not to alienate its audience and an explorative one that wanted to surprise at the same time.

Hollywood was often threatened by novel techniques that did not fit into its classical technique, but part of Hollywood's vitality sprang from the way it incorporated these techniques, picking and choosing among them, using them in such a way that they were subordinated to the classical aesthetic but enlivened it at the same time.

David Bordwell has discussed, for example, in *The Classical Hollywood Cinema*, the way Hollywood incorporated certain arty techniques, such as dissonant music, German Expressionist photographic technique, and Soviet montage, that were, in general, at odds with the conservative Hollywood aesthetic. Dissonant and atonal music became a useful means of conveying alienation or tension. Expressionist photography found its place in Universal's horror films and in those moments where the filmmaker wanted to suggest subjective point of view, psychological disorientation, or dream consciousness. Montage turned out to be a stylish way to collapse time and found its place in moments of great drama when the filmmaker wanted to convey the rushed and frantic way in which people perceive things in moments of drama or horror.

All of these techniques found their place in the Hollywood system but never to the point of disrupting the general system. As Bordwell notes, other aspects of

Expressionist technique, "the more episodic and open-ended narrative, the entirely subjective film, or the slower tempo of story events," did not find their way into the Hollywood aesthetic. Hollywood "took only what could extend and elaborate its principles without challenging them."[1]

German import F.W. Murnau's first American film, *Sunrise*, for example, is often described as an Expressionist masterpiece. Masterpiece it is, but one is struck by how much its Expressionist technique is subordinated to the classical rules of Hollywood storytelling. There are few really alienating angles. Montage and dream effects are used to advance the story. And its most striking moments tend not to be its Expressionist moments. Many of these (the montage sequences, for example) have become so familiar as not to impress greatly, the stuff of future special effects. Where the film most impresses is in its elaborate sets and the uses Murnau put them to in his elegant, long take mise en scène, characterized by the continuity and rhythm characteristic of the greatest Hollywood films.

Hollywood picked and chose from those aesthetics that were alien to its general approach, tuck-pointing new methods into its films where they made sense but not in such quantities that these new methods interfered with Hollywood's central goal, to create a film that was cleanly constructed along classical lines and easily understood by its audience. The result of this process was a quiet, classical cinema, characterized, nevertheless, by a controlled but persistent stylishness.

Hitchcock's *Notorious* is a particularly good example of the way the Hollywood director sought to strike an equilibrium between solid classicism and stylish élan. It would be difficult to find a film that is characterized by more elegant stable structure, a defter example of classical continuity in Hollywood filmmaking. And yet at key moments, for example, when Alyssa wakes up with a hangover and when she is suffering the effects of being slowly poisoned, in other words when she is experiencing states of inebriation, Hitchcock will avail himself of the entire bag of Expressionist tricks: bizarre angles, shadow effects, warped images to express fractured consciousness, and echoing sound effects. In order to convey the menace hidden behind the afternoon tea (at which Sebastian and his mother are serving Alyssa poisoned tea), Hitchcock films Alyssa and her poisoners deep in the background behind a massive close-up of the teacup in the foreground of the image, just one example Hitchcock's penchant for making the quotidian and familiar strange and menacing.

But, as David Bordwell writes, "[i]n Hollywood cinema, there are no subversive films, only subversive moments." Bordwell points out that even Hitchcock's, and perhaps Hollywood's, most subversive film, *Psycho*, is closer in aesthetic to *His Girl Friday* than Bresson's *Diary of a Country Priest* or Godard's *Pierrot le fou*. There is nothing, Bordwell writes, "in any Hollywood auteur film that rivals the idiosyncratic systems of space or time operating in the work of Dreyer, Bresson, Mizoguchi" and other avant-garde directors.[2] Hitchcock would not have had it any other way. Even Hollywood's greatest stylist always prided himself on playing by the rules.

Cukor said that Hitchcock "would make the camera do a dance, but he *knows* what he's doing. When he doesn't want to, the camera is very discreet and just tells the story."[3] Hitchcock was capable of stylistic flourish, certainly a good deal more than Cukor was, but these stylistic pirouettes were accomplished on the firm bedrock of stable, classical film construction. "Don't," he would say, "put a great big close-up there because its loud brass and you mustn't use a loud note unless it's absolutely vital."[4] Powerful images have to be doled out with circumspection and in the context of the larger rhythms of the film. A filmmaker commits the sin of self-indulgence when he no longer thinks out carefully the placement of his expressive shots, when the viewer drowns in deluge of "striking shots." In these cases you have a kind of artsy parallel to the numbing effect of special effects in contemporary action films—in both cases one large, purposeless "effect" after another; in both cases a good deal of sound and fury but, in the end, little significance. It was one of the triumphs of the studio era in Hollywood to create films that were visually striking, stylish but rarely showed off or called attention to themselves pointlessly or excessively. Striking shots, yes, but only when called for.

APPROACHING STYLE WITH CARE

Even directors like Cukor or Wilder, who represent the essence of the quiet classical style in Hollywood, recognized, however, the need for stylistic flourish from time to time. "Occasionally," Cukor said in an interview from the 1960s, "when it's apropos, I do the visual thing, as well. But I try not to make a lot of fancy cuts, and back and forth, which at the moment are very much in vogue. And I think in two years they'll seem awfully old-fashioned."[5] Anyone who has seen a 1960s film by a director drunk on zoom shots understands Cukor's point. Stylistic quirks, like special effects, are loud ingredients that do not necessarily age well. They need to be exercised carefully, subordinated to the structure of the story. Otherwise they threaten to overwhelm the logic and order of a work and to make it look garish.

And yet even the more visually conservative directors like Wilder and Cukor feel compelled occasionally to film in a more stylishly ambitious manner. Cukor's films are studded with lush images built around mirrors, images that balance out multiple reflections and are framed with a good deal of ornate detail. And Wilder could be disingenuous. If he didn't like "fancy-schmancy shots" what are we to make of the opening shot of Billy Wilder's *Sunset Boulevard* in which William Holden's corpse is filmed from below by a camera seemingly placed at the bottom of the swimming pool, the police officers fishing his body out registering as blurred presences above him? Wilder did like a fancy shot, now and then, but it had to be at the right moment. The opening shot of a film allows for some playfulness, existing as it does in a brief period before the exposition of the story needs to be accomplished and before there is anything that the viewer can be distracted from.

Wilder's *A Foreign Affair* is a good example of the way a conservative director quietly works in style. For its first third or so, the film does not exhibit much style. Most of the early scenes, like the several dialogues on the tarmac when the congressmen's plane lands, are unremarkable and expository. But as the film progresses Wilder's style warms and loosens up. By the time we have arrived at the Lorelei nightclub, where Marlene Dietrich's character sings, Wilder is beginning to allow himself some of the von Sternberg and Lubitsch business that he loves. He takes the time to digress from his narrative, though it should be noted that Dietrich's songs, like *Black Market* and *The Ruins of Berlin,* are not just decorative asides but also ironic comments on the themes of the film, such is Wilder's inability to include something that doesn't contribute to the film. During the songs he carves out elegant bits of mise en scène, reminiscent of the business from von Sternberg films. Dietrich, for example, during her act, plucks the cigarette that her beau (played by John Lund) watching the show has just lit. She drags on it as she sings her song, then, slowly gravitating back to piano, leans over the piano and gently places it between the lips of her piano player, played by Frederick Hollander, the film's composer.

And during these sequences Wilder's shot composition gets fancier. Shots of Jean Arthur's table are set up before a window, so that we can watch her scenes and a distant reflection of Marlene, who will be her romantic competition, dancing in the reflection of the window. The visual abundance of the environment, the late night hour, and the postwar nihilism and drunkenness that permeate the place, accommodate a more involved cinematography. It's as if Wilder's camera has had a few drinks at this club as well and is getting slightly loquacious. By this point in the film, most of the exposition has been accomplished. And we've landed in a place that has drawn all the characters together. What's more, that place is musical and full of inebriation. Now it's time to have a little fun with the film.

One of my favorite touches in *A Foreign Affair* comes toward the end of the film. Colonel Plummer (played by Millard Mitchell) has just explained to Jean Arthur's character, Congressman Phoebe Frost, that the man she loves, Captain Pringle (Lund), is not the ne'er-do-well she thought him to be. Phoebe thought Pringle had cruelly dumped her for Dietrich's character, Erika von Shlutow. But Colonel Plummer explains that Pringle has actually been dating Erika in order to track down a high-level Nazi with whom she consorts. Furthermore, he explains, the Nazis are on to Pringle, and he finds himself in harm's way. To dramatize his point, Colonel Plummer draws a bull's-eye on the fogged-up window where the scene takes place. Wilder pans in on the bull's-eye and then dissolves to an image of Captain Pringle, so that in the transition between the two shots Pringle seems trapped in the sight of the bull's-eye.

This is the kind of highly expressive, quasi-cartoonish shot Wilder usually avoids, but it works well here. The shot is effective emotionally because it seems to put into image Arthur's newfound sense of Pringle's vulnerability. He's not a cad; he's in danger. The shot is effective rhythmically, because it kicks off the final scene and climax of the film. Arthur will have to get to him before he's locked in the sights of a real bull's-eye. If there were a moment for this kind of introductory fanfare or visual flourish, it was here. And it is effective because there isn't much of this stuff in Wilder's films, so when it happens it sticks with us. Style needs a neutral background if it is going to stand out effectively.

Interestingly enough, even though the classical predominates over the Expressionist in classical Hollywood film, when contemporary filmmakers try to recapture the power of the classical Hollywood era they often find themselves gravitating to, or imitating, its more stylish or Expressionist films. Since the 1980s there has been a real vogue for Expressionist technique and its attendant phenomenon, film noir. Sharp angles, shadows, fog, atmosphere, cigarette smoke, an atmosphere of evil and corruption—this is technique you can cut through with a knife. It is easier to glom onto than the invisible, seamless style of classical Hollywood. A typical college audience is befuddled by why they should take *Stagecoach* seriously but is much more at home with a noir film like *The Killers*. There is an artistic edginess in the latter film, and a modernist gloom, that automatically justifies itself in the eyes of a modern audience. John Wayne as the Ringo Kid—that's a tougher sell. "The young, particularly," writes Andrew Sarris, "prefer solemnity to hilarity in their cult heroes, which is why Stroheim and Welles have tended to fare better than Lubitsch and Sturges in the textbook histories of film."[6] There is an obvious significance to expressive and lavish technique that suits the modern taste more that the clipped efficiency of classic Hollywood.

Hitchcock too is an easier sell to a modern audience because his style is more overt than other Hollywood directors, and the modern audience often equates overt technique with serious filmmaking. Still, while Hitchcock has spawned a small industry of imitation, few of these films have been great artistic successes, possibly because it is easier to mimic some of Hitchcock's more overt stylistic devices than it is to equal his methodical, careful shot-by-shot construction and his fastidious devotion to unity in his film. The quiet craft of classical Hollywood is harder to return to. When contemporary filmmakers try to duplicate the classical style rather than the Expressionist something goes wrong. They are not as able to arrive at the careful arrangement of shots, the elegant continuity, the solid shot and story construction, the strong sense of unity, the deft and efficient characterization, and the tight script. The buoyant spirit of Hollywood comes out as a facile optimism, the warmth as smarmy treacle. The snappy dialogue comes out as excessively stylized and self-conscious, an homage to something old-fashioned. The film becomes a period piece, a homage or a parody rather than the genuine article.

SIMPLE STORIES

If Hollywood was able to arrive at films that struck a balance between solid, classical construction and, at the same time, a strong sense of style and elegance, it was in no small part due to its insistence that it keep its stories simple and essential. Simple stories provided room, around their margins, for curlicues of style and decoration. Hollywood was attracted to the simple story, first and foremost, because it wanted to reach a wide audience. "We were smart enough to realize," said silent film comedian Harold Lloyd, speaking of silent films in general, "that they had to be understood in India or Tokyo or Holland as well as here, so we tried to make what I consider to be a basic type of humor—that they would understand too. It's not local humor, so it's understood today and is fresh today, if the picture was well made."[7] This is another legacy of the silent era, a tendency to make films that were simple and universal in appeal. And this tendency goes a long way to explaining why Hollywood films are still popular. They avoided, by design, the topical that would tie them to the day and always sought the essential. They dealt with simple little stories that were accessible to large audiences from different cultures and, it turns out, from different times.

Even once dialogue arrived, Hollywood seemed not to lose its desire to reach a global market, to tell simple, essential stories about the human situation that appealed to people in drastically different markets and locales. When Frank Capra was asked why his films had aged well, his immediate response was that it was because "they're probably as humorous now as they were then . . . due to the fact that they stay away from the temporal, from the one-liners of the day. You stick with things that are humorous at all times, under all occasions—generally visual humor."[8]

Simple, universal stories also appealed to Hollywood filmmakers because they provided room for embellishment. As all good rhetoric teachers have taught their students countless times, when you limit your thesis, when you focus, you give yourself time and room to go somewhere, to develop your idea. And this is what Hollywood would do. Hollywood filmmakers kept their stories simple, so that they could do something with them, so they could play with them, decorate them, enrich the atmosphere or characters, fill them with memorable bits of style and business. As Billy Wilder told Volker Schlorndorff in their televised interview, he always preferred a simple story to a complex one because complex stories "lose people," but with simple stories you can take the time to make them "ornate, rich in design."[9]

Paradoxically, though Hollywood arranged its entire industry around the art of storytelling, making every element that went into the film serve the purposes of the story, the best Hollywood films do not make the mistake of confusing a good story with a great deal of plot or action. Excessive plots tend to undermine good stories. If a film is too intricately plotted it often has not taken enough time for the things that give it rich texture, the things that make it memorable: atmosphere, character detail and depth, rhythm. Plot is in many ways hostile to what Hollywood does, which is to "treat" a story, in the sense that you treat a material in order to bring out certain qualities in it, to enrich its texture, deepen its quality. When people cite their favorite moment from Hollywood it is most often the charming bits of decoration, the detail work, the film's bits of "business" that they recall most fondly, the places it lost track of its narrative, not its plot twists and narrative surprises. In this respect, Hollywood is a decorative art. It takes its time in telling a story, stopping along the way to spruce things up, fill in gaps, play games, and in general enrich its texture.

Over and over key directors have emphasized their disinterest in plot. Hawks noted that "little time was spent on the plot" of *To Have and Have Not* and that *Rio Bravo*, too, had "very little in the way of plot— more characterization and the fun of just telling a story," and yet these are two of Hawks' greatest and most characteristic films. It's interesting to note that Hawks thinks of telling a good story as avoiding plot. "Scenes" were what excited Hawks: "We have to have a plot, I suppose, a secondary plot, but it was just an excuse for some scenes. . . . As long as you make good scenes you have a good picture."[10] John Ford makes something of the same point when he says, "I don't like to do books or plays. I prefer to take a short story and expand it, rather than take a novel and try to condense."[11] Hollywood was always more successful at the unpretentious trade of taking a slight story and filling it out than it was at doing justice to serious novel. The story and the play always matched the parameters of film better than the novel. And the short story, in particular, allowed for the marginal doodling that Hawks and Ford liked and which often breathed life into a film. Hawks loved to advertise his disdain for plots, often to the confusion of his coworkers. It was his way of letting them know that he had a subtler idea of what went into a story. When one of the writers of *To Have and Have Not* (he doesn't say which) complained that he wasn't spending enough time on plot scenes, Hawks said to him, "I guess I've been steering away from them because they're so dull." When Hawks called Robert Mitchum to sign him up for *El Dorado*, Mitchum asked what the story was. "Oh—no story, Bob," Mitchum recalls Hawks answering.[12]

Some of the best directors often had to fight to keep their films from being too plot-oriented. What was generally one of Hollywood's strengths, its sense of unity, its sense that everything should contribute to the story, could be a weakness if story was equated with plot, and all that did not contribute to plot was edited out. Orson Welles complained about what happened "when a movie is turned over to the super-editor in the editorial department of the studio. The decision is made on this basis: does it advance the story? And out go all the things that give a movie its real interest." For Welles, as for Hawks, the things that were of real interest were subsidiary scenes, digressions, all of which Welles felt were vital contributions to the story even if they didn't advance the plot. "I like digressions, don't you?" he asked Peter Bogdanovich. "Look at Gogol. Read the first few pages of *Dead Souls* again and you'll see how one mad little digression can give reverberation and density to ordinary narrative."[13]

The best Hollywood directors were adept at the classical style and sympathetic to the efficient standards of the Hollywood studio, but they also tested those standards to a degree and had a propensity for "mad digressions," little bits of eccentricity that brought "reverberation and density" to their work. Here again we see that the best Hollywood films were often not pure products of the studio system but came about from a creative tension between a talented director and the studio.

If Hawks goes to pains to emphasize the difference between plot and story, Hitchcock makes similar points in his repeated emphasis on the difference between mystery and suspense. Hitchcock held mysteries in disdain, as Hawks did plots.

Mystery was to him just a way to keep people interested, keep them turning the page so to speak. Suspense was a form of dramatic irony, where you clue your audience in partially as to what is going on, tell it the things even the protagonist doesn't know, such as a bomb being under a table, and hence make them start to squirm and sweat. Mystery holds a carrot on a stick before the viewers, keeping their interest by holding back the next plot device. Suspense puts its cards on the table. Suspense is not a question of holding back information from the viewers but giving them more knowledge than they can handle. Hitchcock didn't want to just surprise his audience; he wanted them to feel something. He didn't want to forestall their pleasure but to work on them in every scene of the film. "Mystery is an intellectual process, like in a whodunit, while suspense is essentially an emotional process," said Hitchcock. "Many films . . . have mysterious going's on. You don't know what is going on, why the man is doing this or that. You are about a third of the way through the film before you realize what it is all about. To me that is completely wasted footage because there is no emotion in it."[14]

If Hitchcock deemphasized mystery and plot twists, Fred Zinneman deemphasized action. "The fact that somebody shoots a gun is of no interest," said Zinneman. "What I want to know is why he shoots it and what the consequences are—which means that external action is less important than the inner motive through which you get to know what the person's about."[15]

Hawks's, Hitchcock's, and Zinneman's cinemas are all quite different. Hawks wants to take his time along the course of his narrative, play around some in the fringes of the narrative. Hitchcock wants us to feel more, and Zinnneman wants us to take in more deeply the motivations of his characters, but all three are united in their disdain for certain characteristics of the story that are often heralded—plot, mystery, action. All three feel that an excessively wrought, or too busy, story gets in the way of the real business of the film, the depth of emotion and understanding it can arrive at when it has time to do something else other than simply recount a narrative.

Hollywood is notable for the way it turns away from action for its drama. And there is a proportional relationship between its best films and those that are chary with their action. The best Hollywood filmmakers seemed to understand that action falls into that large category of intractable material, like special effects and excessively stylish shots, that can date a film, age it prematurely. Hollywood recognized, also, that extended action sequences rob the film of the time that can be spent making an audience feel more deeply for a character or decorating the film with some pleasant bit of business. Ironically, action can make a film more boring. Action can mask the deficiencies of a film that has not been able to find the ways to make us care about what is happening or that has no idea of how to make itself aesthetically appealing. Hollywood Western director Anthony Mann complained that "the shoot-outs every five minutes" in Sergio Leone's spaghetti Westerns of the 1960s "reveal the director's fear that the audiences get bored because they do not have a character to follow." Mann felt that the director "may not put more than 5 or 6 minutes of 'suspense'" in the story and that too much action interferes with a story's arc, something a director must carefully nurture: "The diagram of emotions must be ascending, and not a kind of electrocardiagram for a clinic case."[16] Too much action, Mann felt, mars the rhythm of a film, deters character development, and weakens the audience's identification with character. It makes an audience care less about a film and less likely to experience the subtler catharsis that is the result of a carefully managed intensification of emotion.

Many of Hollywood's greatest "action" films are memorable for things other than the action. *Angels with Dirty Faces* is one of Cagney's greatest gangster films, but we are less likely to remember the final shootout of the film than we are the marvelous extended shtick earlier in the film, when Cagney violently referees the most slapstick street-tough kids basketball game in film history. The scene is not necessary in advancing the film's action, but it does loads for efficiently deepening the relationship between Cagney and the street toughs, played by The Dead End Kids, whom he befriends. By taking the time to enjoy Cagney's relationship with the boys, director Michael Curtiz and his writers make the final scene, in which Cagney pretends to be a coward at the death chair so as to sacrifice these kids' respect, more meaningful. The basketball game scene represents a "plant" with a huge payoff in the end of the film. Moreover, its just one of many details that describe the tough but vibrant locale of the film. This film is just as much a film about the poetry and vitality of its Hell's Kitchen location as it is a gangster film.

A film about the French Foreign Legion entitled *Morroco* would seem to promise adventure, but the one or two action scenes in von Sternberg's film are the least memorable, and in rewatching the film we find ourselves waiting anxiously, not for the next plot element, but for Marlene Dietrich's next musical number, which will not only give us atmosphere in thick droughts, but which will be interspersed with rich crosscutting and snippets of dialogue that deepen our understanding of the characters involved. We are less interested in the story itself than in von Sternberg's *treatment* of the story, like in the scene in which Dietrich learns that Cooper still loves her by finding her initials ornately composed on the barroom table he has just abandoned. In short we return to this film, not for its plot and action, but for the way von Sternberg dresses up that plot and action, the fun he has dwelling in his world, or the cleverness with which he translates and decorates his slight narrative into sound and image.

Ford's *My Darling Clementine* tells one of the greatest adventure stories of all time, the shootout at the O.K. Corral, but the most memorable scenes from the film are the quietest, for example, the iconic image of a profoundly relaxed Henry Fonda sitting on the wood plank walkway of Tombstone, his feet up on the porch beam in from of him, his chair tilted back, and playing a game in which he balances precariously, shifting from one foot on the beam to another.

Ford handles the final shootout in the film admirably. (He claimed Earp himself described it to him in exact detail.) It's certainly the most cinematically sophisticated and balletic of the many O.K. shootouts in film history, an artful arrangement of fence lines, dust, and cowboy movement. But one gets the sense that Ford's heart in this film is in the small details of the Western culture on the rise: the pretensions of the early version of the barber, the tonsorial shop, for example, and the half-built church that rises majestically before Ford's trademark wide-open sky.

For my money, the most memorable scene in the film is the one in which Fonda offers Clementine his arm and walks her to the inaugural service of the half-constructed church. Ford shoots the couple like a king and queen, as they walk down one of Ford's trademark long porticos leading into the back of the screen. The low angle of the camera mythicizes them against his massive, open sky, dotted with bright clouds. Ford is so famous for his dark, Expressionist shots in films like *The Fugitive* and *The Long Voyage Home* that it is sometimes forgotten that he was equally adept at capturing the freshness of early morning or midday light.

This is the only moment in the film where Earp really enjoys a kind of union with this beloved Clementine, and Sarris rightly refers to it as a consecration of "what is clearly the film's ceremonial high point."[17] Ford lovingly lingers over the details of the church dance: the craggy fiddler and his cowboy speechification, the lovely folk dances, Fonda's mid-American nervousness about dancing, his nervous but stately stride when he does dance—all shot from below in Ford's mythic, sky-oriented way.

This all goes, not to plot, but to story, to character and atmosphere. This is the kind of attention to quaint detail that can exasperate the modern viewer. It certainly has little to do with the Earp legend and contributes very little to the acceleration of the action in the film. But, of course, this is the stuff the Ford devotee, and the Hollywood devotee, comes for. Ford is taking the time to establish setting, atmosphere, and character. He's trading plot detail for emotional depth and a stronger sense of place. He's also tinkering with our sense of time. Few directors can match Ford's ability to dwell in the interstices of his story, to sit back, like Fonda does in his chair (Photo 3), and relax, approaching his story in a leisurely fashion. The purpose of his film seems more to slow us down rather than make our pulses race, to make us conscious of time rather than forget it.

Implicit in this pacing is the idea that film, in the right hands, need not just be blind entertainment. Ford, rather than make us forget the world, often shows show us the world in its best light, its slowest, richest phenomenon. In this respect, Ford often seems the distant cousin of Yasuhiro Ozu, whose aesthetic is quite different than Ford's but whose films have a similar effect of quieting us, heightening our sensitivity to the gentler qualities of the world. And of course both directors represent a substantial argument against those, coming from the *Brave New World* view of film, who see it as a kind of opium, a mindless escape from reality. In the hands of the right filmmaker, film can actually heighten, rather than dull, our sensitivity to the world.

This quality of leisure is one of the essential aspects of Hollywood filmmaking, not just a leisurely pace—with screwball comedy certainly not having that—but also a leisurely approach to filmmaking in general, the notion that a story needs to

Photo 3. Hollywood' simple stories spared room for leisurely schtick, like Fonda's *My Darling Clementine*. Courtesy of Photofest.

be filled in. Hawks, in doing fast-paced screwball comedy, would stop along the way to brainstorm on how to say his lines more elliptically and cleverly. Sturges and Capra make myriad stops along even their most frenzied narratives for little character bits and moments of quiet sentiment.

But the leisurely pace of many Hollywood films is one of the things the modern viewer has trouble adjusting to. This kind of filmmaking results in a cinema that is more vertical than horizontal, more static and monumental than plot-driven and surprising. If you show *My Darling Clementine* to a group of undergraduates, many are befuddled by Ford's preference for churches over shootouts. *Morroco* seems to them to move as slowly as a contemporary art film. Students inevitably balk at the slightly whimsical ending to *To Have and Have Not*, where Lauren Bacall exits the bar with a wiggle of her hips and a limping but enthusiastic Walter Brennan in her train. This strikes them as a laughably abrupt ending to a film that purports to be about a great romance and one tied into the moral issues during World War II. Hollywood endings in particular can seem slight and unsatisfying to an audience that has been trained on film endings that are increasingly long and climactic, sometimes comprising more than half the film. Mysteries require big plot payoffs in the end. Action films require a steady escalation of action. But Hollywood at its best, as Hitchcock emphasized, was never about mystery or, as Zinneman said, about action. Hollywood at its best offered a carefully crafted film from beginning to end. There is no deferred pleasure in Hollywood. The payoff is not in the end but in every scene along the way.

TO HAVE AND HAVE NOT

Howard Hawks's *To Have and Have Not* is a good example of a Hollywood film that pays off along the way, of the way Hollywood is often more about the treatment or decoration of the story than the story itself.

What do we best remember about *To Have and Have Not*? Not its secondhand *Casablanca* plot (a knockoff that in many ways bests the original) and not its themes about Steve's reawakened moral ardor that are a little too explicitly stated at times. Bogart's halo often shines a little too bright in this film. Hawks is always at his most heavy-handed when he is moved by a man's moral redemption. We don't necessarily recall the action scenes in the film or its political intrigue, both of which represent rehashes of standard visuals and themes in 1940s Warner Brothers films. We certainly don't appreciate it as a faithful adaptation of Hemingway's novel. There is very little beyond the first 10 minutes of the film that is recognizable from the novel.

What we tend to appreciate in *To Have and Have Not* isn't its plot so much as the stops it makes along the way of its plot, the way it slows narrative down, takes its time with its story, entertains itself by decorating its story. We remember the rich atmosphere of the nightclub, rendered in lovely composition—in-depth photography and smoky haze right out of the best of von Sternberg and Borzage. We remember Hoagy Carmichael and the way the film stops for three entire songs by him, all of which lend rhythm to the movie, underline or deepen Bogart's relationship with Bacall, and, most of all, establish that cozy, "clean well-lighted café" effect Hawks was so good at arriving at. Hawks had a Hemingway-like ability to carve out a little bit of light in darkness, to describe, in fine detail, a sanctuary of song, drink, and camaraderie that offers some measure of solace to suffering of humans. He often breaks for a song deep into his films, like in *Rio Bravo*, where the four generations of cowboys, huddled in the jailhouse that is surrounded by enemy forces, stop for a duet between Ricky Nelson and Dean Martin, or in *Ball of Fire*, when what often is a fairly broad comedy stops for a lyrical, melancholy rendering of "Sweet Genevieve" by the old professors, all of whom find themselves in melancholy, retrospective mood because of the burgeoning love between Gary Cooper and Barbara Stanwyck. Hawks likes to stop at the cozy center of his films for a little song and camaraderie, as if to say, "Here we are, right in the middle of things. Let's stop, look around, and enjoy this atmosphere I've created." These are the scenes that often sell the worlds Hawks creates. If he was not faithful to Hemingway's story in *To Have and Have Not* he was faithful to the feel of Hemingway's writing, its devotion to those small moments of grace that make life bearable.

What else do we tend to recall fondly in *To Have and Have Not*? We remember the care Hawks takes in delineating Bogart's touching relationship with his rummy sidekick, Walter Brennan, their relationship rendered in the sparest and most elliptical language, never stooping to speechifying background. We remember Brennan's nonsense line, "Was you ever bit by a dead bee," a non sequitur that Brennan trots out every time he meets a stranger. Steve and he look to how the stranger responds to this bit of verbal horseplay as a way of separating who is "one of them." If they respond to Eddie's nonsense with humor and their own word play (as Bacall's character does), they're OK; if they are stuffy and annoyed by Brennan's verbal nonsense, they're not. (The Vichy and the underground, alike, have no sense of humor.)

What people most remember from the film, of course, is the extended foreplay between Humphrey Bogart and Lauren Bacall, whose real-life attraction to each other was branded on the screen. It's striking how long Hawks takes in developing this relationship. Everyone remembers Bacall's famous line about whistling, but the extended dialogue leading up to that line is packed with all sorts of clever elliptical pitter-patter during which Slim and Steve skirmish for position in the first stages of romance. Back and forth they go between each other's rooms carrying a single bottle of wine to each other, the drinking of which seems eternally postponed, a classic Hollywood bit of business in which the consummation of their relationship is invested in a concrete object.

This is the stuff we remember from *To Have and Have Not*: the bar, Hoagy Carmicheal's funky rendition of "Hong Kong Blues," Brennan's "Was you ever bit by a dead bee," Bacall's simmering "You know how to whistle, don't you, Steve," the bottle of wine they keep threatening to drink. All of this is a great deal more evocative and memorable than the political intrigue and the quasi-existential themes of reawakened moral ardor, all handled pretty well here but all pretty much the standard fare of *Casablanca*-like war films and noir loner films.

The huge number of successful touches in *To Have and Have Not* are a consequence of Hawks's desire to always have "an attitude towards the scene." Hawks had a playful approach to filmmaking. He tended, when circumstances allowed, to take his time with his dialogue, sitting around with writers like Ben Hecht and

Charlie MacArthur translating the existing script into more evocative prose. He recalled working with Hecht and MacArthur on the comedy *Twentieth Century* and how, when the script was finished, "they figured they were all done." But for Hawks the real fun was just beginning. "Now we start on new different ways of saying things," he told them. "We had more fun for three days just twisting things around. I asked them, 'How do you say this—'Oh, you're just in love'? Ben came up with 'You've broken out in monkey bites.'"[18] It seems likely that Walter Brennan's nonsense lines about dead bees were born from similar brainstorming.

Hawks also recalled playing around with small gestures as well as bits of dialogue until he got it right. He remembered struggling over a scene in *Bringing up Baby*, where he felt Cary Grant was too conventional in his expression of anger. "'Let's find some different way of getting mad," he recalls saying to Grant. "And we started trying different ways, and then somebody said, 'I know a fellow who when he got mad used to whinny like a horse.' Cary said, 'That's fine, I'll do that.' That's what I call an attitude towards a scene."[19]

Anecdotes like these tell us something about Hawks's, and Hollywood's, art. First they reflect the Hollywood director's passion, born from the industry's cult of unity, for every part of the film, even the smallest, to do its job, to be memorable, to make a splash, to lodge memorably with the audience. There is a wonderful sense of craftsmanship in this attitude that sees bits of dialogue and small gestures as problems begging for a solution, as puzzles to be figured out. Hawks is not the director who seems most indebted to Lubitsch, but the spirit of Lubitsch seems to preside over his productions nonetheless, guided as they were by a commitment to coming up with little bits of creative business, even on the smallest scale. Sam Raphaelson wrote that Lubitsch, when selecting which plays he wanted to film, "chose material for its possibilities, material that left us free for rampages of invention." Raphaelson recalled fondly the brainstorming sessions with Lubitsch and the "certain kind of nonsense that delighted him." He learned early on that for Lubitsch, "these conversational doodlings were serious business."[20]

Raphaelson's phrases, "rampages of invention," "delightful nonsense," "conversational doodlings," apply to Hawks's films as well as Lubitsch's, as does the idea of taking doodling seriously. These comments touch on the spirit of invention and experimentation that is at the heart of the freshness in the Hollywood film. We're used to accounts of Hollywood technicians experimenting with their equipment, grinding new lens, for example, and adding appendages to their machinery, in the experimental hothouse that was the Hollywood studio system. There is something of the same in Hawks's approach to filmmaking as he experiments, brainstorms, plays around with his dialogue and gestures. Hawks prized Julius Furthman as a writer because "if there were five ways to play a scene, Furthman will always come up with a sixth."[21] Harold Jack Bloom, who helped write Hawks's *Land of the Pharoahs*, said that if you gave Hawks twenty pages of script, he'd use one or two and that if you only handed four or five pages for a scene, he'd complain, "You're not giving me any choices."[22] Comments like these testify to a lot of turning up of stones on Hawks's part, a restless desire on his and his writers' part to come up with new ways of saying things in film.

All accounts of the making of *To Have and Have Not* make it sound like an exhilarating experience. Hawks biographer Todd McCarthy writes that "even more than with most Hawks shoots, the filming was leisurely and very often rare, uproarious fun."[23] A good deal of that fun is imprinted on the screen. *To Have and Have Not* reads so nicely now in no small part because it captures some of the freshness of Hawks's improvisational technique. You sense the actors are having fun with this one, and you sense the collaborative nature of the Hollywood film. The community of the production finds evidence in the community represented on the screen. Years later after the studio production era passed, Hawks would complain of how much time he spent drumming up money and chasing producers and how little time that left for filmmaking. *To Have and Have Not* is a film that reflects the leisure of the Hollywood craft, the freedom cast and crew had—despite mind-boggling time limitations—to concentrate on the film, to experiment and play around with gesture and dialogue, to make each moment count.

And even though Hawks's productions were characterized by greater artistic freedom, independence, and inspiration than the average Hollywood film, there is no indication that the kind of spontaneous, inventive mood that was on his set was unusual in Hollywood. Even an in-house studio director like MGM's George Sydney would say, "[T]his was a period in Hollywood when we kind of made up those pictures as we went, and that was fun. I'd get up in the morning and say, 'Gee, what are we going to do today? Let's do this and that.'" As we've seen, Hollywood directors, in general were loath to trumpet the artistic merits of their film, but they would often make comments like Sydney did of his musical *Anchors Aweigh*, that "a lot of new things went into that picture." The Hollywood director took great pride in his spirit of inventiveness, in whatever clever and original bits of business he was able to come up with in the hurried process of making a film. If the hectic pace of filmmaking in the studio era could be oppressive, it could also be inspirational. And the rapidity with which the studio film was made resulted in a kind of light attitude to filmmaking, a breezy spirit of inventiveness that is often imprinted, as in the case of *To Have and Have Not*, in the film. It's one of Hollywood's most important, if least, tangible qualities: a spirit of lighthearted fun. "You go to Europe and to film seminars in this country," Sydney observed, "and they talk about the classic days of the MGM musical. But at the time we were too busy, day and night, making those pictures to think we were making a classic anything. Far from it. We enjoyed the work, it was great fun."[24] Sydney's comments recall, of course, Hawks's own two-word summary of Hollywood filmmaking, mentioned earlier, "Business, fun."

SIGNATURE STYLES

All of the great directors, then, are adherents of, and proficient in, the classical style. And all of them, in their interviews, take great pride in creating films that are seamless in their art and quiet in their authorial presence. Mastery of the classical style is a prerequisite for making a strong film in Hollywood. It represents the canvas on which filmmakers toil. Rarely do they deviate from the cult of the simple story to which all aspects of the filmmaking contribute.

Of course some directors are so proficient at the classical technique that they distinguish themselves from others, Billy Wilder, for example, in his story construction and Hitchcock in his careful editing that carefully controls our point of view and moves us with such clarity and careful pacing to what he wants us to see in the end.

And yet, in the end, what really distinguishes filmmakers from one another is their style, the little bits of business with which they filled the margins of their films, what they did when the engine of narrative paused, and they had the time to play with set and atmosphere, to introduce musical effects, little bits of comic business, or character touches and shadings. All of the Hollywood masters had mastered the smooth continuity of the Hollywood narrative and well-made story, but their signature is the particular way in which they play with that story. All of these directors are most known by their asides. Adept as they were at the classical system, it is the way they deviate from the system, their small, quiet embellishments, that provided their savor.

Preston Sturges, for example, loved to carve out great spaces in his narrative for his huge number of subsidiary character roles. Even when Sturges's films aren't road films, like *The Palm Beach Story* and *Sullivan's Travels* are, they have the feeling of road films, accumulating all sorts of eccentric characters as they develop. Ford likes to stop for sentimental interludes, Von Sternberg for rich, exotic atmosphere. Lubitsch takes the time to stop and think how he can convey his information in the most elliptical way, so that the audience can be tickled with themselves when they figure it out. Hawks arrests his narratives, so his lovers can circle warily around each other, alternately insulting and drawing closer to each other, an all in a language that is so elliptical that it rewards several viewings

Hitchcock is particularly notable for his set pieces that represent large deviations from the narrative. Hitchcock often seems to have thought of his films as a series of striking ideas rather than in terms of conventional narrative. Ernest Lehman spoke of the challenge of writing for Hitchcock who would tell him the fanciful ideas he hoped to include in *North by Northwest* and then leave Lehman to figure out how to make them fit in the script. Hitchcock wanted a chase scene across the face of Mt. Rushmore; he wanted to do the longest dolly scene in film history, taking place at the assembly line of the Ford Motor Company, which would document the step by step process of a car being built, culminating with a dead body found in the back seat as it comes off the assembly line. He wanted to do a scene at a UN convention, where, during session, the secretary general instructs someone to wake up the sleeping ambassador from Peru only to find that he's dead, etc. Hitchcock thought in these set pieces first and narrative structure afterward, in general. Edith Head told Hitchcock biographer Donald Spoto that Hitchcock's efforts to tighten up the rambling narrative of *To Catch a Thief* was impeded by his desire to showcase Grace Kelly and her graceful sense of fashion. "He had," Spoto recounts, "his heart set on an elaborately vulgar costume ball sequence for the finale, the sole purpose of which was to show off his leading lady in shimmering gold."[25]

Stories like these have led credence to the criticism that Hitchcock would sacrifice narrative integrity for showy sequences, that his films could be loosely tied set pieces. The second *The Man Who Knew Too Much* sometimes seems like a second-rate Hitchcock film, leading up to one perfect Hitchcock set piece, the scene at the Royal Albert Hall. Hitchcock was a man of operatic visions who had to fight the inclination to deviate too far from his story and indulge in elaborate "set pieces."

Of course *To Catch a Thief* and the second *The Man Who Knew Too Much* are probably not Hitchcock's strongest films. In his best films, *Rear Window* and *Notorious*, for example, Hitchcock was able to execute his imaginative set pieces without losing grip of the tight overall structure of the film. He was a master of classical Hollywood construction as well as prone to these elaborate set pieces. But even in his tightest, most conservative films there is always something a little operatic about Hitchcock, something of the pageant. He was always resisting the dictates of plot and plausibility which he described as "the easiest thing, so why bother?" His films testify to the Hollywood director's desire to not only tell a story but also to tell it in a creative way, to "sell" the story.

This is the showman side of the Hollywood filmmaker, the other side of the coin of the classical filmmaker. The Hollywood filmmaker is a two-natured creature. On the one hand the careful classicist, working from a simple story, making sure every element in the film contributes to that story; on the other hand the showman, who sets himself the challenge of doing something with those elements, having some fun with them—on the one hand careful construction; on the other a delight in style. These are the essential twin ingredients of the Hollywood film.

8

The Artificiality of the Hollywood Film

One of the reasons a person coming to classic Hollywood has trouble taking it seriously is that, by today's standards, it seems rather unrealistic. "Fakey" and "cheesy" are words I often hear when I teach these films to undergraduates. Fortunately, this perception affords the pleasure as well as the frustration in teaching these films, because when you bring in a sequence of shots from a classic Hollywood film into class and amplify Hollywood's quiet but very deliberate structure, it quickly becomes apparent to students that there is more here than immediately meets their eye. *Stagecoach*, for example, looks like something from another planet to many students today, who have as little experience with Westerns as they do with classic Hollywood in general. For some students, the first associations of Ford's stirring images of Monument Valley are clichéd poster images of the West in computer games with Western themes that they played when they were younger. If you show *Stagecoach* to college freshmen without properly introducing it or providing context for their viewing, this film that Orson Welles respected so much that he made it his principal object of study in preparing to shoot *Citizen Kane*, can appear to the student as tinny and clichéd, a laughable B film.

The impression that classic Hollywood films are "fakey" remains fairly strong, even among those who like Hollywood films but tend to think of them as dated pleasures. According to this attitude, these films have a kind of antique charm, but it should not be seriously advanced that they are the equal of contemporary films, blessed, as the latter are, with manifold improvements in technologies and funding in the hundreds of millions of dollars. This attitude is a subset of the larger one, quite common in America, that progress is the equivalent of improvements in technology.

Over years of teaching Hollywood classics I have learned that there are certain moments that modern audiences have trouble getting by when watching older films. In the fight sequence between Robert Mitchum and his detective partner in *Out of the Past*, just before Jane Greer shoots the partner, I see some nifty noir shadow play; my students notice the accelerated motion meant to depict heightened action and the unrealistic way in which blows are landed. I think *My Darling Clementine* to be one of the most perfect films Hollywood has to offer, but my students have trouble getting by Linda Darnell's portrayal of Conchita, the Mexican saloon girl. I have to admit Darnell does not bring the slightest Mexican air to her depiction of Conchita, and her hair looks like it would be more at home in an Abbot and Costello movie than in the nineteenth century West. Throw into that mix the very plausible opinion that Linda Darnell was not a very good actress, and I have to confess my students have a point.

I remember attending a Christmas-time screening of Frank Capra's *It's a Wonderful Life* at a revival. But even among this appreciative crowd I was struck by the hoots of derision at certain moments in the film that by contemporary standards are rather "fakey": the scenes, for example, in which Capra depicts some of the men from Bedford Falls in the battlefields of World War II by superimposing their image on stock war footage, and the scene during Jimmy Stewart's vision of what life would be without him, in which the police, chasing Jeff, shoot wildly and indiscriminately into the crowd in such a way that we know to be laughably unrealistic.

My point is not that the audience is wrong to notice these glitches or that they do not exist. The faults are there, and my guess is that if Capra or Ford or Tourneur had the money, time, or the benefit of hindsight they would have tried to render these moments more effectively. But I would suggest that the modern audience emphasizes these glitches too much. It is these glitches that lead those that are new to classic Hollywood to dismiss these films, and which leads even those who are sympathetic to these films to condescend to them, to see them as less sophisticated works, the touching product of a more primitive era.

And yet, the faults in realism in *It's a Wonderful Life* are pretty small stuff in comparison to the huge accomplishments of the film. *It's a Wonderful Life* displays what made the Hollywood film great in spades. It has a sharp, witty script filled with many of the allusive jokes and rich poetic slang that represent the best of Hollywood writing. It has, as all of Capra's best films do, a lively, quick pace and solid sense of structure. It mixes tones in complicated ways, combining a strong sense of sentimentality with a disturbingly cynical view of human nature. The shot composition in the film is close to flawless, displaying Capra's and cinematographer Joseph Walker's gift for expressive set design (the Baileys' home, Potter's office) and for rich tumultuous crowd scenes that seem to almost spill out of the screen. When we look at the scene shot by shot, the glitches in verisimilitude seem to shrink in significance.

But that is not the way the modern viewers often see a film like this. What is invisible to them is the classical technique which, by its very nature, refuses to call attention to itself and acts as a kind of anonymous background to what they *do* see, glaring deficiencies in realism.

Ironically, the devotee of classic Hollywood is likely to have the converse experience in watching a contemporary film. In the modern film, the realism may be very persuasive. Bullets whiz by as, presumably, bullets really do. Spent shells clatter to the ground in an authentic manner. Intestines spill out from open wounds with gruesomely literal accuracy. But what someone who has dwelt in the cinematic universe of Hollywood might notice is that the filmmakers have often only gotten right that one thing that classic Hollywood got wrong: verisimilitude. Many of the other things that Hollywood got right are missing. The script of the film might be expository rather than allusive, adolescent rather than wise and worldly. There might be an alarming lack of continuity in space in the action scenes. The scenes with extras are laughable, with large groups of costumed people milling around trying to look like they belong there. The sets are purposeless travelogue backdrops rather than significant means of expression in their own right.

I don't mean to lapse into an old fogy's lament of the degeneration of film; I simply want to emphasize that realism is of such paramount importance to the contemporary audience that it sometimes leads them to be unduly harsh to films that are less realistic and, at the same time, also leads them to be blind to the flaws, the lack of art in films that have a convincing verisimilitude.

What is ironic is that though the modern audience is jaded and cynical when it comes to estimating realism in old Hollywood, it is naive as a baby in its gullibility to contemporary tricks of realism. The same audience that finds the fight sequence in *Out of the Past* laughable for its sped-up motion is unquestioningly satisfied with the ludicrously unrealistic amplifications of sound in its own fist fights. The same audience that snickers at the studio era's quaint matting effects buys wholesale cartoonish computer graphics. Hollywood, in the past and present, appears at its most laughable in its moments of action and special effects. Why? Because special effects are laughable. They impress only their generation, and it takes only a few years for their ludicrousness to become apparent. Witness how generic to the age all those slimy beasts with several rows of teeth are to 1980s action movies. Special effects are always tied into the technology of the age and will last only as long as the technology does, which is to say, not very long. They have the same shelf life as a generation's fashion.

GOOD "FAKEY" AND BAD "FAKEY"

Modern audiences, then, are not entirely wrong to laugh at some of Hollywood's antique special effects. I, for one, cringe most every time a classic Hollywood film incorporates a ski sequence, so comical are the ill-fitted inserts of stars matted on to Alpine landscapes and edited into far shots of professional skiers flying down the mountain. And yet it's remarkable how fond Hollywood was of turning to this effect in the climax of even its "A films." (Hitchcock's *Spellbound* and Borzage's *The Mortal Storm* are just two examples.)

Like my students, I've never liked the technique of literally speeding up film stock in order to ratchet up the action of a scene. There is only one special effect I find dated or ineffective in *Rear Window* and that is when the murderer is attacking Jimmy Stewart in his apartment and his entire complex rushes to their balconies in sped-up time to see what is happening.

And my students are right to laugh at Linda Darnell's hair. They seem to have intuited that Fox foisted Darnell on John Ford "to the point," as Andrew Sarris notes, "of clogging his continuity with mystifying close-ups." Ford seems to have only enjoyed filming Darnell in the scene where Henry Fonda dumps her into a horse trough filled with water. Otherwise, she's a fairly distracting presence. Hairstyles often date period pieces that otherwise are meticulously detailed in their realism. The number of films that get everything right except the hair is a testimony to how stubbornly we hold to the particular styles of our time, and to how important hairstyles are to a time.

And if there are some eras in classic Hollywood, like 1930s MGM, that are charming in their artifice, there are others where that artifice is stultifying. During the boom era of the wartime and just after the war, for example, Hollywood churned out more than its usual amount of hard-to-justify fare, and this fare was characterized by an almost uncomfortable studio gloss. This was the era where, as Capra expressed it "quality went out the window to meet the demand of quantity."[1] As Robert Sklar notes, the great demand for film meant even more exterior scenes shot inside sound stages. Hollywood's increasing skill in recording realistic images had, Sklar explains, the "paradoxical effect of giving American movies an unintended surreal look.... It was as if the technological skills of studio filmmaking had developed to a point of diminishing return."[2] Many of the films in the 1940s are characterized by a bright, lifeless sheen. It was in this era that the naturalism of neorealism seemed to offer such a breath of fresh air, an escape from too confining an artificiality.

So, at times, Hollywood's artifice is too artificial. But there are many times where Hollywood sacrifices realism and chooses artifice, with good reason and to good effect. Not all of Hollywood's fakiness is bad.

The ending of *Rear Window* is a case in point. Students tend to like *Rear Window* quite a bit. Hitchcock, like Wilder, is one of the few easy sells to a modern audience, and *Rear Window* is one of the easiest of Hitchcock sells. But even students who like this film complain about the ending of the film, which they find patently unrealistic. They rebel, in particular, against the scenes where Jimmy Stewart defends himself from a murderous Raymond Burr with the flashes of his camera and to the shot of Stewart falling from his window, both rendered in a distinctly unrealistic manner.

Now putting aside, momentarily, that scores of critics have celebrated these two scenes in particular as quintessential to Hitchcock's technique, the students' complaints are worth trying to understand. In a sense, they are right. The effects Hitchcock employs in these scenes are strikingly unrealistic, particularly from the point of view of a filmgoer today, well schooled in the naturalistic effects that have represented the hallmark of cinema since the decline of Hollywood.

In the scene in which Stewart defends himself with camera flashes, circular bands of bright orange engulf the frame as Hitchcock tries to convey, subjectively, the experience of Raymond Burr's killer, blinded by the flash of Jimmy Stewart's camera. Jeff's fall has a cartoonish effect also. The matting of Jeff on to his background is obvious. And Hitchcock simultaneously zooms forward with his camera lens while tracking back with his camera giving the fall an exaggerated tunnel like effect. Hitchcock's indifference to hiding his matting technique often earned him criticism. For example, the patently artificial look of *Marnie*'s Baltimore harborside neighborhood has often been cited by those who would argue that Hitchcock is not quite the perfectionist in craft his proponents make him out to be. The artificiality of scenes like these often persuades contemporary filmgoers that the argument that classic Hollywood represents superior filmmaking is indefensible. How could that be, when the craft is so crude? And in a sense this viewer is right. Hitchcock asks for a good deal of suspension of belief in these moments, more than the modern viewer is sometimes willing to give.

But the mistake the modern viewer makes is in his approach to film as something that is successful only in proportion to how realistic it is. Given that criterion the film falters in these scenes. But if the scenes are judged by the criteria that were important to Hollywood—visual expressiveness, clarity of expression, and a sense of unity, just to name a few—the scenes are quite successful.

Take, for example, the scene from *Rear Window* in which Jimmy Stewart tries to defend himself from a killer by blinding the killer with flashes from his camera. Hitchcock, as I have found occasion to mention several times in this book, had a mania for unity. Since this film was going to be about a photographer, and one with a tendency toward voyeurism, Hitchcock realized that Jeff's camera was a pretty potent symbol in the film. Throughout the film, Hitchcock works so many scenes and lines around Jeff's prying camera that the film becomes a study of voyeurism on many levels, the voyeurism of photography, of filmmaking, of filmgoing. The camera is at the heart of the film. So Jeff defending himself with his camera may be a tad ludicrous from a point of view of realism (though Hitchcock goes to some lengths to make it plausible that this is the only means at his disposal), but it is rather clever in it contribution to the film's unity and in the way it ties together its themes. Here is Jeff, who, like we have seen, prefers to look at the world through a photo lens than to actually live in it (for example, spying on scantily clad women but avoiding actual commitment to the real woman in his life), trying desperately to keep reality at bay with his camera. The voyeur is getting his comeuppance. The scene is the climactic action scene of the film, but that does not stop it from also commenting on the principal character of the film and doing so with mischievous humor. The trick here is to judge the scene in terms of, not its realism, but its cleverness and ingenuity, the part the scene plays in the over all structure of the film. The trick here is also to see a film not simply as a duplication of reality but a reshaping of reality into a harmonious whole.

Hitchcock was often willing to strain the limits of plausibility for the sake of cleverness and unity. One of my favorite bits of implausibility in *Rear Window* is that Jimmy Stewart and Grace Kelly are convinced that the wedding ring of the woman the suspect murdered would be substantial enough evidence to convince the police to arrest her husband for murder, because, as both Thelma Ritter's character Stella and Grace Kelly's character Lisa Fremont agree, a woman would never leave her wedding ring behind if, as her husband has suggested, she is simply away on a trip. Now this is patent nonsense from the point of view of realistic jurisprudence. What court of law is going to issue a warrant of arrest because a woman never takes her wedding ring off? But in terms of contributing to the unity of the film and in terms of making the plot elements of the film reflect the larger ideas of the film, making the murdered woman's wedding ring the principal piece of evidence is clever. *Rear Window* is about a roving photographer who likes to view the world through a lens, who prefers the world of fantasy to reality and refuses to return the love of the one woman who cares deeply for him. When that woman sneaks into the murderer's apartment, finds the dead wife's wedding ring, and displays if for Jeff, who has been watching from his apartment by means of (typically) the telephoto lens of his camera, she is saying two things to him: first, that she has found the evidence that will prove a murder occurred and, second, that he might want to consider marrying her.

Similarly, the orange circles that wash over the screen, conveying the killer's blindness, may not be strictly realistic but they are very effective in conveying the *sense* of what it would feel like to be blinded by flashbulbs. Hitchcock's intention is not to realistically convey what is going on at this moment but to render, as intensely as he could, the confused consciousness of the killer. In this sense Hitchcock is, at this moment, no different than the Expressionist painters he fancied in his art collection at home, who set it as their goal not to realistically depict a scene but to render the feeling of the moment. In this moment Hitchcock wants us, as he so often does, to get inside the consciousness of his killer.

Moreover, Hitchcock might ask, when is he allowed to be stylishly extravagant if not at his film's climax? *Rear Window* is characterized, for the most part, by a careful classical construction. But when the action ramps up, so does the technique. Now is the moment for bolder statements. The action dictates, or allows, a more stylish and extravagant approach. The orange washing across the screen reflects both the consciousness of the killer and the climactic nature of the scene.

Jeff's fall through his window is, similarly, both highly unrealistic and highly expressive and significant. Hitchcock's scenes depicting falls are rarely realistic, and yet they are among his most vaunted and imitated shots. Certainly the technology existed at Hitchcock's time to create a convincing fall. But Hitchcock's goal was not to record a fall that was realistic but one that made you feel the actual horror of falling from great heights. The matting in Hitchcock's falls allows you tend to stay close to the victims' faces as they fall. He wanted to maintain a psychological intensity in the scene that would be lost if you shot the fall more realistically and from a greater distance. If you film a body falling the way it really does, such stylistic and Expressionist devices are not available to you. To render a fall accurately is to create a documentary effect, something of no interest to Hitchcock who wanted his images to be expressive in an immediate way. In *Psycho*, he matted a close-up image of Martin Balsam screaming and waving his arms on to a background shot that descends down a staircase. The effect is ludicrously and wonderfully unrealistic. Balsam's fall seems to take forever, and we are there to absorb every detail of his stunned emotions in glorious close-up. In *Vertigo*, as in *Rear Window*, Hitchcock accentuates Scottie's fear of heights in *Vertigo* by zooming forward and tracking backwards, as he does in Jeff's fall in *Rear Window*. The effect is to make the bell tower stairs much more nightmarish and to give the shot an Escher-like feeling of moving into two directions at once.

Despite its allegiance to a realistic, transparent aesthetic, Hollywood was willing to dip into artificial technique if clarity was to be gained by that artificiality. Hitchcock often cited his boredom with barroom brawl scenes from Westerns because they were so often shot from a distance. The scale of the event would overwhelm the filmmaker who would then just plop his camera down from some distance and record. The trick to making that brawl interesting, from Hitchcock's point of view, was to cut open that scene, get inside it with inserts that register points of view and the immediacy of action. These inserts can lead to some awkwardness—excessively posed shots, clumsiness in continuity—but what is obtained in psychological immediacy, story involvement, visual expressiveness, clarity of detail, and purposefulness of shot makes it worthwhile.

According to this style of filmmaking, even those inserts during ski scenes that bother me are warranted. Those shots are more strikingly artificial than other shots in the film, but they reflect Hollywood's allegiance to a story that has an immediate effect and images that are crystal clear. They keep one close to the scene, make clear the protagonist's psychology, and clearly present the information to be gathered.

It helps also, in viewing Hollywood films, to remember how much closer these films were to the theatrical and stage traditions that preceded them than films are today. There is a memory of, and affection for, the striking stage background, the evocative backdrop, not realistic of course but all the more visually alive for not being realistic. There is a patience, in this filmmaking, with effects that are stagy if they are also clear and visually strong, a dash of theatrical inventiveness with which these filmmakers were comfortable. A screenful of information could be less realistic if it was poetically arranged, visually informative and evocative.

Those scenes in Hitchcock films that, to many modern viewers, are so unrealistic as to call Hitchcock's craft in question are often the very scenes that, to the Hitchcock devotee, represent the visual highpoint of the film. Critics have documented over an over again how Hitchcock's falls, for example—almost all of which are expressive and unrealistic—represent a principal symbol in Hitchcock's lexicon of ideas. Fear of height is often a stand-in, in his films, for more general fears in life, often fears of sexuality and human commitment. Scenes of great mountain chasms and heights are often, in Hitchcock, exteriorizations of the chasms characters experience within themselves, and his scenes involving heights and falls are often those in which the heroes finally cross a kind of moral boundary within themselves.

The mistake of the modern viewer is to judge the film by its realism rather than the criteria that mattered to Hitchcock and the rest of Hollywood in the classic era. Hitchcock's goal here was not realism. Rather, he wanted a scene that was expressive, in its conveyance of both the killer and the victim's psychology, and he wanted a scene that tied into the persistent themes of the movie and of his work as a whole, a scene that contributed to the unity of the film. And though he could play the classical game of invisible style as well as any Hollywood tradesman, he felt that the climax of the film justified a more extravagant technique. This is one of those moments he often referred to when comparing filmmaking to composing music that required a loud horn flourish.

I have taken, when teaching *Rear Window*, to warning my students of those sections that they are going to find unrealistic. I talk a little about Hitchcock's history of filming falls and ask them when they see a scene in the film that seems unrealistic to ask themselves why Hitchcock shot it that way rather than condemning that scene in a knee-jerk fashion. I point out contemporary filmmakers, like Brian De Palma and Spike Lee, who have imitated Hitchcock's "fakey" mat work, who find his artificial means of rendering falls and movement more inspiring than realistic depictions of falls and movement that aim for nothing more than the record of movement. I find that this warning makes all the difference in how they perceive the film. Rather than arriving in class feeling they have "found out" the film, spied weaknesses that disqualify it, they arrive having already begun to explore why the film is shot the way it is, thinking over what Hitchcock was after in his more expressive shots. They are interested in how these shots express Hitchcock's ideas and how they tie into the film's taut unity. It doesn't take much to get an audience to stop judging a film for its plausibility and to start judging it for its expressiveness and for the solidness and complexity of its structure. On the first count, the best of classic Hollywood is bound to fail, on the second it's bound to succeed.

HEIGHTENED REALISM

Despite its adherence to a realistic aesthetic, a studiously invisible style that did not call attention to itself or distract the viewer from his or her apprehension of the story, *ultimately* Hollywood did not aim for realism. I don't want to lean on that old hoary truism that Hollywood was a dream factory. That is a fallacy in its own right—that we plug into Hollywood films as we might an opium den, for pure fantasy and escape. Hollywood, it strikes me, is too grounded in reality, too cynical at times, too conscious of the earthly plight of humans at others, to be adequately summarized as a dream factory.

On the other hand Hollywood never, needless to say, aimed at a strictly realistic depiction of the world. Ernst Lubitsch said, famously, "[T]here is Paramount Paris and Metro Paris, and of course the real Paris. Paramount's is the most Parisian of all."[3] Hollywood offers idealized worlds, environments reduced to their essences. Hollywood does adhere to certain rules of realism. It offers a realistic three-dimensional space and follows laws of continuity in the way it renders space and edits what we see. But in the long run if it is interested in realism it is so only to the extent that realism makes us buy its marvelous and improbable worlds. As

MGM screenwriter Francis Marion put it, realism "exists in the photoplay merely as an auxiliary to significance, not as an object in itself." Realism is Hollywood's means of making us buy its dream. David Bordwell, paraphrasing Gerard Genette, similarly points out that "the classical theory of the *vraisemblable* depends upon a distinction between things as they are and things as they should ideally be; only the latter is fit for artistic imitation." And only the latter is fit subject matter for Hollywood. Hollywood tries to render physically "things as they should ideally be."[4]

The realism Hollywood goes for is a realism that is just a little more perfect than reality, our world in much of its precise detail but just a little better, a little more attractive or heightened in its charge. If only life moved with the urbane inanity of a screwball comedy. If only pratfalls and sophistication were so happily wed. If only we could spit out the machine gun pitter-patter of the journalist in the Columbia newspaper film or the gangster film from Warner Brothers. If only life moved at the Rossini-like eccentric pace of Sturges films. If only the late-night hours were filled with the sensual ease and understanding of a Lubitsch film or we could drop into Howard Hawks's or Joseph von Sternberg's crowded, smoke-filled bars. If only the world were characterized by Ford's sublime mixture of sadness and sentiment or if small towns were actually peopled by Capra's character actors, all deftly shaded and all adding up to an ideal of community. Hollywood offers one artificial paradise after another, a host of visions of our world at its best and most intense. Hollywood had a realist aesthetic but never simply reproduced reality just as it was. When filmmaking came to be more about a documentary registration of the reality being filmed, about things as they are rather than as they might ideally be, in the films of Stanley Kramer or Elia Kazan in the 1950s, for example, that was one of the many moments that spelled Hollywood's demise.

Ironically, the original audience for Hollywood films, despite its reputation for an innocent and naive appreciation of film, sometimes seems more sophisticated in its approach to film than do contemporary audiences. There was a touch of modernism to classic Hollywood films, a dash of what the academics like to call "self-reflexivity." The classical Hollywood film is willing to let its artifice show. It speaks to an audience that knows it is at a film, having an artificial experience. It didn't presuppose that an audience could be so silly as to confuse this artifice with reality, nor did it seek, as its primary goal, to go as far as it could in convincing its audience that what it was seeing was real. Rather it looked for a healthy dual-mindedness in its audience, a willingness to playfully enter into the reality of the film without ever losing sight that it was a film. Far from being simply a dream factory, Hollywood liked its audiences to keep its wits about it, to approach the film with a certain ironic distance. The Hollywood film asks its audience to give itself to a film but remain conscious, charmed not only by the experience of the film but also by how charming that experience is.

Hitchcock complained to Truffaut about "dullards" who were unduly concerned with plausibility, which he said, "was the easiest part so why bother."[5] Hitchcock preferred the audiences in the earlier days of filmmaking, when he worked in

Britain. He said to Bogdanovich, "[In the mid-1930s] the audience would accept more, the films of the period were full of fantasy, and one didn't have to worry much about logic or truth. When I came to America the first thing I had to learn was that audiences were more questioning. I'll put it another way. Less avant-garde."[6] Hitchcock's choice of words here is quite telling, because we tend to think of the earliest film audiences as more naive and innocent, whereas Hitchcock suggests they were more sophisticated, more "avant-garde," better able to approach a film with that double consciousness that enjoys being lost in an illusionary reality but never loses sight that the film is an artificial construction and not actual reality. They had not been subsumed yet in a cult of realism or fallen prey to film's ability to recreate reality with convincing verisimilitude. A demand for realism is one of the forces that eventually destroyed Hollywood, and Hitchcock seemed to sense the onset of that demand even during the classic era.

There is something childish in asking a film simply to reproduce reality as effectively as possible. If this were the highest purpose of cinema then film would have reached its apex in the Omnimax Theater and as a kind of adjunct to the world of science. Hollywood gives more than a nod to realism and plausibility. It never allows itself the excesses of the art film, but, at the same time, it asks its audience to be a little "avant-garde" to suspend its disbelief, play along with the film, to give the film a little play, to engage itself creatively in the film and not simply sit back, coldly, picking apart its inconsistencies. As Hitchcock says, why bother?

How much playfulness it asks of its audience varies with each film. Obviously, a lot of play is required to watch a frothy musical like Lubitsch's *Merry Widow*, where Maurice Chevalier condemns himself to jail for having been foolish enough to believe in loving one person and where champagne appears in prison cell turnstiles. Here the audience is expected to suspend a good deal of its desire for verisimilitude—though not all, because the development of the love story in this light operetta stays close to some very tough truths about love. Lubitsch biographer Scott Eyman writes that while Lubitsch "never works terribly hard at making us suspend belief, irony and distance are achieved by a complicitous smile, a wink. 'This,' he says to the audience with the genial smile of the master confectioner, 'is artificial, it is candy, and we both know it. But no one makes it like I do."[7] In many of Hollywood's greatest films there is this playfulness of tone, a sense of sharing in a game. A delight in the exercise and the artifice supersedes a desire for convincing realism.

For all the talk of the Hollywood studios as dream factories, of the Hollywood film as pure escapism, it is the modern filmgoer who sometimes seems to be looking more for a dream experience, who seems to enter the theater as one might an opium den or to look for at the cinema an experience comparable to a carnival ride, something that will be so convincingly realistic as to blow them away, erase all traces of conscious thought. *That* is a search for dreams.

The classic Hollywood film was more lucid than that and its audience more conscious. This audience never fully succumbs to the reality being depicted in the film. The reality is never depicted with so much urgency that the audience is called to do so. The classic Hollywood audience approaches the experience in a spirit of play, enjoying the ride but never losing its consciousness, both inside and outside the film at the same time.

At the same time Hollywood tends not to wear its irony on its sleeve. It manages, despite its obvious artificiality, to avoid the mincing self-satisfaction of the film that is too obviously playing a game. When contemporary filmmakers try to duplicate the enthusiasm of Hollywood, its stylized idealism, they often fall flat, accomplishing, not Hollywood's inspired optimism, but something too self-consciously sweet. They seem unable to recreate Hollywood optimism without a certain self-consciousness that destroys the very effect they aim to recreate. They find it impossible to not condescend or parody. George Cukor felt that the thing that was "absolutely invaluable" about silent films was that "they were absolutely on the level. They really believed what they did—they did it without any pretentiousness and without any nonsense." Cukor felt that "the people who'd had silent training—like Ronald Colman—were quite extraordinary. They were sincere. There is some of that tradition remaining."[8]

Cukor aimed for that same sincerity that characterized silent film acting in his own sound films and his own actors, another example of Hollywood defining itself by the virtues established in the silent film era. Hollywood represents a curious mixture, a paradox of artifice and sincerity. It plays a game but not in the arid manner of the art house cinema. It believes in its game. It has a childlike ability to wholly enter into that game. It's this sincerity that is missing in even the most well-meaning attempts to honor or recreate the Hollywood tradition of idealism. A self-consciousness seeps in that spoils the effect, and these films finish by parodying Hollywood's optimism rather than doing justice to it. I would not want to extend this point to sociological observation, to argue that the classical Hollywood era was more innocent (as I don't think people at that time were a lick more innocent) or that our era is more mature or more debauched (equally untrue). I would simply suggest that with the passing of the studio industry we arrived at a point where we could only look at the kind of filmmaking it specialized in from the outside, objectively, and were to a great extent barred, from that moment on, from making films with the same brand of sincerity.

HOLLYWOOD'S IDEALIZED SETS AND MGM

If one of Hollywood's accomplishments is to arrive at a kind of realistic idealism, or marvelous plausibility, much of that effect is accomplished by its set design. One of the most common ways that people express their delight in classic Hollywood films is to say that they feel as though they lose themselves in the film. Certainly all films invite us to be lost in a world, but classic Hollywood seems to have been able to provide a particularly airtight and cozy environment for us to enclose ourselves within. Hollywood seals up its atmospheres tight. Very few films go as far as Hitchcock did in his experiments with single locales, for example, in

Rope, *Rear Window*, and *Lifeboat*, but there is a proportional relationship between many of the best films in Hollywood and a great sense of focus in time and place, something that was not lost on the script advisors and doctors of Hollywood, who always stressed the virtues of simplicity and unity in telling a story. So many great films, Lubitsch's *Shop Around the Corner*, for example, or many of Hawks's films—*To Have and Have Not*, *Only Angels Have Wings*, and *Rio Bravo*— have, if not a single locale, as in *Rear Window*, at least a principal locale which anchors the film and to which the film gravitates back rhythmically. And even when Hollywood strays from a unity of time and place, it is unfailingly devoted to a unity of action, the central tenet of its aesthetic being that everything that enters the film's story—developments, character actors, set design—contribute to the film's central purpose.

The effect of this reverence for unity is not only an airtight, self-enclosed world but also one that is exceedingly well ordered, where things match and are choreographed in a way they would not quite be in real life. Hitchcock's set in *Rear Window*, for example, is so carefully arranged that the one time Miss Lonelyhearts decides to leave the apartment complex for a night out, the café she ends up in is the one spot in the city we can just glimpse from Jeff's window. Of course, it is unlikely that we would have this kind of visual continuity in real life, but we are grateful to Hitchcock for hitting upon a means of arriving at that continuity on the screen. The idea is typical of Hitchcock: at once distinctly implausible and at the same time satisfying, since as viewers we do not really want to leave our cozy set, yet we do want to see what happens to Miss Lonelyhearts. Here, Hitchcock calculates correctly how much we are willing to suspend our disbelief.

Hollywood films in general are like this scene, realistic enough to invite us to suspend our disbelief but, in the end, positing a world that is a great deal more carefully choreographed than our own. To a great extent our sense of being lost in a cozy world when watching a Hollywood film comes from this effort to create a world where everything happens with a certain order and for a reason, a great relief from the haphazardness of life in reality. Our sense, then, that in watching a Hollywood film, we are inhabiting a cozy, self-enclosed world, far from our own is derived not only from meticulous and fanciful set design but also from a tight story structure that keeps us circumscribed within a tightly sealed and organized world.

Of course when we think of sets that idealize the world but do so with a vivid detail that almost makes that idealism plausible, we think of MGM, where set design often vied with actors and directors for principal genius in a film. *Queen Christina*, for example, is a film where the decor competes with actors for top billing. MGM always had great sets even if the sets didn't always have great directors to work with them, MGM being the studio that seemed to care the least about fostering directorial creativity. *Queen Christina* has it all (Photo 4): not only lovely, rich set design by Alexander Toluboff but also a director, Rouben Mamoulian, who had some ideas about what to do with that set. Mamoulian had a particularly gentle but tactile visual touch. "His films," as David Thomson notes,

Photo 4. Greta Garbo in *Queen Christina*. MGM's sets were always lavish, but in the hands of a good director like Rouben Mamoulian they became meaningful as well. Courtesy of Photofest.

"rustle with sound and shimmer with the movement of light on faces, color and decoration."[9] He was an aesthete who knew how to put MGM's art direction to use. *Queen Christina* is, then, a pretty good example of the way Hollywood could establish an idealized environment and bring it to life.

The sequence in which Garbo first arrives at the inn is preceded by lush establishing shots of a wayside inn, more picturesque than any inn could ever be, surrounded by snow up to its frosted windows, and apprehended through a snowfall that sparkles and falls with downy softness. It would be impossible to create the same scene in a naturalistic setting. The setting is too idealized. It represents an evocation of those two or three moments in our lives where we experienced, to the greatest degree, the quiet, fullness, and crystalline clarity of a snow-laden winter night.

Once we are ushered into the fiery warmth of the tavern, with Garbo, we discover a set that represents all that MGM does well. It's characterized by rich plasticity of object and costume and fine detail. Heavy, decoratively carved wooden beams, a massive fireplace roasting a huge spit of meat, several flaring torches echoing the fire, and a rich assortment of coarse peasant faces and fine costume detail create an effect of warmth and abundance. Mamoulian composes the scene in lush Renaissance arrangement of receding diagonal lines, studded with fires a from torches and fireplaces. Thick painterly arrangements of peasants occupy the various receding planes of the scene. The effect of this set, and the way it is introduced, gives us the impression that we are entering into a kind of miniature paradise, a snow scene or dollhouse. The set is more than just decorative backdrop. It interrelates, and conforms, with the characters too much to be just that; it is created too much for the compositional effects which shift with the characters' movement. We get the sense, in scenes like this, that we have walked into a kind of moving tableau, something like a tableau from the stage but one that is more fluid, alive, one that embraces the figures in the frame and constantly shifts and arranges itself around them in new compositions and patterns.

Perhaps the greatest testimony to the evocativeness of Toluboff's set is that the most celebrated scene in this film is not a love scene between Garbo and Gilbert but between Garbo and the room in the inn where she and Gilbert have made love for days. In a lovely extended sequence (which lasts nearly 4 minutes), set to a soft but spirited folk melody on flute, Garbo moves around the room caressing, with her eyes and hands, every object in her path, in an effort to fix in her memory every detail of the room in which she has been so happy. The scene is perhaps the best example of Garbo's unique skill for silently communicating feeling, particularly a woman's rapturous experience of love, so intense in its own private celebration that the man involved seems almost irrelevant.

Garbo caresses everything in her languorous path: a bureau, a candle, a wooden canister, a doorframe, a mirror framed in the bulky carved wood that dominates the inn set. She gently spins the wheel of a loom and embraces a large swath of raw wool hanging near it as though it were a long-lost child. Mamoulian slows the already languorous sequence down even more when she reaches the bed. She half lays across the bed and puts her head on the pillow. Mamoulian treats us to a close-up of Garbo cozying up to the pillow in rapturous comfort, as though she hadn't slept in ages, and then to an even tighter close-up (the kind of luminous shot that defined Garbo's talent) where Garbo, by sheer imaginative energy, conveys the bliss of thoughts of lovemaking.

Mamoulian makes another interesting stop along the way, as Garbo, after getting up from the bed, contemplates a Byzantine tapestry hanging nearby the bed. The shot is so immaculately laid out that the sinuous lines of one of the saints exactly depicted in the tapestry traces Garbo's illuminated profile and seems to reflect the sacred nature of Garbo's experience and thoughts. Then Garbo returns to the sensuality of the bed, where she embraces and caresses one of the bed stands as though it were a man (the shot that set the censors atwitter with its phallic suggestions) before Gilbert asks her what she is doing. "I am remembering this room," she says. "In my future, in my memory, I shall live a great deal in this room," her spiritual memory of the room strangely parallel to that of the viewer for whom, of course, the experience of the room is solely that of the imagination.

Mamoulian approaches here Hitchcock's ideal of what a set should do, which is not only present a vivid backdrop but also a backdrop that contributes to the story, comes to play a significant and expressive part in the film. By the time Garbo has finished her long exploration of the room, all of the objects in the room seem to be invested with, to symbolize the spiritual freshness of, newly discovered love. This is not just a set, it's an ideal, a physical incarnation of sexual intimacy. Mamoulian creates a kind of shrine to love here but one comprised of quotidian physical objects. There is little pretense here, no recourse here to fine words or elaborate metaphysical conceits. The room speaks for itself and, in the end, registers in our memory in a way no speech could.

SETS FROM OTHER STUDIOS

MGM is not alone in crafting meticulous and inviting imaginative worlds in which we take great pleasure in dwelling. Needless to say, Sam Goldwyn, William Wyler, and Gregory Toland conspired to create a different kind of idealized world in Goldwyn's pictures. Here, with Toland's and Wyler's penchant for composition in depth and far shots, the world seems to have greater depth, more dramatic shadows than our own, as though we were always looking through a three-dimensional viewfinder or setting our dramas in the infinite depths of a Baroque painting. Like MGM's sets, it's a rich, satisfying painterly world but not one cluttered with charming detail and fairy tale detritus. It's a more psychological world, a world of "lines and tensions," as Sarris describes it, where the set extends the psychology of the scene more abstractly than concretely.

Warner Brothers proved that Hollywood's desire to idealize does not limit itself to depictions of luxury. The set in Michael Curtiz's *Angels with Dirty Faces*, for example, aims for a realism but, again, a realism in service of the ideal. It's a rich, detailed evocation of Hell's Kitchen, but it is also just a little too perfect too be true. There are a few too many rugs being beaten on fire escapes by a few too many picturesque babushkas; there are a few too many Italian vendors plying their trade. The whole set bustles with a crowded energy that we like to believe is real but we have to admit probably is not. It's how we like to think of New York but not how it really is or maybe how it is but only at our greatest moments of awareness of the poetry of the city. But you would not call it dreamlike. At first glance, it seems to be a perfect evocation of street life. And it is peopled with the plain Depression-era faces that made Warner Brothers the precursor to Italian neorealism. At the same time, we know that street urchins don't say, "Yes, fada," to their parish priest quite as submissively as The Dead End Kids do to Pat O'Brien in *Angels with Dirty Faces*, and God does not spotlight his priests quite as dramatically as Curtiz does Pat O'Brien when O'Brien descends into the boys' lair to call them back into the fold at the end of the film. Hollywood was always reality and dream at the same time, and the audience was always of two minds, playing along by suspending belief but never forgetting it was at the movies.

Lubitsch's claim that Paramount's Paris is the "most Parisian of all" is a pretty boastful one. As lovely as Hans Dreier's Art Deco sets at Paramount were, they were not quite as stunning in their visual clutter as Cedric Gibbons's at MGM's.

Yet, there is still much to Lubitsch's claim because his films remind us that the *"vraisemblable,"* the idealized locale, is not just a question of realistic sets but of charming detail and enthusiasm. As Ethan Mordenn notes, Paramount didn't "have to pile on the class in the visuals because the actors already have it: through direction, script, themselves."[10] Paramount was the intellectual's studio. It didn't have MGM resources, but it did have much better directors, and those directors had ideas on how to convey a setting intensely.

Even when Lubitsch made films for MGM he tended to convey atmosphere through spirited rather than concrete detail. We are likely to remember the Paris depicted in *The Merry Widow*, not because of the fine localized detail of the type we see in *Queen Christina*, but because of the sheer delight Chevalier expresses as he puts on his top hat and tails and sings of the glories of Maxim's. Similarly, when the lonely Mr. Matuschek, played by Frank Morgan, stands outside his department store, in (again!) the gently falling snow, at the end of *The Shop Around the Corner*, describing the meal he is going to buy for the lowly errand boy who has consented to have dinner with him, we get a sense of the redemptive powers of Hungarian cuisine, snowy Budapest and Christmas all rolled up in one. This is an idealized world that comes to us by rich and realistic set design but even more by charming and spirited detail. Lubitsch has a way of convincing us that there is no place we would rather be than the place he is describing at that moment, whether it is dancing at Maxim's in Paris or hunkering down to a Christmas Eve goose in Budapest. His sets are meaningful because he relishes his dreams.

One of the greatest sets in film history came not from MGM but, ironically, from the famously low-budget Columbia Studios, proving that the imaginative effect of Hollywood set design was as much a question of spirit as it was of luxurious detail—though it has to be admitted that Columbia's director George Cukor had already begun to ply his trade at MGM and so perhaps brought some of his MGM flair with him. Often, when people try to summarize why they like MGM's *Holiday* so much they start, not with Cukor's direction or Hepburn's or Grant's acting, but with the room that Hepburn retreats to in rebellion against her stuffy family. The room, though picturesque and teeming with vivid detail like an MGM set might, is not at all MGM-like in its content. It represents a Bohemian paradise of sorts, much more in keeping with one of the studios that placed a higher value on artistic independence.

The room, Katharine Hepburn's character Linda tells us, was the brainchild of her dead mother, who "felt there should be one room in the house where people could have some fun." The room manifests the rebellion that Linda and her brother feel toward their wealthy family, the rebellion also a legacy of their mother. The room is a kind of combined childhood playhouse, gymnasium, and art and music studio, striking a visual claim for all that money neglects in life. It is replete with childhood toys: dolls, a giraffe on wheels , a tricycle Grant rides around a bit, model sailboats, music box carousels, an elaborate puppet theater (employed with great relish by Johnny's Bohemian friends, played by Edward Everett Horton and Jean Dixon.) Many of the objects are put to good metaphorical use. Grant compares a porcelain doll to his fiancée, Julia, not realizing that he is foreshadowing why he will not marry her. She is too vain, fragile, tied to her wealth to live the life Johnny has planned for them. When he picks up a toy giraffe on wheels, Hepburn notes a resemblance between herself and the giraffe, expressing a fetching self-deprecation, a sense of inferiority to her sister's beauty, and an inability to fit into her world—all qualities that will win Johnny over in the end.

Swords, juggling instruments, and a trapeze swing evoke a carnival atmosphere and provide for gymnastic displays that allow Cukor to take advantage of Hepburn's athleticism (as he did in several of his films with her) and Grant's acrobatic past. A covered painting testifies to Linda's frustrated artistic talent, and a variety of musical instruments testify to her brother Neddy's abandonment of his great musical talent at the behest of their money-driven father. Neddy (played with an elegant, acerbic deadpan by Lew Ayres) tends to rummage around the room plucking randomly at the instruments and providing apposite musical underlining to the scenes in the room, as when, with a swoop of his tin whistle and a smack on his drum, he heralds the exit of his stuffy relative, Mrs. Cram, from the room. The sound, causing Mrs. Cram to both look backward and scoot that much more quickly forward, represents a kind of aural kick in the behind.

Some of this design comes from Phillip Barry's stage play that preceded the film, but with film's ability to dwell on objects in greater intimacy and its ability to frame a room from many angle in the manner of an exquisitely composed, three-dimensional, mobile structure, the set takes on that same living, breathing dollhouse effect that the inn in *Queen Christina* does. It becomes the cozy incarnation of a dream, not the dream of sexual intimacy that the inn in *Queen Christina* represents, but, in this case, the dream of spiritual and aesthetic freedom lost in childhood, found in the arts, and sheltered from the materialistic world.

── 9 ──

Hollywood and Sentiment

One of the aspects of the Hollywood film that is essential, but also quite difficult, to discuss is its optimism—essential because Hollywood's buoyant spirit is a large part of its appeal, difficult because its studio enforced optimism often jars the modern sensibility, sounding mawkish or smarmy at times and downright propagandistic at others.

And yet 40 to 50 years of realism have taken their toll on the modern viewer as well, and when audiences find themselves interested once again in classic Hollywood, it is often out of a fatigue with morbid realism. They discover they have a greater thirst for the particular kind of purity Hollywood has to offer.

But it is difficult to define what kind of purity Hollywood has to offer. Defenders of Hollywood often fall into a variety of rhetorical traps. They sound as though they are advocating a retreat to a more civilized or more innocent past. Here they confuse film criticism with a soft kind of sociology and suggest that films were better in the past because *we* were better in the past. Fans of classic Hollywood often find themselves in the unseemly company of unthinking, conservative moralists who find the Hollywood film most useful in illustrating their theories on the degeneration of morals, an attitude that, no matter what your politics are, is insulting to classic Hollywood because it sees the films as reflections of their age, ignoring the careful craft of the films.

Another cliché that we often fall prey to is the notion of Hollywood as a kind of "dream factory," where we can lose ourselves, shut ourselves from reality in frothy spectacles that take us to ethereal grounds far from our sordid reality. But Hollywood, at its best, is too worldly and urban, too conscious of the tough realities of life to be summed up as a "dream factory. It's not the complete story to say that Hollywood is an idealistic art. Rather, Hollywood does idealism well. To do idealism well, a good deal of room has to be given to the darker, less ideal aspects of life. The enemy has to be given its due, and in the best of Hollywood that is done.

Also, we want to be careful not to idealize Hollywood's enforced idealism. Another myth, and again one with a lot of truth in it, is that the seemingly repressive studio system, seeking both to satisfy the public's desire for happy endings and to meet the demands of the production code, turns out to have been Hollywood's salvation, saving its films from a morbidity and artistic indulgence that has become all too apparent to filmgoer's since the demise of classic Hollywood.

But we also know that the production code and Hollywood's pathological optimism lead to some of its sillier moments, love scenes with couples in separate beds, the tacked-on "happy ending" to films like Wyler's *Wuthering Heights*, Borzage's *Three Comrades*, and Vidor's *The Wedding Night* where dead characters beckon to their surviving loves as they march in transparent ethereal glory to heaven. Even in their latter years, when time had given them the perspective to see the taste and discretion in the classic Hollywood films, directors still grumbled at the concessions they had to make and the indignities they had to suffer under the enforced optimism and purity of Hollywood. One of the most repeated clichés about Hollywood is that classic Hollywood filmmakers knew how to depict sex and violence without being crude or childishly explicit. And yet it was fascinating to see the films that Hitchcock, the master of suggesting violence rather than showing it, turned out as soon as the code was lifted, films with as graphic a violence as seen on the screen to that point.

Still, it's hard not to sigh in agreement with Dmitri Tiomkin when he writes, "Hollywood was a wonderful place when I first went there . . . it was a bright dream about a beautiful democracy in a world under the shadow of tyranny. I suppose there were fakes and phonies, but I can't help thinking there was an innocence which has now vanished. Once Hollywood forgot the dream and got down to reality it failed."[1] Tiomkin is right. One of the things that marked the end of classic Hollywood was the advent of realism. World War II brought with it a kind of realism that, even before the divestiture of theaters from studios, signaled the end of Hollywood and manifested itself in more virulent, melodramatic themes, films with social agendas, "film noirs" with bleaker visions and a more dominant sense of the world's corruption. And though these films vary in success, they all represent the end of a certain kind of Hollywood optimism.

For the most part, when Hollywood "got down to reality" it lost its vocation. For every Hitchcock, happy to break free of the restraints, there was a George Cukor who made himself breathless trying to explain to modern audiences that just because Hollywood films were less explicit than modern fare didn't mean they were childish. "I don't know what the hell 'adult films' are; I really, honestly don't," Cukor said when Bogdanovich asked him if he thought that now that censorship had been lifted Hollywood would be able to make "adult films." "You mean going around bare-assed or something. . . . Now don't get me wrong, I'm not a great moralist or anything, I just think it's awfully easy to do that way." In contrast to the equation of nudity with "adult films" Cukor cited the scene from

Camille where "Garbo kissed this young man; and she literally did not touch him—she just very gently kissed his face, moved all over his face—and that was frightfully tantalizing and erotic."[2]

In fact, the opposition between Hitchcock's and Cukor's postcode attitudes is emblematic of the paradoxical feelings of many Hollywood directors who were frustrated by absurd studio restraints but just as, perhaps more, dissatisfied with the cinema that came in their wake, a cinema that seemed to have lost the art of good taste and suggestiveness, and that simplistically defined maturity as openness in sexuality.

IDEALISM WITH AN EDGE

But it is not only the explicit and morbid realism of much of contemporary cinema that drives viewers back to classical Hollywood; it is also the insipidness of "feel-good films" that want to celebrate goodness in the manner of classical cinema but are unwilling to put in the hard work to make goodness effective on the screen and so finish only with a bland and clichéd optimism. Classic Hollywood was an era of innocence and idealism: that is clearly understood. What seems less understood is that there are tricks to conveying innocence and idealism effectively. There is a great deal of sophistication in Hollywood's approach to innocence, and its idealism, when expressed effectively, takes full account of the less idealistic aspects of life. Hollywood aimed at idealism, it's true, but its idealism is subsumed under its larger aesthetic of understatement. The best Hollywood directors thought of idealism as they did of sex and violence, all potent ingredients that needed to be doled out carefully. And they had the sense that idealism, to be effective, had to give room to a certain degree of pessimism.

Samson Raphaelson, one of Hollywood's great screenwriters, wrote that "the so-called happy ending of a high comedy should have a sardonic overtone. . . . because there is no such thing as a happy ending for an intelligent writer."[3] Here, Raphaelson explains why Hollywood, in its best films, was effective in expressing its idealism: because it approached it with a delicate sense of equilibrium. The best Hollywood films were expert in not laying it on too thick. They cut their idealism with a sardonic twist, a certain amount of irony or honest realism.

Many of classic Hollywood's greatest films are the product of a clash between studios enforcing optimism and idealism and independent filmmakers doing their most to test or complicate that idealism—an example of how the greatest Hollywood films tend to be the product of, not just the studio system, but also those who fought the system. In fact, this is another of those litmus tests that separate the wheat from the chaff in Hollywood. The greatest filmmakers were those who could make something of the dictate to be upbeat, who knew how to give their idealism shadows, to create disturbing undercurrents that gave their idealism some kick but were not so strong as to alienate producer or audience.

Here, as is so often, Charlie Chaplin is a prime example. Chaplin's films are frequently derided by unthinking critics for being too sentimental. But a careful study of Chaplin's most serious efforts shows very little sentiment that hasn't been earned through rich character detail or convincingly counterbalanced by an acute sense of the world's cruelty. The sentiment in Chaplin's films is effective because it is shot through with a shocking amorality. In Chaplin's *The Kid*, for example, you would be hard-pressed to find a scene of strong or excessive sentiment up until the scene where the boy is wrenched from Charlie's arms. There are touching scenes, as Charlie warms to the role of the parent, becoming adept at playing both father and mother, but, at the same time, we note how Charlie selfishly reverses the parent–child dynamic by training the kid to take care of his caretaker. It's the boy who prepares pancakes for Charlie, hounds him out of bed, and calls him to the table with the air of a frustrated mother in their famous breakfast scene. And Chaplin always undermines the sentiment of his parenting by stressing its physicality, as for example when he rolls a wash cloth into a fine point so that he can methodically clean each of the boy's nostrils, a kind of comic overstatement of Charlie's responsibility as a parent.

We also note Charlie's many moral lapses as he raises the child. When Charlie finds the child at the outset of the film, for example, he tries to palm it off on others (including an old homeless codger) several times. He would abandon it to the street again were it not for the attentive eye of a policeman. When he finally sits down on the curb, seemingly resigned to assuming responsibility for the child, his cane, as if acting by its own agency, gently lifts a nearby sewer grate, and Charlie contemplates the unspeakable.

And, of course, Charlie is raising his son to a life of crime. The boy is his partner in a con job in which the boy breaks windows by throwing a rock and Charlie, pretending to be a glazier, happens by the frustrated homeowner and offers his services. One of the emblematic scenes in the film is when a policeman has figured out the con and identifies the boy as Charlie's. The kid approaches Charlie enthusiastically, but Charlie, suffering under the policeman's gaze, pretends he has nothing to do with the boy. As they walk away from the cop, Charlie gives quick little furtive sideway kicks to the puzzled boy as you might to a stray dog that wishes to follow you home.

The scene where the kid has a fight with a neighborhood bully is a marvel of the way Charlie floats dexterously between charm and amorality. At first, when he realizes that his son is being picked on by a much larger bully, Charlie rushes to break up the fight. When he sees that his son is winning he not only lets the fight go on but also exults in the battle, playing, as the childish Charlie will, all the roles associated with a boxing match. He referees a little; he kneels down and excitedly places wagers, like a boxing fan; in between rounds he plays the role of his son's manager, spreading the boy's arms out on a neighbor's clothing line, spritzing him with water by drinking and spitting on him, and giving him boxing advice. (From the nature of his gesticulations it is clear that he is advising the kid to kick the other boy in the seat of the pants and strike him below the belt.)

His tone changes though when the bully's enormous brother shows up and informs Charlie, "If your kid beats up my brother, I'll beat you up." Now Charlie wants nothing more than his son's defeat. Watching the fight is an exercise in sweaty misery, as his son continues to dominate. But, at a moment when his son slips to the ground, Charlie takes matters into his own hands, stepping on his son and holding him down with his foot, while raising up his battered adversary's hand in the air and trying as best as he can to give the impression that it is the other boy who is the legitimate victor in the match, not his own son.

These are my students' favorite scenes in the film, and they are immensely important to them in making Charlie's more ideal and sentimental features more palatable. There are few directors who more exemplified the importance Hollywood placed on the classical virtues of balance and equanimity than Chaplin did. His tramp is a hybrid of matched opposites: a scoundrel and a hero; awkward and elegant; a bum and an aristocrat; selfless and loyal one moment, shockingly self-interested and amoral the next; a squalid homeless man repugnant to most women, a knight in shining armor to others; at the bottom of the social pecking order while at the top of the spiritual hierarchy.

Hollywood is most successful in conveying its sentiment and idealism when it follows Chaplin's pattern of giving due measure to the contradictory, darker qualities in life. The moralism of Warner's gangster films, for example, is often balanced out by a strong emphasis on the omnipresence of political corruption. Their gangsters often acquit themselves admirably, if not altogether, when they defend their right to a life of crime, so strong was Warner's sense of the moral relativism occasioned by the injustices of the Great Depression.

Warners' musicals also embody the upbeat, relentlessly forward moving energy of Hollywood, and yet a film like *42nd Street* represents, as Charles Higham notes, "a remarkably frank, savage and earthy picture of the world backstage," replete with chorus girls using their bodies to better their careers and dance directors hiring for sexual opportunity. It's a world, Higham notes, where "money and desire are the only motivations of a life devoid of beauty, wit or culture." The kind of "acid realism" that we find in Warner's 1930s scripts is sorely missing in the glossy war propaganda films, women's pictures and biopics the studio turned out in the 1940s which, as Higham notes, mixed "schmaltz with adeptness in presentation."[4] Earlier Warner's films mix tones more sophisticatedly, despite the madcap production process there. Many of the latter films are prone to the glossy sentimentalism that modern audiences all too often associate with Hollywood in general.

The story of much of Hollywood's success is the story of filmmakers who cut the treacle, stay faithful to Hollywood's essential positive thrust, its distinctive energy, but don't fall prey to a lifeless, unearned optimism. Lubitsch's musicals at Paramount have a lewd vitality, a sexual frankness and worldly cynicism, that saves them from the smarminess that is dangerously endemic to the musical genre. Just look at the difference between Jeannette MacDonald at Paramount, where she exudes a comfortable sexuality, and Jeannette MacDonald at MGM, where she is transformed into a virginal and, as Ethan Mordden writes, "rigid diva." "Once out of Lubitsch's care," writes Mordden, "the MGM MacDonald turned into steel froth, losing the slithery tact of her Chevalier days for a family-show aplomb, squeaky and haughty at once, that makes one wonder whether she glows in the dark."[5] Howard Hawks creates the closest thing to an existential setting in Hollywood, specializing as he does in little cozy spots in the middle of darkness, "clean well-lighted cafés" in the middle of exotic locales with characters of questionable pasts, just on this side of resignation, depression, and alcoholism. Hitchcock took great glee in subverting the Hollywood happy facade, by suggesting the great depth of horror that hides behind normal appearances. Uncle Charlie's speech in *Shadow of a Doubt* about the hell and pigsties that reside within the walls of respectable domiciles and Norman Bates's summary of humans as caged animals clawing at each other in *Psycho* suggest just how dark Hitchcock's vision can be, but his best moments are when he gently implies the peculiar that lies just under the happy and familiar, the scenes, for example, in which both the murderers in *Rear Window* and *Frenzy* conscientiously tend their gardens.

And no one has tried his sentiment with more cynicism than has Billy Wilder, maybe the only director who can wind sentiment and cynicism together with the dexterity of Chaplin. Jack Lemmon's and Shirley MacLaine's romance in *The Apartment* blossoms in a high-rise office milieu characterized by the worst kind of sexual cruelty and pathetic professional ambition, both of which Lemmon, the hero of the film, is initially guilty. Only Wilder could create Marlene Dietrich's character in *Foreign Affair*, ex-Nazi and consort of Hitler but also warbler of German postwar malaise and humiliation, survivor of Russian and American abuse alike, at once the film's villain and its soul. But of course this was Hitchcock's bailiwick, as well, inverting the relationship between hero and villain, so that in the end, the villains in *Notorious* and *North by Northwest* seem more sympathetic, more loving of the film's heroine than the emotionally stunted characters played by Cary Grant.

In short, the great Hollywood directors were sentimental and idealistic. Those ingredients are part of the essential Hollywood concoction. But they also took great pains to complicate that idealism, giving it shadings that allowed it greater depth and more dramatic resonance.

DARK SENTIMENTALISTS

Even those directors who have the greatest reputation for Hollywood hokum, upon closer analysis, give a fairer share to the dark side than they are often acknowledged to have. Capra's reputation for "Capracorn" has given way in recent years to an appreciation of just how fully he documents the forces that challenge his strong idealism. Capra's careful delineation of corrupt political machinery in *Meet John Doe* and *Mr. Smith Goes to Washington* represents a pretty sophisticated sense of the significant fault lines in American democracy. And though we relish the warmth of Capra's redemptive endings, his scenes of quasi-crucifixion, like the one in which a stadium full of devotees turn on John Doe, may stick in our memory more vividly.

Those who find John Doe's idealistic radio speech too clichéd in its populism tend to forget the saving grace of that sequence, John Doe's utterly cynical partner on the bum, "the colonel," played by Walter Brennan, who thinks that everyone who is celebrating John Doe is just a "bunch of helots." (No classical reference here, he just thinks they're a lot of heels.) During the broadcast, the colonel stands, to John's right, near an exit door from the stage where John is delivering his speech. While the audience laps up John's populist message, the colonel remains steadfastly unimpressed. At one point, Capra cuts from the audience, rollicking in appreciation of this everyman's wisdom, to the colonel, biding his time, sewing a button on his tattered jacket. Periodically, during the speech, the colonel catches John's eye and, with a comic deadpan, opens and shuts the exit door as if inspecting how well it works. Then he waves to John to indicate that, yes, it does work and would well provide an escape from all this nonsense.

Despite his reputation for wild-eyed optimism, Capra was also skilled at conveying suffering. Andrew Sarris, for example, feels that critics have failed to appreciate the "force and fury of Stewart's acting" in *It's a Wonderful Life* (Photo 5) and the "pain and sorrow it so eloquently expressed." Sarris cites Stewart's "angry, exasperated, anguished 'proposal'" to Donna Reed in the film as an example of "one of the most sublimely histrionic expressions of passion mingled with the painful knowledge that one's dream of seeing the world outside one's small town vanishing before one's eyes."[6] The scene is a surprising one, one of the most painful and confused marriage proposals in film history, with Stewart viciously, angrily shaking Reed by the arms, exclaiming violently why he'll never get married. Moments later, Reed's anguished expression causes him to break down and embrace her in what constitutes the first moment of their engagement.

Stewart's tantrum at his home on Christmas Eve (the night of his visitation by Clarence the angel) is another example of the darkness of Stewart's performance, and of the film. The moments when Stewart rages at his adoring and bewildered children and verbally abuses Zouzou's teacher over the telephone, blaming her unfairly for his daughter's fever, are uniquely dark moments in both the Hollywood film and the handling of Stewart's persona.

And the scene in which George Bailey contemplates his future over dinner with his father is unlike any other father–son bonding moment that I have seen. The scene finishes with a trademark bit of "Capracorn," as Jimmy Stewart leans toward his father and says in hushed tones, "You want a shock, Pop? I think you're a great guy." This is the kind of sappy moment audiences associate, not just with Capra, but also with Hollywood in general. But this bit of sentiment occurs just moments after George has insulted his father a couple of times and in ways that are painfully familiar to parents. The scene is as noteworthy for its realism as it is for its sentiment.

As they sit down to dinner on the eve of George's departure from Bedford Falls, George's father suggests that he would like George to stay in Bedford Falls and continue to work at his father's savings and loan. George is horrified by the prospect. "I couldn't face being cooped up for the rest of my life in a shabby little

Photo 5. The many dark moments in Frank Capra's greatest films disprove the pejorative "Capracorn" and attest to his films' great sense of balance. Courtesy of Photofest.

office," he explains before realizing how cruel this summary of his father's life is. This is the kind of unthinking moment many parents have suffered at the hands of their children but not the kind we automatically associate with corny Capra. George goes on to further denigrate his father's choice in life, "It's this business of counting nickels and dimes, of spending your whole life trying to save 3 cents and light the pipe." In the end, the father wins George's praise, not by getting him to buy into his placid values, a la Judge Hardy, but by encouraging him to shake the dust of his scruffy little hometown off. "You get your education and get out of here," he concedes. So much for the bliss of small town life.

This conversation is typical of the film's dualism, the way Capra balances the suffocating alienation of small town life and its blissful domestic regularity, for, after all, George will stay in Bedford Falls, and the film represents, in the end, an endorsement of that decision to stay. This and other scenes like it are why Sarris feels that the film's "happy ending never quite compensates for all the suffering that precedes it" and describes the film as "one of the most profoundly pessimistic tales of human existence ever to achieve a lasting popularity."[7]

This strikes me as an overstatement. I agree that in *It's a Wonderful Life*, as in *Meet John Doe*, Capra didn't quite know how to wrap up the film. I've always found the inscription that Clarence the angel left in George Bailey's copy of *Tom Sawyer*, "No one is alone who has friends," inadequate in answering the problems the film raises. The film is about so much more than friendship: it is about ambition and compromises, about failure and the beauty and horror of marriage, children, and small town life. The town's emptying of its coffers on George's desk also strikes me as a literal, and not particularly subtle, answer to the dire emotional straights George finds himself in. These are the kinds of heavy-handed ideas from which long-time writing partner Robert Riskin might have saved Capra had he worked with him on this project as well.

But, in general, Capra's cynicism is more than balanced by the wealth of touching detail that accumulates along the course of the film. Any fan of the film could provide reams of examples, whether it be the scene where taxi driver Ernie and cop Bert abet Donna Reed in creating a faux tropical paradise on her honeymoon night with Stewart or the scene in which the incomparable character actor Dick Elliot chides Stewart for failing to kiss Reed after serenading her late on a summer night, "Oh youth is wasted on the wrong people." The moments of sentiment and idealism are as thick as the exquisite characters actors in the film and more than balance Capra's deep sense of life's failures and compromises. It's the texture of the film as a whole, not any particular message that Capra comes up with, that best balances and refutes the film's deep pessimism.

John Ford is another director whose sentiment can be a bit strong for modern tastes. I would not relish showing the *How Green Was My Valley* to a group of students who weren't well versed in Ford's taste and ideas. Ford's movies, at their most sentimental and indulgent, often remind me of Gregory Hemingway's assessment of his father's novel *The Old Man and the Sea*, "as sickly a bucket of slop as was ever scrubbed off the bar-room floor."

But in his best films, Ford strikes a balance between his taste for sentiment and a dark, forlorn sense of the world. Sergio Leone praised Ford's Westerns for their realistic texture: "He was the first to show us that real Western cowboys did not walk around dressed in clean black on white plucking banjos and batting their eyelashes like gigolos in the manner of Tom Mix and Hopalong Cassidy." Leone cites the mud-caked duster in *My Darling Clementine*, the movement of white clouds over blue cavalries, and the image of a dust-covered John Wayne halting the stagecoach in *Stagecoach* as images that "sacrificed nothing for postcard effects." Ford was, to Leone, "one of the most authentic pioneers of modern realistic cinematography."[8]

And if Ford's world is sentimental, it is just as often melancholy and elegiac. He has a love of not only folk songs and country dances but also the sad exile, for example, the errant merchant marines in *The Long Voyage Home* or the various lost intellectuals—the doctors, newspapermen, actors, and failed Southern gentleman—who stumble out West in his films and lose themselves in the bottle.

And of course, Ford created a particularly moving mixture of gruffness, duty, and solitude in the persona he gradually established for John Wayne. Wayne, in Ford's films, is always dutiful but increasingly finds no place for himself in the world he serves. He is loyal as a dog but also gruff, angry, and bitter to the point of cruelty and self-exile. As Ethan Edwards in *The Searchers*, Wayne, in the final moments of the film, alone and rubbing his arm vulnerably in that famous imitation of Harry Carey, watches everyone else revel in their happiness (for which he is responsible). In *The Man Who Shot Liberty Valance*, Wayne's Tom Donovan burns down the house that he had hoped (before Jimmy Stewart happened by) to live in with Vera Miles, recognizing, bitterly, that both she and the West, in general, are better off with the likes of Stewart's Ransom Stoddard. In *Fort Apache*, Wayne's character swallows the truth about Henry Fonda's foolish, Custer-like suicidal charge, sacrificing both the truth and the honorable role he, himself, played in the story, for the sake of a mythology and the good reputation of a hopeless martinet. Wayne's persona is a nice example of the way in which Ford could make a pretty strong sense of idealism palatable by wedding it to an inevitable loss and sadness.

DOING INNOCENCE WELL

It is also important to note, however, that Ford, Capra, and Hollywood in general did not always need to situate goodness in close proximity to evil in order to effectively communicate goodness. To argue this would be to miss the point that Hollywood often had a pure and simple gift for conveying goodness. I have already examined the scene in *My Darling Clementine* in which Wyatt Earp conducts Clementine to the inaugural church dance as an example of how Ford's films are chock-full of little poetic, meditative moments that concern themselves little with advancing the plot or contributing to the film's action. The scene is also a good example of Ford's ability to simply record ideal moments in vivid and fresh detail.

Here is a scene where a fresh optimism is conveyed in the stark light of the day, without any recourse to shadows or equipoised thoughts of darkness. Ford's noirish collaborations with cinematographers like Gregory Toland and Gabriel Figeroa are so renowned that we often forget he also had the ability to capture the freshness of morning light with greater accuracy than other directors. It may be this characteristic of Ford's filmmaking that Leone had in mind when he wrote that it was the "solar and humanistic West of Ford that had guided . . . [his] route."

Leone was not only impressed by Ford's dusty realism but also "influenced by Ford's honesty and directness."[9]

Honesty and directness would certainly be two words that describe the Sunday morning scene in *My Darling Clementine*. It's a fresh springtime sequence that aims to describe the touching religious stirrings of a new community. It has all the potential to be pure schmaltz. But it isn't. Why? Because of Ford's particular mix of charming detail and moving, reverent mise-en-scène. He fills the sequence with all sort of sorts of quaint business: Fonda's embarrassment over the lilac cologne that was splashed over him at the newfangled tonsorial parlor (itself a touching commentary on the burgeoning civilization); the good-natured chafing he takes over the smell from his brothers (enhanced by our affection for Ford regular Ward Bond); the half-finished church that suggests a religious community before the hypocrisies of organized religion set in; and Fonda's embarrassment in dancing at the founding ceremony, his stride at once awkward and strangely elegant in its long-leggedness. Ford seems to have sought every opportunity to use Fonda's gangling elegance on the dance floor. It seemed to him a touching representation of the chivalry of the raw cowboy bowing to the arrival of civilization.

At the same time the film has a more serious mythic qualities as well: the traveling shot that accompanies them down the long portico that extends deep into the frame, with Ford's trademark composition in depth, and points to the church poised in the back of the frame; the quintessential Ford shot from below of the dancers framed by an enormous sky that makes it impossible to find anything tawdry or quotidian in the scene that is otherwise quite homely. The sequence is never so quaint as to be silly or broad but still has a wealth of humble detail to humanize its elegant and mythic mise-en-scène.

Now, a scene like this is effective not because Ford has shaded his optimism, struck a balance between good and evil, though Hollywood directors could, as we have seen, be quite good at that; the sequence is effective because of its charm and lyricism. I think it's important not to justify Hollywood's idealism by saying it could only be effective when rendered in great proximity to pessimism. Hollywood did not always have to mix its good with bad. It could also be very adept at simply conveying good. Hollywood specializes in exercises of pure, unadulterated freshness, "ceremonies of innocence." It is capable of expressing its idealism simply, "honestly and directly." And this needs to be stated without embarrassment. A cinema of idealism and of sincerity is not de facto a puerile cinema. In fact, the history of art shows us that one of the greatest accomplishments in art is to present goodness in a way that has some blood and substance and is not cloying and propagandistic. The world of art is filled with bland Jesuses and King Arthurs and a great many more intriguing Satans and Lancelots. A depiction of good that is not bloodless is a rare find in the history of art. If a modern audience gravitates back to classical Hollywood it does so, not because it is glutted on the morbid and clinical realism of contemporary films, but because it is unconvinced by their efforts at optimism, their unearned happy endings, their heroism without the gentle shadings and deft touches in which Hollywood specialized.

I am always pleased to note that my students are genuinely moved by the scene in *The Kid* where Charlie Chaplin's adopted son is torn from his arms by heartless government authorities. The sequence is wrenching, with alternating close-ups of Charlie being restrained by the police and the boy being carted off in a truck, clearly crying out "I want my daddy." My students, who are often put off by the emotional demands of scenes far less operatic than this one, are often moved to the point of tears. When I ask them why this scene in particular does not offend them in its strong sentiment, when so many other Hollywood scenes I've shown have struck them as "schmaltzy," they answer that it is because they have come to acutely appreciate the relationship between the tramp and the child. They refer to the countless scenes in the earlier part of the film where Chaplin meticulously denotes the loving relationship between Chaplin and the boy. Invariably, they return to the scene where the boy prepares pancakes for Charlie—an idyll of Sunday morning leisure, replete with all sorts of tiny details that express the love and eccentricity of their relationship, for example, Chaplin shuffling and counting the pancakes like so many cards in a playing deck to insure that both he and the child get the exact same number of pancakes and Charlie playing the role of the paterfamilias and making sure they bow their heads in prayer before they eat, even though the prayer is one of the utmost brevity, a testimony to the breadth of their appetite rather than their faith.

In this film, Chaplin is effective in his evocation of emotion, not by mixing sentiment with cynicism, as he does so masterfully, but simply by doing the hard work of carefully building a relationship. And building a relationship does not mean a bunch of scenes in which characters speechify about their love for each other or a montage of parent–child bonding moments. It means concretizing that relationship in charming and imaginative detail that memorably embodies the characters' affection and loyalty for one another. Hollywood's effective rendering of sentiment, then, is due not only to the way it keeps its eye on the darker side of life but also to the sheer energy and imaginative effort it puts into rendering that idealism into vivid and concrete detail.

FAILURES IN SENTIMENT

All this is not to say that Hollywood doesn't ever miss the mark when it comes to sentiment or idealism. Hollywood produced countless sanctimonious and melodramatic films, and these films come in all sorts of permutations: B film series of the likes of Rin Tin Tin movies at Warner Brothers and the Andy Hardy movies at MGM, 1930s MGM melodramas and 1940s Warner Brothers's women's pictures, preachy biopics, and propagandistic wartime efforts. I've never had the patience others have for Bette Davis's endless sorrows in many of her pictures for Warner. And I find that Hollywood films about doctors are almost always studies in an annoying and endless martyrdom. Here even trustworthy talents like George Stevens (*Vigil in the Night*) and John Ford (*Arrowsmith*) tend to fail. Hollywood falters whenever it's not true to its highest aesthetic, whenever it breaks its own cardinal rule of not saying too much, when it can't, for example, keep its virtue or martyrdom to itself.

I'm sympathetic to the angry invective to which Ethan Mordden, normally a critic with great patience for Hollywood schmaltz, is moved by the Andy Hardy pictures. "The Hardys of Carvel, Idaho," he writes, "are dreary white Protestants who make one feel good to be single, Jewish, or an axe murderer." Mordden has a great deal of fun enumerating the small town clichés in the series, "the man-to-man father–son talks that, no matter what the subject, are always about their mutual affection; . . . the maiden aunt who hangs on at the edges of things, answering the doorbell and making sensitive remarks at dinner; the noble Judge Hardy bucking township consensus on a controversial issue." This series, Mordenn concludes, "isn't just corny and simplistic. It's insidious hogwash. It's blackmail. It's lies."[10] These thoughts, registered by a critic who is an absolute sucker for the most outlandish artifice of Ernst Lubitsch, testify to the fact that all sentiment in Hollywood is not alike.

The relationship between Andy Hardy and his father, for example, represents a useful contrast to the father–son relationship in *It's a Wonderful Life.* Judge Hardy represents everything a father should be and consequently most of what fathers are not. Here ideals become oppressive. The father in *It's a Wonderful Life* incorporates a good deal of rumpled failure. George Bailey's reverence for the father is very idealized. But the tired, less impressive spectacle of the father makes that reverence more touching. Hollywood, as a whole, is very sentimental, but in its successful communication of that sentiment, there are scores of distinctions to be made.

Hollywood does not just falter in its weakest films alone. Even Hollywood's best films have clunky moments. *To Have and Have Not*, a near-perfect film, stumbles when the French Resistance fighters feel the need to make sure we understand just how heroic Humphrey Bogart is, since he won't let on. Hawks's *Only Angels Have Wings* falls short of being one of his best films because it overplays its male bonding. The expressions of mutual respect by the men in this film lack Hawks's usual obliqueness. By contrast we are never in doubt of Hildy Johnson and Walter's passion for each other in *His Girl Friday*, though they go more or less throughout the entire film without saying a kind word to each other. Even the most ardent apologist for Capra has to admit that at times he loses sight of the creative way to get his point across and just spells it out in speeches that go on a little too long and are just a little too aw-shucks in their populism. Even the greatest Hollywood directors weren't always capable of reaching that perfect blend of sentiment and cynicism.

CAMILLE AND *A FAREWELL TO ARMS*:
TWO SENTIMENTAL ENDINGS

The ending to Frank Borzage's *A Farewell to Arms*, a film with many lovely touches, may be a good example of how easily sentiment degenerates into treacle, even in the best Hollywood films. *A Farewell to Arms* has a lot to recommend it, particularly the scenes of early courtship between Gary Cooper and Helen Hayes, which are typical of what Sarris saw as Borzage's great talent for expressing "a genuine concern with the wondrous inner life of lovers in the midst of adversity."[11] But Helen Hayes's death scene at the end of the film always puts me in mind of Oscar Wilde's famous quip: "You'd have to have a heart of stone to read the death of little Nell without laughing." The scene is set to the swelling love theme of *Tristan and Isolde*, an unfortunate choice to begin with, not just because it represents a kind of cliché of romantic love in movie soundtracks, but because it hadn't been so long before this film that Luis Bunuel had sent up the romanticism of the piece in *Chien Andalou.*

The death scene culminates with Cooper and Hayes sharing a kind of prayer or marital vow that reaches its apex just as the theme from Wagner's opera does. "I'm not afraid. I'm free," exults Hayes, as the music swells to its famous climax. Meanwhile, bells outside announce the armistice at the end of World War I, and Borzage ratchets up the lighting, bathing Hayes in white. A montage follows that describes news of the armistice, and then Borzage cuts back to the hospital. Cooper has picked up his lover's dead body. Silhouetted dramatically before the window with its alpine landscape, holding Hayes's body in the manner of a pieta, Cooper dramatically exclaims, "Peace, peace." The final shot is of doves ascending to the skies, maybe a purely abstract symbol for peace, maybe doves that have been awoken by the sound of the bells.

The scene is not without its operatic sweep. I particularly like the way that Borzage arranges Hayes's sheets so that when Cooper picks her up, the sheets fan out like an elaborate funeral shroud or gown—a lovely, decorative effect. But, all in all, you're going to have to have an enormous tolerance for sentiment to endure this scene.

I think the final scene of *Camille*, similar in so many details to the end of *A Farewell to Arms* compares favorably and shows why Cukor's hallmark is his good taste while Borzage's reputation has had to defend itself against charges of an excessive sentimentalism. The contrast also highlights the techniques a great Hollywood filmmaker like Cukor availed himself of in order to take the mickey out of his sentiment.

In some ways comparing the two is unfair because Cukor had Garbo for his film, while Borzage had Helen Hayes, who, for all her dignity on the stage, was a wooden presence on the screen. Here, excessive makeup accentuating the sharp angles of her face, she gives the impression of a dying marionette. Cukor, on the other hand, only had to keep the camera on Garbo and let it soak her up, while she did what she did best, writhe in the bliss and agony of her intense love.

But, at the same time, Cukor does all sorts of things that make the sentiment in his scene more effective and less bombastic. Both endings turn on the same charming little conceit, the stock detail of the woman, at death's door, touchingly seeking to apply some makeup before her lover enters the room for their final farewell. But Borzage is much more ham-handed in how he uses this detail. When Catherine asks for her handbag so that she might make herself more presentable for her lover, Frederick, the nurses that flank her bed exchange glances that say, "How tragic!" Cukor doesn't underline Marguerite's martyrdom so obviously in *Camille*. Moreover he evades the problem of having strangers by her bedside altogether. Marguerite's deathbed is presided over by her loyal servant, Nanine, a character whose dogged devotion to Marguerite has been well documented throughout the film. Like Chaplin, Cukor does the preparatory work that earns our emotions. Nanine is the filmic equivalent to the Harlot's loyal servant, when all others have abandoned her, in Hogarth's *A Harlot's Progress*. She's not only a well-developed part of the movie but also touches on traditions in this genre of the story. She has a kind of traditional painterly quality. Cukor avoids handing important moments to anonymous characters. And he keeps the sterile presence of nurses and doctors with their professional sympathy out of his love scene. In fact, when Armand calls for a doctor, Marguerite laughs at him. "If you can't save me, how could they?" she says teasingly. Cukor understands that doctors and nurses are superfluous in a love scene.

Cukor's choice of music is telling in *Camille*. He doesn't make the mistake of trying to charge his love scene, from the outside, with a turbo blast of operatic passion like *Tristan and Isolde*. Rather, the scene plays to a quiet waltz that takes us back to Marguerite and Armand's first times together in the demimonde of Parisian courtesans. It is a Lubitsch-like choice to convey the romance, steeped in Paris and champagne, that is particular to their love. Cukor never takes his eye off the love relationship in this scene. Borzage seems to think the love between his two characters is not enough and broadens out the scene to encompass world peace, the end of World War I, and the Christian concept of heaven. Hayes is given lines that amplify her martyrdom, as she makes the doctors admit she's dying, puts on a brave front for Cooper, falters a little, but then recovers in a triumphant prayer. Garbo wants only to gaze at her lover's face in her few remaining moments.

Camille's dialogue is far more touching than that of *A Farewell to Arms*, because Robert Taylor's character, Gaston, unaware of how sick Garbo is, starts to prepare to take her to the country, and Garbo, so entranced by the dream of returning to the country with Gaston, plays along with the charade just to spend her last moments in a dream of love. Only when she looks into the troubled eyes of her servant, Nanine, does she falter a little in her illusion. The fantasy of the retreat to the country offers a touching counterpoint to the reality and proximity of her death. No triumphant speeches here, no resolution to the problem of death and lost love, only a momentary dream of escaping her fate. Garbo dies, not with words of triumph on her lips, but wrapped in the embrace of a lovely lie.

And whereas Frederick in *A Farewell to Arms*, like a kind of death counselor, provides Catherine with her final lines, coaching her to her final expression of utter confidence, Armand is completely taken aback by Catherine's death. Not until the last moments did he realize how sick she was. His final words to her, "Marguerite come back, Marguerite don't leave," are moving because his dream of being with Marguerite has come to such an abrupt end and because he realizes now that he waited too long to return to her. The scene is more effective because there is not a frantic attempt to make the death successful or all for the good. We are frustrated, not soothed, by Marguerite's death. Fortunately, Cukor and Garbo convey their rapprochement with such fullness that our frustration is tempered. At least they, unlike Frederick and Catherine, didn't waste their final moments in prayers and mystical gobbledygook. Rather, they finished in a luxurious dream of love.

QUIET SENTIMENT

Even classic Hollywood's greatest practitioners, like Borzage, then, found it difficult to convey sentiment effectively, without recourse to cliché or excessive emphasis. When Hollywood did fail to convey sentiment effectively it was usually because it wasn't faithful to its own aesthetic—that of presenting its most serious ideas elliptically and avoiding whenever possible stating things outright.

When classic Hollywood hit the mark, when its determination to represent goodness on the screen was matched by a filmmaker's or actor's ability to deftly register that goodness, then it reached levels unmatched by other cinemas. The Hollywood studio film was not too cool for its own good. Hollywood was willing to ascend heights of sentiment that other film eras, governed more tyrannically by the dictates of naturalism and realism, are not. The classic Hollywood film is an interesting mixture of deeply emotional cinema conveyed through an aesthetic of restraint. At its best it wants to make us feel, but it also wants to avoid the obvious and to avoid being craven in manipulating our emotions.

In the best Hollywood films the heroes are not allowed to express their own valor or explain themselves. Humphrey Bogart, in *Casablanca* and *To Have and Have Not*, is so convinced of his own dissolution and so convinced of the futility of life that he doesn't want to make an ass of himself by pretending to be more virtuous than he is or that he can be of more use to the world then he can. Others are going to have to extract his heroism like a painful tooth. And he's going to deny his virtue all the way through the film, not just out of false modesty but also almost out of disgust at making the mistake of believing in himself and in the world again. If Gary Cooper is forced to articulate his good intentions he gets tongue-tied. John Wayne gets angry. Cary Grant does not want to let on that he is anything more than a roué. So many of Grant's films are based on the question of whether or not you can trust this charming ne'er-do-well. Of course you invariably can, but he's going to make it as challenging as possible to believe that there is a consistently loyal heart beating beneath that roguish exterior.

Hollywood writers, at their best, treat sentiment and idealism as they do other potent ingredients like sex, violence, and explicit ideas—as things to be doled out with the minimum of words, as things so potent in force that they need to be checked by cross-forces if they are not going to overwhelm the picture.

THE DINER SCENE IN *THE GRAPES OF WRATH*

Take for one final example of Hollywood's gift in conveying idealism, the scene in John Ford's *The Grapes of Wrath*, one of my favorites in all of Ford's oeuvre, where Pa Joad enters a diner, hoping to buy a loaf of bread for a dime. Inside the diner are two truckers eating pie, a somewhat crabby waitress, and a gruff short-order cook frying hamburgers, the stubby remains of a cigar in his mouth. The waitress angrily tells the grandfather they don't sell loaves of bread at diners and asks him why he doesn't buy a sandwich instead. Pa Joad responds with that slow, carefully reasoned country rhetoric so typical of Ford's best scripts and so well-articulated by a Ford veteran like Russell Simpson, who seems born to speak the folksy verse to which Ford was partial: "I sure would like to, Ma'am, but the fact is that we ain't got but a dime for it. It's all figured out, I mean, towards the trip."

The waitress is unmoved by Joad's careful explanations and continues to testily deny his request until the short-order cook, and seeming boss of the place, rudely interrupts her. "Give 'em the loaf," he barks angrily at her. Confused, she protests that they might run out before their next shipment of bread, to which the cook responds, just as testily, "All right. Then we run out."

The cook is charitable here, but there is nothing simpering in this expression of charity. In fact, the cook's charity is nicely contrasted with his gruff demeanor; he seems to be charitable more out of anger with his waitress than out of sympathy for the Joads. And there's poetry in his curtness. He doesn't go on to explain his point of view, that turning these people away would be worse than running out of bread at the end of the day.

As the waitress goes to the back of the diner to fetch the loaf, the two Joad children warily enter the diner, like careful aliens entering a foreign terrain. They head to their dad, holding on to him for security and then gravitate toward the forbidden fruits of the candy counter at the cash register. Ford gives us a near shot of one of the truckers watching them. The trucker's expression is entirely neutral as he watches the child.

When the waitress brings out the 15-cent loaf of bread, Pa Joad tests her patience even further by asking if she might cut off 10 cents worth. Before she can object, the cook, a man of few words, barks out again, "Give 'em the loaf." Pa Joad objects that he doesn't want charity, and the cook now barks at *him* angrily, "Go on; it's yesterday's bread."

Now for the first time the waitress seems to warm to the situation. She seems to realize that she has found herself in a charitable situation. Her voice softens and her face is confused as she says, "Go ahead; Bert says to take it." Still, to Ford's credit, when Joad thanks her, again explaining the tight budget of the family, she does not respond with a look of understanding or a warm smile. She just looks blank as if she were still figuring out what was going on or calculating what was required of her.

As Pa Joad readies to leave, he notices his children eyeing the candy. He asks the waitress if the striped candy sticks the children covet are penny candies. When the waitress does a double take and haltingly tells him that, actually, they are two for a penny, we know she is lying, and that the candy is more expensive than she is letting on, and that she is aiming for her own act of charity here. The truck drivers exchange wry glances; they see through her ruse. Their expressions, though, are not cloying but close to neutral, almost more derisive than appreciative, as if they have spied the waitress in a moment of weakness. They seem to find her new charitable instincts a bit comical. After the Joads leave, they tease the waitress. "Them ain't 2-cent candies," one says, almost menacingly. "What's it to you," she says defensively, as if caught out in a shameful act. "Them's 5-cent candies," the trucker adds, finishing his point.

The truckers take that moment as their cue to leave, and as they walk out the door, they drop their payment in a dish by the cash register. The waitress looks at the money in astonishment and calls to them as they are almost out the door: "Hey wait a minute, you've got change coming to you." "What's it to you," says one of the truckers, throwing the waitress's own words back at her. Again, the truckers' act is charitable, but the motivation seems to be to tease the waitress as much as it is to be kind.

The truckers gone, the waitress stares at the money for a moment, as if she can't decide whether the truckers have been mean or charitable, then calls to Bert, the cook, holding out the money in the palm of her hand for him to see. Ford cuts to a comical shot of the crabby faced Bert, cigar in mouth, looking blankly at her. He says nothing; he only stares at her and pats his sizzling hamburger loudly three times. The effect is almost musical, giving an aural dimension to the moment as he reflects on what he's seeing in a slow-witted manner. Ford cuts back to the perplexed waitress who finishes the scenes with two words that she expresses with chuckling, affectionate derision: "Truck drivers."

It would be too difficult to convey charity, an emotion that has elicited a good deal of heavy-handed technique, with greater understatement than Ford does in this sequence. No one in this scene calls attention to his or her charity or puts it into words. In fact all of them do whatever they can to deflect attention from their charity, as if they were embarrassed for it to be seen in public. Ford provides us with the motivation for the truck-drivers' charity in the shot of the one watching the children ogle the candy and in the humorous expression they exchange when the waitress starts to be charitable. But the truckers never let on to their emotions. In the end they pick up the tab for the entire event, but they do it with a cocky deadpan.

The waitress and the cook also deflect attention from their charity, expressing it in a crabby, confused way that suggests they don't enjoy being called out in the open this way, that something of this kind of emotional delicacy is something they would rather keep to themselves. In many ways, the scene is less about people being charitable than it is about how people behave when they have to think on the spot, when they are met with moral exigencies outside of their normal routine. It's a scene about the trickiness of charity, the confusion that often surrounds an act of charity.

In the end, both the deadpan truckers and the crabby waitstaff are examples of Ford's ideal of humility, of the American puritan attitude that does not let the left hand know what the right hand is doing. The scene is remarkable for its austerity, its reluctance to pat itself on the back. Ford allows only two words of praise for any of his characters in this scene, and those words, "Truck drivers," are terse, allusive, and short on obvious sentiment. Ford and Nunnally Johnson's shorthand dialogue here is good because it doesn't explain itself. It seems suitable to people who aren't by nature communicative, and it seems suitable to a scene that is about the significance of actions not words.

The scene conveys a variety of ideals, some of them highly debatable in the end but all conveyed as effectively as they could be by Ford's quiet technique: that diner owners in the Depression would take a loss in profits to help wayfarers, that truckers are the salt of the earth, that we tend to pay forward the charity others show us. Ford conveys all these ideas without words, through a combination of concrete actions and searching expressions. The scene is characterized by two of the most important aspects of the Hollywood film: a willingness to be emotional, sentimental, idealistic in content and also a determination to convey that sentiment and idealism through an aesthetic characterized by reserve, understatement, and ellipticalness. It would be difficult to decide which of these two qualities is more important to Hollywood, its sincerity or its understatement. The best Hollywood films are great because they are subtle and also because they aim high.

It is Hollywood's willingness to aim high, to be idealistic that drew French film critic and future filmmaker Erich Rohmer's appreciation, when he was writing for *Cahiers du Cinema*. Classic Hollywood, Rohmer writes, "touched, not my schoolboy's heart with its ardor for Gide or Breton, but the innate taste that we French never lose for a moment—beyond all changes of fashion—for the art of the moralist." Morality is certainly a loaded word to throw around, but we have to remember that Rohmer is also the critic who praised Hollywood as an art of dignified gesture. The morality Rohmer responds to is not one that is spoken explicitly but one that is inscribed in the actions of the film and the gestures of its characters. And it's worth noting that Rohmer does not find Hollywood's idealism puerile but, on the contrary, a sign of its maturity. Classic Hollywood did not cater to the modern schoolboy's taste for romantic poses and existential despair. At its best, it is what Leone (another European) described Ford's films as: "solar and humanistic." Characterized by "a language that was open, yet without a hint of coarseness," classic Hollywood was, to Rohmer, "the most civilized of creatures."[12]

—— 10 ——

Hollywood Acting

ONE PERSONA

There is a school of criticism that values versatility in actors. According to this school, the highest praise that can be accorded actors is to say they are expert in inhabiting different personalities and that they are never the same in any two roles. Correspondingly, this line of thinking tends to downgrade actors who seem always to be the same from role to role.

Hollywood, in contrast, did not really believe that actors could transform themselves from movie to movie. Or, at least, Hollywood did not prize that quality in actors. There were a few exceptions such as Lon Chaney and Bette Davis, who were marketed for their versatility. But it would be a difficult to find an actress more powerfully herself from film to film than Davis, despite her tendency to bounce between good girl and bad girl roles. And Lon Chaney might be Phroso Deadlegs, paralysis victim in *West of Zanzibar* and Alonzo the Armless in *The Unknown*, but what made him one of the greatest Hollywood actors was not his mastery of disguises or his great physical stunts but his Garbo-like vulnerability before the camera, the way he had of making us feel so deeply and immediately for the pitiable monsters he played.

Hollywood prized actors, not for their versatility, but for their consistency, the depth of their personality, the audience's familiarity with them and not for how much they could change with each role. Versatility in an actor, the ability to change like a chameleon with each role, is a virtue more suited to the stage than to the cinema. Film is a mechanical medium. The camera records, in close-up, the reality of a person, the musculature of the face, the quirkiness of his or her gait. When one tries to gin that up with face paints the performance is obfuscated. Most great directors, avant-garde and commercial alike, have come to the conclusion that in film the real goal is to get actors to strip away technique and let the camera find who they really are. Directors as different as Hitchcock, Robert Bresson, and Sergio Leone have all asked their actors to unlearn their technique, to calm their features and let the camera discover things behind the mask—in the glint of the eye, the twitch of a smile, in the eccentricity of an actor's stride. This objectivity of the camera is why nonactors have had so much success in films, for example in the neorealist films of Vittorio De Sica and Bresson's experiments with nonprofessionals. These actors have no acting ability, but they have something fresh and unmannered that the camera drinks up. Technique does not get between them and the camera.

The same might be said about many of the classic Hollywood film stars, who were successful, not because of subtle acting skills, learned on the stage, but because film registered something of them that reverberated with huge amounts of people. Gary Cooper might be considered the quintessential Hollywood actor. If you were to judge him by the yardstick of serious theater he would fail all around. He moves and speaks stiffly. There is an overstated childishness in his sense of humor. He sometimes reminds one of summer stock theater productions in the awkwardness of his technique. But his eyes turned out to be extraordinary receptacles of light, and the camera found a dignity and grandeur in each deep groove in his face, no matter how common a man he played.

Cooper's success was not just a photogenic miracle either. His awkward mannerisms and halting speech, the folksy resonance of his voice, elicited empathy and trust immediately. He also had a natural grace in build and movement. No one wore a suit as beautifully as Gary Cooper; Cary Grant looks stocky and indistinct by comparison. Cooper was unable to find bad lighting or to strike an angle that did not reveal a perfectly distinct mixture of elegance and sturdy reliability. He was Cary Grant's continental elegance and Jimmy Stewart's middle-American likeability rolled into one package, the consummate Hollywood star. Cooper was a tremendous film presence, not because he could act particularly well, not at least by standards of theater, and not because of the versatility of his roles, but because he registered magnificently on the screen, both in image and in sound.

Once Hollywood discovered what actors did well, how their physical and emotional presence best imprinted on the screen, they tended to stick with that quality. Hollywood was prone, once it discovered a good thing, not to waste it but to use it again and again. So Gary Cooper was a great Hollywood actor for that very quality that modern tastes are likely to see as a fault: he was always Gary Cooper. Hollywood had great respect for the camera, for what it revealed. If Gary Cooper was so good as Gary Cooper, why interfere? And so Gary Cooper was more or less the same character, whether he played a baseball player in *The Lou Gehrig Story*, a homeless drifter in *Meet John Doe*, or a college professor in *Ball of Fire*. The same goes for most great actors in Hollywood. How much does Marlene Dietrich vary from role to role? How much do we want her to?

Hollywood history is filled with the debris of those films where actors, infected by the bug of self-seriousness, strayed from their set persona in a quest for greater respect. We love Cary Grant for those roles in which he is most Cary Grant—*The*

Awful Truth and *His Girl Friday*, for example—not for his "stretch" performance as a street cockney in the stultifying and serious Clifford Odets film, *None But the Lonely Heart*. That may have been Grant's favorite role, but it is not ours. It may even be (and here is where the question of what the camera captures gets pretty complicated) closer to what Cary Grant was like offscreen. Grant and those close to him always emphasized that he was much more middle-class and much less sophisticated than the image he projected on screen. But that is not what the camera caught. The camera caught a charmer with the devil in his eye, who never took things seriously, liked to have a good time, appreciated a good kidder, wouldn't even let a fairly significant thing like a divorce get to him down but who, in the end, had a pretty good sense of who was who and what was what. That's the Grant the camera caught, and that's the Grant we wanted. It's the charmer in him that danced for the camera.

THE IMPORTANCE OF CASTING

Hollywood did not see the downside to actors always playing the same role. Just because the actor had the same persona from film to film didn't mean you couldn't play with that persona some, tweak it here, deepen it there. Hollywood directors did not see their actors' set personas as limitations but as something that freed them, gave them more room in which to move and improvise. The familiarity of the audience with an actor meant the directors could bypass all sorts of tedious expository background or character building. Now they could go right to the subtler stuff, play with the persona a little, shade it the way they wanted, do a little something with an actor that hadn't been done before, without, of course, sacrificing or being untrue to the essential nature of the actor's persona.

Hitchcock and Anthony Mann are often praised for seeing something different in the Jimmy Stewart who returned from the war a decorated veteran and for, consequently, drawing out darker aspects of his nature in their many films with him. Hitchcock was someone who instinctively understood an actor's persona—so well in fact that he could work marvels of improvisation on that persona without every losing grasp of its essential core meaning. He found an obsessiveness lingering in the background of Jimmy Stewart's middle-American persona, after the war, that he was able to bring out in *Rear Window* and *Vertigo* without damaging Stewart's essentially likeable characters. It is often remarked that casting Jimmy Stewart was essential in maintaining the audience's sympathy with the hero of *Rear Window*, whose voyeurism would trouble us too much were it any other actor. Using Stewart as an actor allowed Hitchcock to go further than he would have been able to with another actor in making a raw, almost autobiographical statement about the dark, obsessive nature of someone who is compelled to live in a world of romantic fantasy, both in *Vertigo* and *Rear Window*.

Hitchcock's variations on, and explorations of, Cary Grant's persona approach the virtuosic. In *Suspicion* Hitchcock asks whether there is not something sinister behind the playful bounder Grant often portrayed, a dark side under

Grant's sly humor that women would be well advised to watch out for. In *North by Northwest* he found and accentuated a mommy's boy quality in Grant's suave and just a little bit coddled persona that nevertheless does not undermine our appreciation of Grant's cool elegance in that film and only adds a little shading to his character. Hitchcock cuts against the grain of Grant's persona in *Notorious* also, making him grim and judgmental toward the female lead, whereas Grant, in his greatest films is irrepressibly playful and charming and particularly unwilling to draw conventional boundaries in his relationship with women. *Notorious* comes close to making Grant too dour, and for Grant fans it is hard to see him so condemning of Bergman's character, when what we often love about Grant is his easygoing way, the smile he has trouble repressing even in moments of high seriousness. But in the end it's interesting to see Grant a little vulnerable and insecure in love in this film. And the final intimate scenes with Bergman are moving because we have actually seen Grant suffer a little for once.

In many ways, one of the principal litmus tests of the Hollywood filmmaker, a deciding factor in determining how successful a director is, is how well he capitalizes on, or plays with, the personas that come his way. Marlene Dietrich always represented a great opportunity for a director to inject a film with musical style, a hard-bitten, European, and sophisticated charm, and a certain moral ambiguity. Von Sternberg, of course, created the Dietrich effect in his many films with her. But the better directors knew how to take advantage of what von Sternberg had created. Billy Wilder's *A Foreign Affair*, Welles's *Touch of Evil*, and Hitchcock's *Stage Fright* are all films that are immensely improved by their understanding of Dietrich's persona and the way they make that persona central to the purposes of the film.

In *Touch of Evil*, Dietrich floats in the background of the film, a kind of one-woman Greek chorus, commenting, with equal parts boredom and nostalgia, on the inevitable demise of Welles's corrupt cop, Hank Quinlan. *A Foreign Affair* includes Dietrich numbers that, as in von Sternberg's films, lend an elegant rhythm to the film and provide Dietrich's effect in its richest dollops. Both *Stage Fright* and *A Foreign Affair* also take advantage of a certain moral ambiguity in Dietrich by casting her as a villain, who nonetheless evokes great sympathy from the audience. It is interesting that though she has a more subsidiary role in these films than in her star vehicles (all of them being from the latter part of her career) she is always sent off, at the end of the film, with the kind of stylish exit reserved for the greatest of stars. Welles rewards her with the famous last line in *Touch of Evil*: "He was some kind of man. What does it matter what you say about people." In her final scene in *Foreign Affair*, Dietrich distracts the MP (military police officer) designated to escort her to jail by straightening her stocking, forcing Millard Mitchell's character, Colonel Plummer, to assign another MP to watch the MP who is watching Dietrich. She walks off with both MPs in her wake and the audience gravely unsure that she will be brought to justice.

Hitchcock is not as closely associated with Dietrich's mystique as some other directors, and yet her final scene in *Stage Fright* is, for my money, one of the greatest Dietrich moments on the screen. Her character, Charlotte Inwood, has just been caught on tape confessing to being an accessory in her husband's murder. An unfailingly polite policeman named Melish has been assigned to guard her. Charlotte's confession has taken place in a theater (in this film which represents Hitchcock's most Shakespearean rumination on the nature of acting), and so circumstances are such that the policeman finds her a temporary perch on the stage of the theater. In this way, Hitchcock strikes upon a final scene with Dietrich that is filtered through the least amount of fictional context. The scene plays as though Dietrich were sitting down for a screen test.

The policeman places the chair in a beam of light that finds itself on the stage, and Dietrich takes the seat, her face unerringly finding the light. A bright white stole resting on her right shoulder and her pearl necklace glitter, MGM style, in the light. (It's not Hitchcock's accustomed mode of lighting. This is lighting for Dietrich.) Dietrich pulls a cigarette from an elegant case, and the policeman lights it. All the Dietrich elements are in place for this little coda in which Charlotte will offer some final words on why she killed her husband. It's a typically clever and hardened little speech, delivered with Dietrich's typical world-weary suaveness. But toward its end, she falters just a little: "When I give all my love and get back treachery and hatred, it's . . ." Here, Dietrich pauses and her eyes go just a little soft. Her voice quavers almost undetectably: "It's as if my mother had slapped me in the face." Her face quickly regains its customary control as she turns to the cop and says, "Do you understand that Melish?" Melish's response is cold and slightly male chauvinistic: "I've heard it takes some of them that way."

Hitchcock then cuts to a lavish, lovely close-up of Dietrich. It's reminiscent of the close-up of Claude Rains in *Notorious* when he confesses, at his mother's bedside, that his wife is an American spy. Hitchcock shoots Dietrich in tight close-up from an angle slightly tilted from above. She raises her face to the camera and, of course, to the light which pours over her. As she does she exhales from her cigarette, filling the screen with silky smoke. "Yes," she says to Melish flatly, with a mixture of vulnerability and bitterness, "it takes some of them that way." Here, Hitchcock, as he so often does in his films, reserves his moments of greatest expressiveness and sympathy for his criminals. It's people like Melish he holds in disdain, "good people" who have little understanding of the dark subterranean passageways of love, how much a person can love, how deeply he or she can be wounded in love. And he packages this quintessential Hitchcock moment in a loving homage to Dietrich: pearls, fur, cigarette holder, a hardened woman hiding deep feelings, and, above all, the face in all that misty smoke tilted to a flooding light.

The best directors recognized that when they were dealing with Dietrich, they were dealing with rich material and with a rich history, which, if used carefully, could give their films greater depth and resonance. They knew how to tap into the drama of Dietrich's legacy. Dietrich was an actress who, whether she had a small or a big role, had such a complex and forceful presence that it begged to be at the heart of the film's drama and poetry.

On the other hand, even though she is accorded some time for numbers in *Destry Rides Again* and even though those numbers are by longtime collaborator Frederich Hollander, George Marshall's use of her there does not satisfy the Dietrich fan. The film, and she, are too American. Her bouncing version of "See What the Boys in the Backroom Will Have," replete with odd sound effects, does not tap into her worldly pathos as well as, say, "What Am I Bid for My Apples" in von Sternberg's *Morocco* and "Black Market" in *A Foreign Affair.* And she is a little too vulnerable to Jimmy Stewart's goodness, a little too good herself. She doesn't hold back, as she does in her greater films, evincing that attitude that she does so well that she, alone, will decide her moral tack, that she alone has a feel for the dark complexities of the world. She lacks the dark melancholy strains of her other films. Marshall's use of Dietrich is just one example of why this film, gorgeously shot by Hal Mohr and as pretty as any film you could find in Hollywood, has the paradoxical effect of looking like one of Hollywood's greatest films but never quite delivering as such.

Visual style only carries one so far in Hollywood. Knowing how to use the recognizable actors who fell in a director's way was crucial to the director's ability to create a film of great resonance. Great Hollywood films were not just the result of artistic sensibilities and visual flair but also of knowing how to play the game of Hollywood, how to take full advantage of the peculiar assets of the studio system. Each actor, even the smallest character actor, represents a little case of "tradition and the individual talent," in which the director had to respect the tradition of that character's persona but, at the same time, effect some variation on that character, do something new with it, stamp it with his personal touch. The system is one of mutual enrichment. The film is deepened by the actor's history, and the actor is further enriched and complicated by this new touch on his or her persona. In the end, creatures like John Wayne, Humphrey Bogart, Marlene Dietrich, Walter Brennan, and Thomas Mitchell, hoary and barnacle-strewn actors, dragging immense case histories behind them, have only to appear on screen to evoke deep feelings from the audience. These are actors who have been steeped in, and treated by, so many films and so many directors that they have arrived at the very finest and most authentic of grain and texture and become, in themselves, works of art.

AN ART OF QUIET GESTURE

Hollywood recognized, then, that an actor is only capable of being one thing onscreen, that which he or she is. Gregory Peck, for example, experienced a great deal of frustration when he worked for Hitchcock, who he found unresponsive to his technique: "In answer to my questions about mood or expression, he would simply say that I was to drain myself of all expression and he would photograph me."[1] Hitchcock felt that the more actors quieted their technique, the less they got in his way. He got along marvelously with Hollywood professionals like Carol Lombard and Jimmy Stewart, who were good at putting themselves in his hands.

But he often struggled with stage actors, like Charles Laughton and John Gielgud, who were proud of the technique that they brought from the stage and balked at the more modest demands film made of their vocal register.

Hitchcock had a particular impatience with the convolutions of "method actors," finding Montgomery Clift "too obscure"[2] and endlessly repeating his complaints about working with Paul Newman in *Torn Curtain* in his interviews: "I wasn't too happy with the way Paul Newman played it. As you know, he's a 'method' actor, and he found it hard to just give me one of those neutral looks I needed to cut from his point of view."[3] This is the kind of story Hitchcock liked to trot out to make it look as if he held actors in disdain, but in reality, actors for the most part enjoyed working with Hitchcock, in no small measure because they looked so good in his films. And they looked good because he had a searching camera, which, particularly when they stopped emoting excessively, could find interesting things in their presence to register that no other director's camera saw. He may sound rather pleased with himself, but no one is likely to disagree with Hitchcock when he notes that Grace Kelly "was rather mousy in *High Noon*. She blossomed out for me."[4] Kelly really owes her legacy and greatest success to Hitchcock's sparkling entertainments, not to the more "socially relevant" films she was in, like *High Noon* and *Country Girl*. *Country Girl* is to Kelly what *None But the Lonely Heart* was to Cary Grant, one of those "stretch" roles actors do that allow them to dress down, show their serious side, and often, as was the case with Kelly, earn Academy Awards. But *Country Girl* has not contributed to Kelly's mystique nearly as much as the frothy *To Catch a Thief*, a slight film which gave full play to her extraordinary mixture of elegance, haute couture, and light comic ease.

Hitchcock was not the only director to register his annoyance with method actors. Hawks felt that, starting with *Dawn Patrol*, he brought a kind of understatement or casual approach to acting that caught on until "Kazan came along with Brando and Jimmy Dean and started going way up again."[5] Hawks spoke often of his efforts to get actors to stop acting. He had to fight, for example, what he saw as a tendency in John Wayne toward corniness during the filming of *Red River*. "What are you trying to do—play *Uncle Tom's Cabin*?" Hawks recalled saying to Wayne. "I was just trying to get something in the scene," Wayne responded. "Well," Hawks said, "this is one of those scenes where you don't try to get anything in. Just say the lines and get on out."[6] Hawks was, of all the Hollywood directors, most suspicious of pretension, and most acutely sensitive to melodrama, pious clichés, and overstatement. It was a big part of his technique to get his actors to take it down a notch, pitch their performance to a level that awoke rather than overwhelmed the camera.

Hollywood acting, despite many descents into melodrama in its weaker films, is, at its best, an art of understatement. Several directors told the same story of directing Gary Cooper, of how they thought his performance was awful until they saw it in rushes and realized he was doing all sorts of small things that only the camera, with its careful eye, would pick up. "You'd see him working on the set

Photo 6. Gary Cooper. "You'd see the rushes," said Orson Welles, "and he'd fill the screen." Courtesy of Photofest.

and you'd think, 'My God, they're going to have to retake that one. He almost didn't seem to be there' " Orson Welles said. "And then you'd see the rushes, and he'd fill the screen."[7] This is what French director Robert Bresson means when he refers to the camera as that "prodigious, heaven-sent machine," an instrument not just of recording but also of revelation, showing us what we can't normally see or, more precisely, what is so small or quiet that we don't take the time to see.[8] Welles compared the camera to a "Geiger counter of mental energy. It registers something that's only vaguely, suppositionally detectable to the naked eye, registers it clear and strong: thought. Every time an actor thinks it goes right on the film." Laurence Olivier would no doubt blow Gary Cooper off the stage, but he did not have Cooper's talent for registering thought on a camera. Cooper was able to still himself in ways that Olivier, jittery with stage technique, was not. Light caught Cooper's eyes better (Photo 6), and he knew how to pitch and time his performance to the camera which, in turn, recorded what his eyes were expressing more than it did Olivier's. "Who knows more about technique than Olivier?" Welles asked. "And yet, fine as he's been in films, he's never been more than a shadow of that electric presence which commands the stage. Why does the camera seem to diminish him? And enlarge Gary Cooper—who knew nothing of technique."

Hollywood acting had less to do with stage technique than it did with a consciousness of the camera, an intuitive relationship with the camera, a knowledge of what kinds of minutiae it picked up, and an ability to play to that silent, mechanical audience. Claudia Cardinale spoke of how she warmed to the many close-ups in Sergio Leone's *Once Upon a Time in the West*, remarking, "[The camera] became like a friend to me: the way it hums is familiar to me, and I can feel it at once if it is set up well or not."[9] One senses this sense of friendship or intimacy with the camera in the performances of many of Hollywood's greatest actors—Cooper, Jimmy Stewart, Ingrid Bergman, Greta Garbo. All of these actors have a very intimate relationship with the camera; they pitch their performance to the camera. Bresson described cinema as an art of hands and eyes, citing those two aspects of humans that are least subject to the brain's control, most involuntarily expressive of a person's interior life. Great Hollywood actors seemed to instinctively intuit the camera's aliveness to movements of the hands and eyes. Think of those hushed scenes of mental turmoil that Jimmy Stewart was so adept at playing, where his face would be composed, but his eyes would dart around in agitation or where he would, in a trademark gesture, anxiously gnaw at his fingers, which nervously played over his face.

Garbo, like Gary Cooper, is another actress who if judged solely by acting ability as it is conventionally defined on the stage would not be judged too well. Even her best performances are inconsistent. She's manic in *Grand Hotel*, amateurishly stentorian in *Queen Christina*. But when she nestles into the arms of her lovers in any of her films, it's a different matter entirely. Here she stills herself, abandons conventional technique entirely and quivers in a flurry of fleeting expressions and small gestures made for the camera alone. Here she is not so much acting as moving in intuitive correspondence to the camera.

We see the same skill, the acute consciousness of the camera's attention to the minute in Charlie Chaplin's films. One of Chaplin's most impressive accomplishments was to recognize, so early on in the history of cinema, how small a detail the camera could catch and how, often, the smaller the details in the film, the more riveted the audience was. Whether it was a tiny bit in an elaborate gag, a fleeting expression, or an obscure *trompe d'oeil*, he always taxed his audience's visual acuity.

In *The Gold Rush*, for example, Charlie brushes up against a woman with whom he is smitten in the midst of the crowded saloon. The woman does not even register Charlie's presence, but as she nears him, Charlie's body stiffens electrically. He becomes immobile as a statue, only his eyes making occasional nervous, darting forays to catch quick looks at the woman to his side. He is the personification of the stealthy voyeurism that sneaks out of our stony facades everyday in crowds. The gestures here are remarkably small, bordering on the immobile. And here we really are reminded of Bresson's sense of a good film actor as "a gathering into himself, of keeping, of not letting anything get out. A certain configuration common to them all. Eyes."[10] Chaplin knew how to take full advantage of immobility, how to quiet his technique, so that the quietest gesture could be seen. And though he could use his entire body for rocketing comic effects he often stilled that body and turned to his eyes to get across his subtlest moments of humor or pathos.

This is the aspect of Chaplin that is often underestimated in the modern tendency to rate Buster Keaton's films more highly, and as more filmic, than Chaplin's because Keaton's are more physical and mobile, more large-scale in their visions. Keaton's vision was macrocosmic, Chaplin's microcosmic. Chaplin's great art was one of intimacy; he sculpted on the minutest level. One of his great accomplishments was capitalizing on film's ability to register, in ways no other art form had ever been able to, the small and delicate gesture. Chaplin's acting is an example of that quality that Allan Dwan praised in D.W. Griffith's actors, "an economy of gesture," an ability to excite more of a response in an audience by doing less, that ability to "sit dead still" and make the audience read one's thoughts. Chaplin was able to, as Robert Bresson advises, "use to the full all that is communicated by immobility and silence."[11]

The best Hollywood filmmakers had something of Chaplin's or Griffith's discretion. They knew how to sit back on their heels some and save their actors, when they could, from their own acting. The look the truckers exchange over the waitress' act of charity in that diner scene from *The Grapes of Wrath*, which I analyzed in Chapter 9, is effective as much for what it doesn't express as for what it does. It is effective because it is neutral. The truckers don't betray their emotion or signal to us in a highly defined way what they are thinking. Their eyes are more expressive in proportion to how little their faces move. We see a twinkle in the eyes of one, though we can't quite tell if the eyes are smiling in appreciation of the waitress' action or in mockery of it.

On the other hand, the look of profound pity and mutual understanding the nurses exchange over Catherine's bed in *A Farewell to Arms*, when the dying Catherine asks for her handbag to put on her makeup before seeing Frederick, just about kills off any ambiguity as to its meaning and any effort we need make to read the scene or intuit the emotions of the characters. It's a look that wears its intention on its sleeve, thereby missing the reserve and dignity of the truckers' expression.

There is a power and dignity in neutral expressions, a mystery and subtlety, that is killed off when the actor signals his or her attention too glaringly. One of the most famous neutral shots in the classical Hollywood era has to be the close-up of Greta Garbo at the end of *Queen Christina*. Garbo's lover, for whom she has relinquished her throne, is dead, and she has decided to sail to his native country of Spain rather than return to her kingdom in Sweden. Director Rouben Mamoulian was not sure how to shoot Garbo in this final scene of the film. "What do you play?" he remembered asking himself. "Do you cry? Do you have little glycerin tears? Do you smile for no reason, or do you laugh?" He resolved finally to have Garbo strike all emotion from her face, filming her in close-up, on the prow of the ship with the wind blowing her hair and an utterly neutral look on her face, and for the duration of one of Hollywood's lengthiest close-ups ever. "Don't act," he told Garbo. "'Do nothing. You don't have a thought. In fact, try not to blink your eyes. Just wear a mask.' And she did just that for ninety feet of film."[12] The result is one of the most striking sequences of Garbo's career.

What Mamoulian found was that camera could sustain a great deal of interest in Garbo's face for a great deal of time, without her moving a muscle. In fact, moving a muscle would have broken the spell, given us too strong a clue as to what she was thinking, interrupted our fascinated gaze. Christina's decision to carry on with her journey, despite the death of her lover, conveys plenty of nobility and perseverance itself. The suffering in such a situation is self-evident. We are also well aware of the freedom Christina feels, having seen her hanker the entire film for escape from her throne. Garbo doesn't need to underline any of these feelings; the more she holds those feelings back, the more we search for them in the depth of her eyes and the set of her jaw; the more we imagine her feelings rather than having them pantomimed for us, the more eloquent she seems in her immobility.

The success of this moment then comes from "not acting," according to Mamoulian, from "wearing a mask" rather than from versatility of technique. It's striking how many of Hollywood's greatest actors—Bogart, John Wayne, Marlene Dietrich—wore a kind of mask, had a kind of inflexibility of acting technique, a proud hauteur that did not allow their faces a good deal of mobility. Wayne's face almost seems to be in pain from the strain of smiling the few times he does in his films, so set is it in a kind of craggy stoicism. These actors appeal to us in the ways they hold themselves back.

At times, even neutrality isn't enough. Howard Hawks was so conscious of the prying eye of the camera that he often sought means to obscure his actors' performance. He felt, for example, that one scene in *Scarface*, between the quasi-incestuous brother and sister, was too intimate to be filmed. "You shouldn't be able to see their faces when you hear lines like that," he told his cinematographer Lee Garmes, who, Hawks said, "sent for a pair of curtains that had a pronounced pattern so the light barely came through. He turned out all of the front light and just shot it in backlight. Made a really good scene out of it." Lesson learned, according to Hawks? "If you're ever stuck and get into a scene you don't think should be exposed to people—shoot it so they can't be seen too well."[13]

Hawks makes a couple of points here: First, that scenes of greater emotion demand a proportional restraint in technique. And second, that acting has to be quieted for the camera, even obscured or covered at times, to be effective. When Hawks noticed that the spindly Montgomery Clift was having trouble coming off as tough next to John Wayne in *Red River* ("Wayne blows people like that off the screen"), he told Clift to "take a coffee cup and be drinking it and we'll see just your eyes. They won't know whether you're smiling or what's happening."[14] Over and over, we see instances like this in Hollywood where directors and actors conspired to give less and less to the camera, which responded, paradoxically, by searching for more and more.

Sessue Hayakawa, an actor in Thomas Ince Westerns, compared the burgeoning art of silent film acting to acting in Kabuki theater, where "intensity of emotion was conveyed by the concentrated visible act of holding back rather than booming forth; the audience became enthralled not by large gestures and broad expressions, but by small movements of eyes, face, body and hands, an interest enhanced by the absence of voice in silent movies."[15] Hayakawa, like Dwan, was thinking of Griffith's actors, but his summary of the acting in Griffith's films represents a pretty nice summary of Hollywood acting at its best, whether it's the acting of Chaplin, Cooper, Garbo, Dietrich, Wayne, Bogart, or Stewart. All of these actors were expert at holding back rather than booming forth, all expert at a cinema of "small movements of eyes, face, body and hands."

It's this cinema of small movements that Eric Rohmer also often cited when he wanted to explain what he liked about American cinema. Hollywood was a cinema "more sparing of gesture" than French cinema with its huge romantic themes of gothic tragedy and devotion. Rohmer liked the quiet unpretentiousness of Hollywood, its way of avoiding drama, of achieving the maximum of cool with the minimum of gestures. Hawks's genius was "a sensitivity to the precise delineation of the gesture and its duration."[16] And he praised Hawks and Griffith (thus joining Hayakawa) for their "elegant restraint" which conferred "on human gesture a grandeur that is not inflated." The beauty of Hawks's *To Have and Have Not*, as I emphasized in my earlier analysis of that film, is not in its ideas but in its actions, particularly in some of its smallest actions. Much of the film's lasting quality is due, not to its rendering of the issues of World War II resistance, but to the way that Lauren Bacall tosses back Humphrey Bogart's lighter when they first meet, the way she gently slaps him on the face when she says "sometimes you're just a stinker," the way she literally walks around him to show she understands there will be no strings attached to their relationship, the way she strikes a match and lights his cigarette just at the moment he's about to slug the tourist Johnson and in doing so dissipates Bogart's anger and brings a sly, appreciative smile to his face. Hollywood doesn't aim for the big ideas; it settles for the small, telling gesture, the memorably concrete action that sticks in your crop. For fans of Hollywood, like Rohmer, it is in its lack of inflation, its "elegant restraint" and "sensitive delineation of its gestures," that Hollywood finds its grandeur.

— 11 —

Character Actors

One of the great signature traits of the studio years in Hollywood was its wealth of character actors. This was a beneficent effect of the sheer quantity of films made in Hollywood during these years and its precise, machinelike division of labor. Once Hollywood discovered what an actor did well, it capitalized on that talent over and over again, until certain actors, and their types, were as familiar to the public as old aunts, uncles, and ne'er-do-wells in their own families. The great array of character actors represented a significant tool in the arsenal of the Hollywood filmmaker. Hollywood filmmakers had, at their disposal, a wide variety of clearly defined types to choose from in telling and casting their stories, and these types came with ready-made backstories. Casting was extremely important in Hollywood because through casting alone directors could achieve great variety, precision, depth, and familiarity in characterization.

The kind of film Hollywood made was conducive to a rich and varied characterization as well. Hollywood, rather than speaking volumes about its characters, liked to define them through a few tics, traits, or leitmotifs—a physical gesture, a nickname, a habit. It favored a deft, efficient visual expression of character that allowed a director to fill his or her canvas with a good many characters.

Moreover, Hollywood favored a simple, accessible story over a highly convoluted or plotted one. It liked to take its time in relating its narrative, leaving itself open to little digressions and stylistic moments, songs, for example, and little bits of comic or stylish business. Character actors were one of these bits of business. Many of Hollywood's character actors had been vaudeville actors and brought their respective bits of vaudeville shtick to film. And as the power of Hollywood coalesced, it drew character types from across the world, not only Vaudeville stars with their great variety of types and gags but also clever comedic prigs from the British stage or comedians of great comic pathos from the film and stage world of Germany.

And Hollywood's devotion to unity served the character actor as well, guaranteeing that if he or she were brought into the film it would not be simply as a comic digression and that his or her presence would be significant to the significance of the film. It was a precept of Hollywood that whatever entered the film, be it locale, prop, or character actor, should be used and should in some way reflect the central purpose of the film. The best directors, then, worked hard to bring out some depth in their character actors, to take whatever these actors did well and use it to deepen the central significance of the film.

How a director used his character actors is one of those things that separate the great directors from the weaker ones. The greatest directors seemed to be expert in their evaluation and use of character actors. They knew how to capitalize on the audience's knowledge of, and affection for, these characters, and they did little things with these actors' personas that made them just a little better than they were in other films, that capitalized best on what these actors could do.

CAPRA AND *IT'S A WONDERFUL LIFE*

Frank Capra's *It's a Wonderful Life* is an excellent example of how much can be accomplished in a film by virtue of a sharp estimation and acute casting of the talent available. Capra's films, like those of Preston Sturges, are remarkable for the sheer quantity of talent assembled, but even more for the use that talent is put to. Great character actors were available in spades to any Hollywood director. Knowing how to get the maximum effect from them was the challenge. Capra had an eye for the best character actors, but even more important was his genius for knowing what to do with each of these characters.

Certainly, *It's a Wonderful Life* is noteworthy for drawing career performances from many of its topflight character actors. I cannot think of any film that has been more successful in bringing out the cranky rhythms of Lionel Barrymore's diction than this one. Barrymore, like his brother John, always delivered an interesting performance but also often one that, in its immensity, could overwhelm a film. Capra had Howard Hawks's talent for quieting performances. It's striking how often this director who could convey the excitement of crowds better than any other Hollywood director also liked to shoot scenes where the dialogue is hushed to a near whisper. Beulah Bondi is always a great character actor, but we detect her art particularly well in those quiet teasing scenes on the Baileys's front porch the night she encourages George to call on Mary, sensing that love is the only thing that will settle his disgruntled spirit. Bondi specialized in gentle, often long-suffering, slightly beatific mothers, but this scene particularly registers her talents because of its quiet intimacy and the nice rapport with Stewart, another actor who tends to convey more, the quieter things get. (Bondi also gets a turn in another of her specialties, "the old bat," in George's vision of what his mother's life would have been like were he not born.)

Thomas Mitchell's Uncle Billy is one of his greater roles, a softer drunk than he usually plays, a little gentler and more melancholy, not the cantankerous drunk spoiling for a confrontation he plays in so many other films. I can't find another film that taps into Henry Travers's befuddled charm as well as this one in which he plays Clarence the angel. Ward Bond and Gloria Grahame, two character actors who had a nose for finding their way to good directors and films, are both used to great effect. Grahame flounces through the film with that springtime fresh coquetry she had that gives loose women a good name. Bond (Bert the cop) teamed with Frank Faylen (Ernie the taxi driver) has several of the moments we look for when we watch the film, for example, the scenes in which he and Faylen, with a kind of slapstick antic kindness, stage a fake Polynesian honeymoon for George and Mary on their wedding night.

And Bond gets, as he so often does in Ford films, one of the earthier moments in the film. Bert, Ernie, and George have all run into Gloria Grahame's Violet Bick out in the streets of Bedford Falls. All three stand stock-still watching her pass by in a revealing spring frock, transformed into three statues by the swish of her gait. "How would you like . . . ," Ernie the taxi driver begins to ask. "Yes," George answers, before the question is even out, a testimony to the like-mindedness of their thoughts. Bond's character, Bert the cop, is the most troubled of all by what he's seen. When Ernie asks Bert if he wants to come with them for a ride, Bert looks down at his watch and then back at Grahame, a troubled look on his face the entire time, before deciding, "No thanks. I think I'll go home and see what the wife's doing."

Capra is just as impressive in the aptness of his casting in the tiniest roles in his films as he is in the larger character roles. Beyond the major-league character actors mentioned above, the film boasts a host of smaller professionals, each doing their jobs remarkably well: Sheldon Leonard, with his inimitable gangster accent, as Nick the bartender; former silent star H.M. Warner as the shattered druggist, Mr. Gower; Ellen Corby (the future Grandma Walton on television), who specialized in meek country spinsters, as the gentle woman who won't take George's money during the run on the bank; Charles Lang, the actor everyone knows by face and voice but none by name, as the sharp-voiced accountant advising Potter to watch out for an up and coming George Bailey; Charles Halton as the bespectacled, personality-less bank examiner who plagues George on Christmas Eve; and the dignified Samuel Hinds as George's careworn father. Hinds's scene with Stewart at the dinner table where they talk over George's future is, like Stewart's scene with Bondi, a model of understatement, the dialogue at times sinking nearly to whispers and Hinds, remarkably, shot almost entirely in profile, head down, in a kind of Lincolnesque pose of humble suffering.

These are small-time character actors who don't register in the public consciousness as explicitly as Lionel Barrymore and Thomas Mitchell did, but what they do in the film is just as carefully defined, and Capra paid close attention to these small but precise personas, matching them to his dialogue so carefully that after the film we still recall Sheldon Leonard ringing up his register and saying in his famous New York mobster intonation, "Hey get me, I'm giving out wings." We remember the always-irritated Charles Lang saying, "It's no skin off my back, but one of these days this bright young man is going to be asking George Bailey for a job." We remember the way Charles Halton blinks stupidly and intones in his best middle-American accent, "I want to spend Christmas in Elmira with my family." This is poetry on a small scale. Capra's script is successful, not just because it is well written, but because Capra took such care in choosing the right messengers to deliver his lines.

Capra's attention to small character roles has a couple of beneficent effects. First, the film is energetic even in its smallest machinations. Everyone seems to be doing his or her part with intensity. Even the smallest engines of the film seem to be firing. The consequence is a film that is characterized by an enormous amount of energy.

Secondly, the film is characterized by a great variety of types. Capra's films fairly burst at the seams with characters, a real parade of democracy far more effective than some of his lapses into political didacticism. When Dmitri Tiomkin refers to the studio era as a period characterized by "a bright dream about a beautiful democracy" it might strike some that he is making a rather conservative statement, expressing appreciation for the propagandistic rhetoric of Hollywood, the kind of rhetoric Capra is often associated with. But I think what Tiomkin is referring to, and what we find in Capra, is something different than propaganda, something subtler—a democratic population or culture, a democratic texture to the film. Capra's films are, in the end, convincingly democratic in the countless small and varied details of human life they register more than in the populist speeches in which he didactically enunciates his ideas—though these speeches can be quite well realized.

Capra's success as a filmmaker is due more to his attention to small detail than to his interest in large ideas. Character roles are treated with the same attention as star roles, bit roles with the same attention as character roles. Even Capra's use of extras is more distinctive than that of the average director. It's difficult to find any films in Hollywood in which crowd scenes fill the canvas as well as, or pop with more energy, and excitement than Capra's. Capra's success with large-scale crowd scenes is due, to a great extent, to his excellent pictorial sense. He and cinematographer Joseph Walker were expert at crowding the parameters of the frame, filling a frame to bursting. Capra composed well on a large scale, with huge crowds, but he was even more adept at suggesting crowds through bursting arrangements of figures. His films prove that there is never a need for what we often see in other films (particularly during the decline of classic Hollywood and after): a listless mulling of extras, surrounded by an empty space that reveals all too obviously the paucity of their numbers.

But Capra's success with extras also has to do with the care with which he treated them. Capra's extras are more animate than those in other films, not only because of how he arranged them but also because he encouraged them to act. Capra explained, in his memoir, that he was able to create effective crowd scenes because he gave each extra a little something to act out: "Extras walking on sidewalks as backgrounds to a scene can walk through as a flock of sheep or as real pedestrians depending on the wit of the director. He must give each one an identity. One extra is late for a dentist's appointment, another is looking for the address of his wife's lawyer. That one is going to a poker game. This woman is shopping for her kid's shoes. It doesn't matter who the director tells them they are, as long as they are *somebody* as they walk through the background. One simple detail changes the scene from the ersatz to the real."[1] This kind of attention to specific persons explains, in part, the kineticism of Capra's crowd scenes, why they burst off the screen, whereas in other films the extras in crowd scenes move around with a laughable aimlessness.

Capra's success is due not simply to an easy to swallow populism, a corny spirit easily available to mass audiences but to the kind of hard work evident in his handling of actors. Whether it was his stars, his character actors, his bit roles, or his extras, he worked hard to make sure that everyone in his frame had a reason for being there, the result being an unusually purposeful and energetic cinema.

PRESTON STURGES

If we were to cite one director who took the most advantage of the superabundance of character actors in the Hollywood studio system, it would have to be Preston Sturges. His films teem with a rogue's gallery of eccentrics that represents Hollywood's A list of character actors, and the turns they take in Sturges's films are often their best. He had a knack for using these actors more memorably than other directors. Sturges had a slier, more sophisticated veneer than Capra, but in the end, like Capra, he is one of Hollywood's great populists and in no small measure due to his virtuosic handling of character actors.

In addition, Sturges was one of Hollywood's greatest screenwriters, for Sarris, "the wittiest scriptwriter the English-speaking cinema has known."[2] He not only had a good feel for Hollywood's best character actors but also was able to feed them their best lines. And so characters actors who could be nondescript in other directors' films shone in Sturges's films. Sarris cites Eric Blore as an actor who is always good but rarely as sublime as he is with Sturges. *The Lady Eve* is good from stem to stern, but one waits in keen anticipation for the moment when Blore appears as the good-natured conman posing as English nobility, specifically, Sir Alfred McGlennon Keith, R.F.D, a character he plays with exuberant, elegant, lisping, mincing, highly articulate self-satisfaction. The pleasure he takes in being a con oozes from every one of his felicitously concocted lines. When Barbara Stanwyck's character, looking to con Henry Fonda's industrialist family, the Pikes, asks Blore if he's familiar with this family, Blore responds with a childish glee that expresses the profound pleasure he takes in fleecing Connecticut's industrial elite. "My dear," he says with his trademark lisp, "I positively swim in their ale."

The scene in which Blore's conman recounts the bogus history of Barbara Stanwyck's family, "the sorrow of Sidwich, the secret of the century" (a summary that again takes full advantage of Blore's lisp), is one of the best in the film, with Blore gushing out his lurid melodrama in ludicrously heightened language ("There was a coachman on the estate, a gay dog, a great hand with horses and ladies") and stopping every few moments in mock paranoia to grab Fonda's face and hush him dramatically, even though the doltish Fonda isn't saying a word. It's a tour de force performance, and Fonda is such an easy prey that we can't help believing that the conman's performance is as much for his own entertainment as it is to trick Fonda.

Sturges had been raised, in good part, by an impetuous mother who dragged him around Europe in pursuit of a bohemian, vagabond sort of life (with her best friend, Isadora Duncan), but he was much happier with his stints in America with his father. His background was different than other Hollywood writers, more European, more cultured, and, at the same time, determinedly democratic. He was as conversant in street lingo as he was in the highfalutin falderal he could put in the mouths of actors like Blore. The result is a funny mixture of diction that can be both street tough and highly poeticized. His films are filled with palookas who are capable of astonishing turns of phrase. Edgar Kennedy embodies this odd mix when, for example, playing a bartender asked to serve a customer who had never had a drink before, he announces, "Sir, you arouse the artist in me." In *Unfaithfully Yours,* orchestra conductor Rex Harrison merely thought he had hired, in Kennedy, a coarse private detective to track his wife but finds, to his great frustration, that the detective is also his biggest fan and a blue-collar critic of sorts. "No one handles Handel like you handle Handel," Kennedy croaks ingenuously.

Sturges was less likely than Capra to give upbeat speeches about the common man. (Though as the ending to *Sullivan's Travels* suggests, he wasn't immune to that temptation.) His films are more overtly cynical than Capra's. But in Sturges, as in Capra, there is something inherently democratic in his fascination with the smallest characters in his films, his distinctly American oddballs. He not only uses these characters for comic effect but also seems fascinated by what they reveal about the hidden depths of the most common person. This is a democratic attitude that has nothing to do with political rhetoric. It expresses itself in a fine appreciation for the warp and weave of American life and its belief in the poetry and significance of the stray oddball.

One of Sturges's great talents was his ability to introduce a wide variety of eccentric characters and scenes without losing the central thread of his narrative. His films recount a moving central narrative (as he had a great hand at romantic dialogue) while tolerating the maximum of digressions. These digressions finish by being, in many ways, the meat of the film. I like every inch of *The Palm Beach Story*, but I look forward with particular anticipation to the appearance of Rudy Vallee, as John D. Hackensacker III, the most gentlemanly doormat who ever unsuccessfully wooed a woman, a man who apologizes to *you* when you step on, and crush, his pince-nez. I look forward to the scenes with "The Ale and Quail Club" (Photo 7), a pack of middle-aged hunters who adopt Claubert, in Snow White fashion, on a train to Palm Beach, before forgetting her altogether in a drunken frenzy during which they, literally, shoot their train car apart. There are

Photo 7. No films drew more successfully from Hollywood's stable of great character actors than Preston Sturges's did. Here Sturges (center of picture) is surrounded by "The Ale and Quail Club" from *The Palm Beach Story*. Courtesy of Photofest.

few greater celebrations of anarchy in Hollywood. The scene represents a kind of homage, right out of Maupassant, to the middle-aged huntsman's blind pursuit of his own pleasure.

I probably most look forward to the scenes with the Weenie King, a wealthy magnate from the Midwest who made his fortune out of the "Texas Weenie." ("Lay off em," he tells Claudette Colbert, "you'll live longer.") The Weenie King is a myopic, nearly deaf old man, prone to loud monotonous orations, who takes a lustful liking to Colbert, showering her with money just when she and her broke husband need it most. Sturges regular Robert Dudley plays the Weenie King with a hilarious obtuse deadpan, barking out his lines like a third grader doing an oral recitation for his teacher. That said, the Weenie King gets off some great lines, the literacy of which belie his bland American gothic demeanor. "Cold are the hands of time," he intones, realizing that Colbert is too young to return his affections, "that creep along relentlessly, destroying slowly but without pity that which yesterday was young. Alone our memories resist this destruction and grow more lovely with the passing years." The Weenie King is as wise as he is ludicrous, a testimony to one of the recurrent ideas in Sturges's democratic cinema, that smarts turns up in the oddest places.

The Weenie King is a stock character, the hopelessly provincial Midwestern magnate, drawn to New York by a socially ambitious wife. But Sturges adds a few deft touches that make him best of the type. "You'll get over it," the Weenie King says to Claubert when he finds out she's broke. "You'll get over being young too. Someday you'll find everything behind you. Gives you quite a turn. Makes you feel sorry for a few of the things you didn't do while you could." These words read a great deal more sentimentally on the page than they do on the screen where Dudley blares them out with his dull monotone that makes you wonder whether the sentiments could apply to the man who utters them. Here the Weenie King suggests the motivation for his generosity; he's a romantic old coot, nursing his own regrets. "The delicate mechanism of a Sturges scenario," writes Sarris, "cannot be considered a laugh machine. The dramatic structure is too intricate and convoluted, the mood invariably mixed. In the very midst of a loud guffaw one is surprised to find a lump in one's throat and tears in one's eye." Sturges could veer from broad comedy to touching sentiment in the blink of the eye and then just as quickly return to the fast track of his central narrative. It's this ability to quickly make something moving and substantial of the quiekest little digression that makes his films rich and his use of character actors the gold standard.

TROUPES

Sturges was not the only director in Hollywood to have a troupe or family of actors. A great part of Hollywood's success in general is that each studio represented a family of actors with which the American public became quite familiar. Warner Brothers, for example, took great pride in the fact that while it didn't have MGM's money or stars, at least it had a greater stable of character actors, the real meat and potatoes of Hollywood. "MGM had far more glamorous people than we did," said veteran Warner Brothers director Irving Rapper, "but we had the actors."[3]

But certain directors like Sturges, Ford, and Lubitsch created their own families within their studios' families. There are a couple of positive effects to working, film after film, with the same family of actors. First, the camera appreciates the familiarity actors have with one another. Walter Brennan and Gary Cooper worked together so often that by the time a film like Wyler's *The Westerner* and Capra's *Meet John Doe* they appeared to have achieved the easy relationship of teammates.

Also, an audience gains a familiarity with a troupe of actors. Directors like Ford and Sturges who went back to the same actors time after time were only accentuating, or taking advantage of, one of Hollywood's great qualities, its deep fund of recognizable personas and types. By limiting themselves to a few of these personas, these directors were exercising judgment as to which actors best meshed with their worldview. By using them over and over again, they were creating a cozier, more enclosed world and a richer, denser symbolic pattern in their films. With each film, we gain a richer appreciation for the actor and a greater comfort with the director's world. Everything deepens.

Ward Bond, for example, is a very consoling presence in a John Ford film. When he shows up, we are pleased. We know that we are in Ford's world. In fact, he is so much part and parcel of Ford's world that when he plays for other directors he seems to bring a piece of Ford's world with him. We know Bond as a large bluff man, often teased, easily moved to angry frustration but rarely violent. He's good for comic background but has a kind of strength of character that seems writ in his strong body that lends the kind of depth of character to him that the greatest character actors had. You can turn to him for a little humor, but even more importantly, you can deepen that humor into something touching or meaningful. And our relationship with Bond deepens with each film. *The Searchers* has many a serious and moving scene and theme, but I'm not sure I take more pleasure in any scene than the ones in which Bond is smacked on the behind by a woman and erupts with his trademark horse whinny. No, the scene itself is not deep, but our relationship with Bond, and our familiarity with his character, is. We have a history and depth of experience with this character, after the umpteenth Ford film in which he has been such a stalwart presence, that makes a scene like this more wryly humorous. Ward's presence grounds a film, gives it depth, calls for an immediate emotional investment. By this time in our relationship with Bond, he can do less than anyone else in the film and call forth the deepest response.

The use of a family or troupe of actors is not limited to classic Hollywood. Contemporary directors, like British filmmaker Mike Leigh and the American filmmakers the Coen brothers, use a family of actors and both to good effect. Using a family of actors is one way of recreating, in the contemporary film situation, a certain kind of atmosphere that was central to the success of Hollywood. Even the most jaundiced actors from the studio era in Hollywood came to long, after the studios had died off, for the sense of community or family that the studios offered. That sense of being among family, of the actors' familiarity with one another, translates onto the screen, where their ease and comfort with each other, a certain organic communication between them, are manifest, just as they were in Hollywood. Also, the ability to work with the same director, to participate in the same kind of filmmaking, to finesse the same persona, means that the actors get repeat experiences, as they did in Hollywood—an opportunity to hone their specific art. Howard Hawks defended the way he would famously plagiarize his own films for themes and patches of dialogue by arguing that this kind of repetition was part of the beauty of working in Hollywood: if one didn't pull off an effect the first time, one might be able to the second or third; one could experiment, repeat, and develop the material. The sheer quantity of films produced allowed for greater experimentation and refinement of those experiments. Likewise, the sheer quantity of films produced, coupled with an astute attention to the personas actors were developing, allowed actors to get good at what they were doing by doing it over and over again, to hone a film presence.

This is not to say that a troupe of actors à la Ford and Sturges is necessary to use character actors well. Hitchcock, for example, went to the same well often for his stars (using Jimmy Stewart and Cary Grant in four films each and Ingrid Bergman three times) but not so often for his character actors. Character actor Leo G. Carroll worked in six Hitchcock's films, but Hitchcock did not do anything particularly memorable in shaping a persona for Carroll. We don't have a sense of Hitchcock delighting or trusting in a troop of actors the way Ford and Sturges did.

But Hitchcock was, nonetheless, adept, in his own way, at getting the most out of his character actors. With his strong sense of the ubiquity of evil and his particular sympathy for those who struggled with evil, Hitchcock took particular care in shaping his villains, who were often such charming and complex characters that they elicited more sympathy from the audience than Hitchcock's male leads. It has often been noted that one feels a great sense of sympathy for Claude Rains's Nazi conspirator in *Notorious* and James Mason's Communist spy in *North by Northwest*. Both, despite their evil, are characterized by a kind of sorrowful puppy love for the film's heroine, while the film's protagonist, Cary Grant in both films, is often cold and judgmental toward her. Hitchcock used characters actors to convey one of his central ideas, that the weak and evil are often more sympathetic than the complacently good.

One often notes a Capra-like attention to detail in Hitchcock when dealing with even the smallest of his heavies. Evil inspired him as warmth and sentiment did Capra. Reggie Nalder, for example, the character actor with a death mask of a face, who played the very small role of the assassin in the 1956 version of *The Man Who Knew Too Much*, recalled Hitchcock advising him to "look lovingly" at the man he was going to kill as if he were "glancing at a beautiful woman."[4] This represents a different kind of motivational idea than we are likely to find in Capra, but the same recognition of giving purpose, and poetry, to the smallest roles in your film.

TAKING SMALL ROLES SERIOUSLY

What is striking in Hollywood films, whether they are characterized by a family of actors or not, is how seriously filmmakers took their subsidiary roles and character actors. There seems to be an inherent understanding that the small roles in a film could make or break the film. Significant roles are not always proportional to the size of the role. Orson Welles often spoke of his fondness for playing characters that were introduced late in a film or play, characters, like Harry Lime in *The Third Man*, that everyone was always talking about, so that when they arrived the pump had been fully primed for the maximum impact or characters that were small but important, who made a quick powerful impression and then parted before overstaying their welcome. Welles loved to point to the famous stage role of Mr. Wu as the quintessential example of the power inherent in the brief role. "All the other actors," Welles said, "boil around the stage for about an hour shrieking, 'What will happen when Mr. Wu arrives?' 'What is he like this Mr. Wu?' and so on. Finally a great gong is beaten, and slowly crossing over a Chinese bridge comes Mister Wu himself in full Mandarin robes. Peach Blossom (or whatever her name is) falls on her face and a lot of coolies yell, 'Mr. Wu!!!' The curtain comes down, the audience goes wild, and everybody says, 'Isn't that guy playing Mr. Wu

Photo 8. Character great Thomas Mitchell (center) cadges drinks from the hapless Donald Meek (right) in Ford's *Stagecoach*. Ford regular John Carradine sits by. Courtesy of Photofest.

a great actor.'" The important thing about a role like that, Welles concluded, "isn't how many lines you have but how few."[5]

John Ford seems to have had a particular sensitivity to the significance of small roles. His character roles are great, not just because of our familiarity with his troupe of actors but also because he challenged himself to make something significant of even the smallest roles in his films. For example, in *Stagecoach*, Ford and screenwriter Dudley Nichols hit upon a comic gambit that could have been annoying if played to excess. Town drunk Doc Boone (played by Thomas Mitchell) befriends a timid whisky drummer (played by Donald Meek) with whom he shares the stagecoach. For the duration of the film Boone will comically bum drinks from the salesman's sample case (Photo 8).

Now, classic Hollywood was littered with bits of shtick just like this one that were run into the ground in the course of the film. Defining character actors through a tiny bit of business or eccentric trait is generally one of Hollywood's strengths. Hollywood was good at quick, deft, efficient definition of character, at making one remember and feel for a character without resorting to lengthy dialogue or speeches. But even shtick has to go somewhere. As Billy Wilder said, first you plant a gag, then return to it, and then you pay it off. Too often directors would assign a "charming" detail to a character than repeat it ad nauseam throughout the film. The sheriff in *Destry Rides Again,* played by Charles Winninger, for example, has a habit of untucking his shirt in confused frustration at his moments of greatest pique, a detail that is a great deal more charming and amusing the first time than the fourth. Once a gag is created, it has to go somewhere.

Ford was good at going somewhere with his gags. Instead of just soaking the relationship between the drunk and the whiskey salesman for relentless comic effect, Ford develops the relationship between the two a bit, elevating it along the way from coarse comedy to delicate pathos. And he does so despite having very little time to do much with these characters at all.

Of course Ford's effective characterization begins with his sound casting. Mitchell specialized in cantankerous, loquacious drunks like this one, as hopeless as they are intelligent and with a great deal of fun in their eyes. Donald Meek specialized in timid types (few actors have been so aptly named), small, frightened men who are easily pushed around and are always mousing about, looking for an exit from whatever trouble they find themselves in. His character's name here, Peacock, seems only to comically underline his timidity. Peacock, the whisky salesman, is such a timid fellow that the other characters in the film keep mistaking him for a minister, setting up a comical counterpoint between his parsonlike manner and what he does for a living.

Boone, out of money and liquor, takes to Peacock like a long-lost buddy and courts him like a suitor as he filches drink after drink from Peacock's sample case during their long, dusty ride together on the stagecoach. Mitchell and Meek work well together, with Mitchell bluffly bullying Meek and Meek putting up with it all, wearing a sad neutral expression reminiscent of Stan Laurel. The effectiveness of the scenes is due to Meek's patient deadpan as much as it is due to Mitchell's trademark devilish drunk. In one scene, Doc Boone wraps Peacock's scarf around Peacock's head and neck and dabs gently at his eyes that are watering from the assault of wind and dust during the stagecoach ride, as though he were ministering to an invalid aunt. Meek bears the indignity with the infinite patience of a dog that is being dressed up by children.

The relationship between the two takes a more serious turn about halfway through the film. The stagecoach has been on the road for sometime now, and everyone in the coach, including the drunk doctor and timid whiskey drummer, is covered in dust and depressed by fatigue. Dust, as it so often does in Ford's film, literally swims in the air of the stagecoach. As Doc Boone reaches for a liquor sample for the umpteenth time, Peacock, uncharacteristically, stays Boone's hand. It is as though Peacock's fatigue has overthrown his timidity. "Please, brother," is all he says, quietly imploring Boone to stop drinking. The scene surprises us because usually Meek isn't usually called to rise above comic relief. But Meek, like so many character actors, is a fuller bodied creature in a Ford film.

Doc Boone looks into Peacock's eyes with the expression of grim, humorous menace Mitchell specialized in when playing his combative drunks. He seems both surprised by Meek's assertiveness and touched by his concern, but at the same time he remains (in keeping with the Ford drunk) unswervingly committed to his self-obliteration. He brushes aside Peacock's hand, downs the bottle, and tosses it out the window. His face takes on a harder, meaner, more miserable expression before his head lolls forward and drops onto his lap.

This scene isn't played for laughs. It's a kind of sadly lyrical evocation of self-destruction and, in itself, typical of the way Ford could scatter quiet little bits of poetry along his narrative. But it's also an example of his quick and deft characterization, the way he could elevate the smallest and most subsidiary characters into something significant in his film. The scene represents a surprising turn in a relationship that has been, up till now, played for laughs—though played well by these two consummate professionals. Doc Boone's drinking no longer seems comic but sad and nihilistic. Meek's timidity gently gives way to empathy and moral assertiveness. Stirrings of serious friendship arise from the two men's forced intimacy and shared discomfort. Comic relief begins to transform into interesting character study.

This scene also sets up nicely the latter one in which Doc Boone is asked to wake from his drunken stupor in order to deliver Mrs. Mallory's baby. Ford sets up the shots in these scenes so that Doc Boone's reawakened moral ardor is tied, visually, to Peacock. When Boone realizes that he will deliver the baby, he puts a stopper in the whisky bottle he's been drinking from at a bar in a wayside inn at which they've stopped. Meek's character is the only other one in the frame. He stands to Mitchell's lower right just around the corner of the bar. His back is against a wall and the light casts a strong shadow to his right. As Doc Boone stops the bottle and calls for coffee, Peacock just stares at him intently. Smaller than Boone, and situated along the receding line of the bar, he seem to be a kind of Jiminy Cricket, a visualization of Boone's conscience or moral fortitude. As Boone leaves the screen to the left, Ford holds the camera on Peacock whose eyes follow Boone offscreen. This is one of those moments in Ford's cinema where he seemed to have had an intuitive idea of just what was called for, allowing us to contemplate Boone's moral awakening through the eyes of the man who has been closest to his dissolution and most interested in his redemption. And it's effective, again, because of Meek's deadpan. He doesn't go soft in the face with adoration; he just continues to stare at Boone with an intensity and severity that seems out of keeping with his normally meek nature. His look represents the consolidation of energy that's occurring at the moment.

When Doc Boone returns triumphant from delivering the baby, it's Peacock who clears a path for him to the bar. Mitchell downs a glass of whiskey with the pleasure a man might experience if he drank water for the first time in a week. Peacock remains at his side, again like a dog, only this time a loyal, alert one. When, twice, the others begin to speak, Peacock yells, "Quiet!" as though nothing were of more sacred importance than that the might doctor enjoy his drink. The moment is humorous not only because of Peacock's new tolerance for Boone's drinking but also because of the stern attitude the mild-mannered man has developed in his new role as Boone's protector and moral guardian.

What has to be kept in mind in contemplating these scenes involving Boone and Peacock is how far down they are in the pecking order of the film's concerns. These are minor characters, whose time together on the screen represents, altogether, only a few minutes. Certainly the relationships between Ringo and Dallas, Mrs. Mallory and Hatfield, Ringo and Curly, and Mrs. Mallory and Dallas are more central to the film and developed in greater detail. But the effectiveness of the scenes with Boone and Peacock reminds us that a significant part of Ford's success is due to the seriousness with which he approached his smallest roles in the film, the deft, efficient way he could develop characters and relationships, and his Chaplin-like ability to build pathos into small bits that other directors would have been satisfied to use for simple comic effect. Ford seemed incapable of letting the smallest of roles go by without doing something memorable with them. This accumulation of small glories is a part of what makes his films seem so crammed with significance.

It is striking how much emotional freight a small character role can bear. There's a funny way in which small character roles often become the richest emotional deposit of the classic Hollywood film. Hollywood liked character actors for the opportunity they provided to get ideas or feelings across obliquely, in a way slightly removed from the stars or from the central narrative of the film. Directors often saw the best character actor as a reliable place in which to stow their film's meaning.

Character great James Gleason, for example, has a very similar role in two films, Vincent Minnelli's superb *The Clock* and Henry Koster's not-so-bad *The Bishop's Wife*. In both films, Gleason plays a blue-collar guy, a working stiff who becomes a mascot of sorts for a young couple out on the town having the day of their life. In *The Clock*, he's a milkman who gives the couple a lift in the middle of the night and who's so convivial the couple ends up helping him on his milk rounds. In *The Bishop's Wife*, he's a cabbie who the couple find so amusing they invite him along to ice skate with them.

Gleason was in many ways emblematic of the Hollywood character actor. Gruff, slangy in diction but gentle and good-hearted, he seemed to incarnate the ideal of the morally centered, good-natured urban workingman, the idealized spirit of New York City. I can't think of any actor who more characterized the mixture of buoyant energy and gritty urban texture that Hollywood character actors specialized in.

When Gleason meets the couples in these films, he becomes their chaperone, their pet, their comic entertainment. He offers them a kind of workingman's christening of their relationship. It's typical of Hollywood's uniquely earthy textures that cupid here is played by a New York City cabdriver or milkman. The eccentricity of Gleason's character seems to capture the fortuitous spontaneity of the young lovers' day, the sense that anything that comes their way is fun and meaningful. He's the first to see them as couple and thus becomes significant in their personal mythology, an externalization of their love. He starts by giving them a lift but finishes by becoming a kind of guiding spirit for, and benediction of, their love. He's only on screen for a short time, gone almost as soon as he arrives, but somehow he comes to represent the beauty (if we can use that word with the craggy Gleason) of their day in the city.

It's in this manner that the best character actors deepened their persona film by film. By the time of these two films, the veteran Gleason's talent for gruff, loyal, ingenuous charm, his good-natured ease with himself, his sensitivity to the spectacle of young love had deepened to the point where this old vaudeville comedian had become a kind of personification of the best in human nature, a guy one turned to for the soul of the film.

One indication of just how seriously Hollywood took its character actors is how often it chose to finish its films with its subsidiary players rather than its stars. That's Claude Rains walking off into the dark, arm in arm with Humphrey Bogart at the end of *Casablanca*, not Ingrid Bergman. And that's Claude Rains walking up the steps to certain death in the lovely operatic finale to *Notorious*. That's William Demarest in the final frame of *The Lady Eve*, slipping out of Henry Fonda's stateroom, sticking his mug in front of the camera and saying, "Positively the same dame." That's Walter Brennan doing a little jig, the last one out the door, in *To Have and Have Not*.

Capra chooses to finish *Mr. Smith Goes to Washington* not with the principals, Jimmy Stewart and Jean Arthur, but with the Senate president (and sole ally to Jefferson Smith in the Senate) played by silent film star Harry Carey. The Senate having broken into chaos after learning of Claude Rains's suicide attempt, Carey's character attempts to bring calm to the chamber with his gavel but pretty quickly gives up. Tossing the gavel up and catching it playfully, he leans back in his chair, puts his hands behind his head in leisurely fashion, and settles back to enjoy the show. It's a lovely character touch to end the film on, as we know that the vice president was rooting for Smith and is letting his affection for the young Senator get the best of his sense of decorum. But the gesture rings even more richly due to our affection for the great silent star Carey and due to what we know is Capra's affection and respect for Carey in giving him this final gesture and also because the laconic gesture is in keeping with the persona that Carey developed in the silent film Westerns he made for Ford.

In each of these films, the directors, paradoxically, chose to lodge a good deal of the films' deepest emotion in some of the films' smaller players. The best Hollywood filmmakers knew how to take advantage of Hollywood's stable of character actors. They knew which one had the solidness of persona, the long-standing familiarity with the public to bear the film's emotional import.

And these filmmakers and their writers had enough storytelling savvy to know that at times it was important to deviate from the main narrative and give it a breather. When one has secondary actors who can carry the ball, and they existed in spades in Hollywood, use them. Counterpoint is a big part of the art of the Hollywood story, knowing how to take the pressure off the central narrative by shifting the burden at key points to the supporting player. Hollywood knew how to share the wealth in its films. And many Hollywood directors seemed to understand Welles's feeling that less is more, that sometimes the most moving and enticing characters in a story are the ones we see the least. Couple this bit of standard story-building wisdom with a great stable of actors who can register with the audience just by appearing, and the result was the plethora of significant character roles that represents one of the chief glories of the studio era.

— 12 —

Hollywood Writing

SEPARATING FILM FROM LITERATURE

In the 120 or so years that film has been around it has taken quite a beating at the hands of the higher arts, the practitioners of which tend to sneer at its gross sensationalism and popularity. Film has suffered in particular by comparison to literature. The wordsmiths have always sniped at film the most. Hollywood, in its heyday, invited a host of the world's greatest writers to its studios. An exhaustive list of respected writers who worked in Hollywood would consume too much space, but at one time or another Thomas Mann, William Faulkner, F. Scott Fitzgerald, Dorothy Parker, Bertolt Brecht, S.J. Perelman, Upton Sinclair, Gertrude Stein, Rebecca West, Thornton Wilder, P.G. Wodehouse, Stefan Zweig, Arnold Bennet, Somerset Maugham, Hugh Walpole, Aldous Huxley, and Maurice Maeterlink all worked on Hollywood scripts. Some warmed to the role with generous humor. Faulkner saw Hollywood as a pleasing holiday that came with a check. Some languished for months at a time without writing a word before taking a quiet departure. Some, like S.J. Perelman, found their revenge in penning vicious satires on Hollywood. Almost all, though, shared a disdain for writing in Hollywood and sneered at the notion that what they did there had anything to do with art. And their collective attitude has defined much of our attitude toward Hollywood writing.

Hollywood unwittingly affirmed these writers' condescension toward Hollywood by, in an effort to elevate film's status, translating great works of literature into film or by creating films with obvious content or social relevance. In hindsight, these films look like some of Hollywood's most leaden and pretentious works. Hollywood seldom looked more foolish than when it strove to be serious. One of the most glaring deficiencies in the arguments of those, like Thomas Schatz, who would raise the status of the Hollywood producer to semi-auteur, is the producer's middlebrow taste. Ironically, Samuel Goldwyn, credited with coining the most familiar dictum of Hollywood (and one that most succinctly summarizes its craft), "If I want a message, I'll call Western Union," was one of the most vulnerable to the lure of "high culture." But even the boy genius Irving Thalberg, that moniker of good taste, the one man who supposedly came closest to getting down the "whole equation" of Hollywood films, is associated mostly with films that bear traces of the MGM's trademark stuffiness, a stuffiness that is, in part, an expression of his notion of what makes film "art."

On the other hand, many of the works that seemed light and frivolous at the time now represent Hollywood's crown jewels. Hollywood's great success is what many deemed, originally, its greatest weakness: its studious lack of content, its light touch, and its glancing way of dealing with its subject matter.

Hollywood has probably failed the most in taking on, and suffered the most by comparison to, the novel—particularly the great novel, the sanctified classic. Because the novel and film are two favorite forms of entertainment in the modern era, the idea occurred early in film history that the two should be conjoined, despite the fact that condensing hundreds of pages of text into 2 hours of dialogue (which moreover contends for space with music and visual images) defies common sense. The history of novels turned into films is a sordid one, a story of one failure after another. These films are doubly cursed. Not only are they bad films, but they also tend to represent insults to the work they translate. Just as annoying as the films themselves is the cackle, left in their wake, of indignant literati voicing the eternal truism that the film is not as good as the book. Perhaps the most damaging effect of the novel turned into film is how successfully it confirms our sense of film as an inferior art form in general and compared to literature in particular.

The most successful film adaptations of novels are those where the director and screenwriters had the guts to bowdlerize the novel, to find the slight, glancing take on the novel that would fit the abbreviated nature of film. Filmic adaptations of novels tend to resemble critical essays on novels more than the novels themselves. They only have enough time to represent a slight take on the work. *To Have and Have Not* is one of the great novels turned into film. Why? Because Howard Hawks kept the atmosphere of the book and threw everything else out. On the other hand, it is a pretty arduous task to summon the name of a film that was faithful to the book *and* a good film. Even making films of exorbitant length is not a guarantee of success. Sergei Bondarchuk's justly vaunted version of Tolstoy's *War and Peace* is 507 minutes long in its fullest version, and though one of the most breathtaking spectacles in film history, it skitters along the surface of Tolstoy's tome. It seems more an expression of a lush 1960s mysticism than a representation of anything Tolstoy had to say.

In the world of literature turned to film, Francois Truffaut's dictum that good books make bad films and vice versa seems to hold eternally true. Film creators are more comfortable eviscerating less venerated novels and contouring them to the limitations of the film medium. Good novels turned into film result in numbing genuflection, lumbering pacing, and an annoying preponderance of British accents.

The marriage of cinema and the stage is also more fortuitous. In many ways, Hollywood built itself around the goals and traditions of the theater, making particular study of the efficient streamlined product that was the nineteenth century "well-made play." Much of what is truly satisfying in Hollywood film, much of its clean classical style comes from the well-made play, where sacred attention was paid to unity and the arc of narrative, where every element in the play was meant to serve a dominant theme or purpose. Plays, like film, take place in a continuous time to which we have to subordinate ourselves. And we often feel the same pleasure after a film that we do after a play, that of having been put through a refreshing exercise, of having experienced a couple of hours of graceful, rich, and well-ordered time.

That said, the history of cinema has, at the same time, been one of slow disassociation from the theater, which is responsible for many of Hollywood's more static films. Film had to wean itself from the proscenium arch, to learn that it had means to carve up time and space, a kind of zip and energy that theater did not. In the meantime, scores of plays turned into films had littered the Hollywood landscape, some with interesting bits of film business but most unable to capitalize on film's potential for packaging time and space in its new, more lightning quick, more intimate way. As Andrew Sarris has pointed out, few "cult classics emerged from adaptations of popular plays."[1] Theater on film turns out to be a lumbering affair for the most part. Whatever film does is close to theater but quite different as well.

The relationship between film and literature starts to seem more valid the more we scale it down. The lighter or more compact the literary form, the better it seems to match up to film. Sarris is right that few cult classics emerged from prominent plays. But when Hollywood avoided prominence, when it drew from theater's lighter fare the odds for a success increased. From the very beginning of the sound film, Hollywood turned to light comedies of manners that were distinguished by the cleverness of their dialogue more than the seriousness of their content. When we listen to dialogue in Shaw and Wilde, it's impossible not to hear the eccentric rhythms of what will become (when it mixes with Hollywood's more slangy, populist lingo) screwball comedy. The goals of clever theatrical comedy and the Hollywood film are very similar: to create a lively entertainment that, though veering from topical seriousness, manages, at its best, to imbue its material with some significance. Both value an almost musical rhythm that aims to satisfy, not by the depth of its content, but by the elegance of its form. Both aim for a kind of Dionysian experience that elevates and refreshes rather than turns us toward sober reflection. And here, in translating sophisticated theatrical comedy to film, the wits, intellectuals, theatrical pros, and jazz age veterans that the Hollywood studios had stocked themselves with came in handy. Charming cynics like Dorothy Parker and Noel Coward had a place in this world that, if not quite knowing what to do with serious theater, seemed to move happily to the jaunty rhythms of Cole Porter.

Hollywood's ties to another slight literary form, the short story, may be even stronger than its connections to theater. As Kristin Thompson has pointed out, though voluminous attention has been paid to the relationship between film and both the novel and the theater, the influence of the short story on Hollywood has been "largely overlooked." Thompson describes the first decade of the new century as "the era of the short-story handbook." Poe's ideas on the short story and its suitability to classical virtues—his notion of a story as something that could be read in one sitting and therefore lent itself to a great unity, his sense that every element in a story contributed to a "unity of effect or impression"—held great sway at the time.[2] There was also a boom at the time in short stories in popular fiction magazines, and many of the early screen writers and screenwriting coaches were steeped in Poe's theories and trained in the art of these popular magazines. The short story meshed nicely with the Hollywood film. Its brevity matched that of the film. Like a film, it could be taken down in one gulp. Characterization in a short story, as in a film, was something that had to be taken care of quickly and efficiently, with deft but striking and memorable touches.

If the influence of the short story on film has been neglected, the relationship between film and poetry has been virtually ignored. And yet there are fruitful comparisons to be made between Hollywood language and poetry. Both are spare. Language, in film, has to compete with images and sound, two things that many film purists say represent the real substance of film. Language takes a more subordinate role in film. It tends to be then sparer and more allusive. No time here for great ponderous speeches.

And Hollywood dialogue, like poetry, tends to be stylized. Though Hollywood followed some naturalistic traditions, for example, the way in which it could, in the manner of Flaubert, summarize a character by a single, telling physical detail, its diction was rarely naturalistic. Whether in high-pitched melodrama or slangy street film, Hollywood's language was always idealized, a little more emotional, a little slangier and wittier than in real life. The history of screenwriting is the history of great lines like—to cite the first two on the hit parade—"Here's looking at you, kid" and "You know how to whistle, don't you?" Hollywood has its own kind of poetic diction, though one that tends to avoid formality and ornateness. The greatest screenwriters were those who knew how to insert a telling line or catchy phrase, to accent a scene, rather than overwhelm it, with words.

It is, then, in the sparer literary forms—the breezy comedy, the operetta, the short story, the poetic aphorism—that we see a more fortuitous marriage of film and literature. On the other hand, when Hollywood took on the large and ponderous, the weighty novel, for example, it embarrassed itself. And this new art form, light and breezy, accessible and yet chock-full of wisdom came, then, to be ashamed of itself.

FILM WRITING

That Hollywood screenwriting was an art unto itself, and a tricky one at that, is evidenced by the fact that so many of the serious writers Hollywood were incapable of managing it. As Thomas Schatz has noted, very few eastern writers were successful in Hollywood. The most successful transition, Schatz notes, was made by journalists like Ben Hecht, Robert Benchley, and Charles MacArthur, "who were accustomed to deadlines and copy editors and writing for an anonymous public that liked its information meted out in economical and dramatic doses." Moreover, Schatz notes, journalists "shared with veteran screenwriters a tendency to think of their work more as a craft than an art."[3]

Here again we see the connection between film writing and the lighter literary crafts. The Hollywood screenwriter, like the journalist, plies his trade within a commercial context and consequently suffers less from the self-aggrandizement characteristic of the "artiste." Both professions, filmwriting and journalism, aim at a terse, economical prose that is accessible and gets to the point fast. Both aim for a certain naturalism, an objectivity in rendering their stories, so that the public is as little aware as possible of authorship, a situation again contributive to a certain artistic humility.

The other successful practitioner of the Hollywood script was the band Schatz alludes to as the "veteran screenwriters," those who came to screenwriting through the world of film itself, not from outside, those who had an inherent instinct for how words fit into cinema and were not naive about the subordinate nature, or at least altered significance, of words in cinema.

During the rise of feature films in the teens, Kristin Thompson notes, Hollywood increasingly relied on staff writers to translate novels and plays into films. These writers would work from synopsis, which they would, in turn, break down into shots, so that in the end, Thompson writes, "one would be hard put to look at *The Eagle's Mate* (Kirkwood, 1914, Famous Players) next to *Girl of the Golden West* (Cecil B. DeMille, 1915, Lasky) and know which came from a novel and which from a play."[4] Writers like Francis Marion and Anita Loos at MGM, Schatz writes, "honed their skills in the silent era, when writing simply meant talking through a story idea with a director. Their skills developed along with the studio system, as story ideas gave way to scenarios and then to shooting scripts and dialogue continuities."[5] These writers' development was organic to, and concomitant with, the development of the Hollywood screenplay. They understood where words fit in it. They had an enormous advantage in working in the silent era because they had the experience of seeing the things that were important to cinema aside from words, rhythm, for example, or expressing things visually rather than verbally. They were loyal to these values after sound came into cinema, recognizing the primacy of film as a visual medium, recognizing that pacing was a question of editing as well as story rhythm, recognizing that there was just not the same room for words in this medium that there had been in theater.

Anita Loos, for example, felt awful when she ended up replacing F. Scott Fitzgerald on MGM's *Red Headed Woman*, but she also recognized that Fitzgerald's writing just wouldn't play. "She knew," Schatz writes, "Thalberg wanted the kind of sexual banter and playful eroticism that had become her trademark and she delivered that for the Harlow vehicle." Loos had the light touch Hollywood needed, an instinctive talent for light repartee that filled in a film without weighing it down and an instinctive sense of what the studios wanted from language in the films.

Still, even directors who had cherished relationships with writers emphasize over and over again that the screenplay had to be absorbed into the film, not vice versa. Hitchcock complained that the studio system had it backward. Ideally, the director would hand the screenwriter a treatment, talk to him about the goals of the film, and then leave the screenwriter to add the dialogue, which is essentially the practice Hitchcock arrived at in the end anyway. "The writer," Hitchcock said, "thinks he's done a wonderful thing when he writes 'close-up,' but that's ridiculous and stupid. It is a bad system because strictly speaking a writer should be given a treatment written by the director. I usually work with the writer on the treatment. Now, when I say treatment, it is really a description of the film. It describes exactly what is coming on that screen. There are indication of shots in it and so forth. Then you give that to the writer and let him go off."[6] Raoul Walsh too joked about throwing out all of the shot suggestions that came with the screenplay. Both his and Hitchcock's comments point to a glitch in the famously economical studio system because they would end up reinventing the script during shooting, meaning that there was a great deal of wasted effort in the writing department. Of course, this wasted effort led to a great deal of frustration on writers' part with the Hollywood process. They rightly came to understand that in this town the word did not rule.

Rarely do we come across great directors being handed a script and working straight from it. Jacques Rivette probably exaggerated (as the *Cahiers du Cinema* critics tended to) when he said, in 1957, "[W]e now know for sure there isn't a single one of the great American directors who doesn't work on the scenario himself right from the beginning."[7] But it does seem to be a cardinal trait of the best Hollywood filmmakers to be in on the scriptwriting whenever possible and to shape the script, as much as possible, to their own designs. Hawks is famous for exhausting his writers and actors with constant brainstorming sessions, improvisations, and rewrites during the course of his films. Samson Raphaelson, we recall, spoke of the "serious business" of his "conversational doodlings" with Ernst Lubitsch and of how he (Raphaelson) learned to become expert in "a certain kind of nonsense that delighted" Lubitsch. Ford is famous for tearing pages of dialogue out of his scripts and finding a silent, visual way of getting across the meaning at hand. All the best directors were always on the lookout for ways of making their scripts more efficient and of finding translations in images for the words handed them. All worked at paring the script down under the dictates of the film, not vice versa.

Film writing is subordinate to the creation of the film as a whole; it has to arrange itself around or react to the film. It doesn't dictate its demands but tries to understand the demands of the film and the director. But the word "subordinate" doesn't seem to adequately describe the work of the best screenwriters in Hollywood. Because a talent like Loos's and Hecht's, a knowledge of how to slip language into a film, was rare. And too many of Hollywood's films come out of great director–screenwriter duos for screenwriting to be seen as a subordinate process. In fact, as I emphasized in the second chapter, the director–screenwriter partnership may be the collaboration that is responsible for the greatest number of classics in Hollywood. And there are too many stories of spirited collaborations between the director and screenwriter on the set to suggest the screenwriter was anything but central to the creativity of these great films. Even Hitchcock, who might be said to control his writers the most, to put them to his use, finds his best films where he finds his best writers, Ben Hecht and *Notorious*, for example, Jeffrey Michael Hayes and the trilogy of films he made with Hitchcock, Ernst Lehman and *North by Northwest*, and Samuel Taylor and *Vertigo*.

In the end, the skewering of Hollywood by the insulted literati who toiled there make great reads for their sharp invective. They ably satirize the foolish waste of the studio system and the imbecilic pretensions of the studios' producers, directors, and actors. Hollywood was not an intellectual town or one that really understood much about literature. But these writings are notable for their own lack of understanding of the Hollywood process. The writers had a pretty large blind spot themselves, one that has become more apparent, as many of these studio films have aged as well as they have. And so, as much as we enjoy the witty invective of, say, an S.J. Perelman, we marvel that more didn't have the humility of John Collier, one of the few vaunted writers, who blamed himself for his lack of success there. "I still wish I'd had enough sense to let Cukor teach me more," Collier wrote. "But at that time I was too ignorant and, I suppose, too obstinate to take advantage of such a wonderful opportunity to learn about filmmaking." Cukor, he went on to say, "was a man of great talent and wonderful expressiveness. He would be the person from whom one could acquire a great deal of pragmatic knowledge."[8] Collier's comments are unusually modest for a member of Hollywood's prideful literary elite. He suggests that there might actually have been something to learn in Hollywood, that his failure might have had more to do with his pride than the vacuousness of the enterprise, that being a good screenwriter meant understanding the director's craft. He acknowledges that film is an art of visual expressiveness, not just of words, that to learn it one has to humble oneself to a great deal of "pragmatic knowledge" and that the Hollywood film tended to veer away from vaunted literary expression in its effort to arrive at clever, practical ways of getting its point across.

ANTI-INTELLECTUAL

Hollywood is best, and most itself, not when it seeks to placate the intellectuals but when it pokes its finger in their eye. There is a rich tradition, in Hollywood, of films that take intellectuals to task. Certainly the tradition of poking fun at intellectuals is richer than the one in which Hollywood tries to incarnate, seriously and respectfully, the intellectual world. Those films tend to be sophomoric and rich in unintentionally hilarious lines. The one time Hitchcock was not able to make good use of Jimmy Stewart's persona was when he cast him as a professor with a bent for Nietzschean ideology in *Rope*. Vincent Minnelli's *Some Came Running* is an excellent film, but we still look away in embarrassment during those scenes where Frank Sinatra has to actually speak lines intended to illustrate that he is a great American novelist. And the scenes in which Sinatra's love interest, a college literature professor played by Martha Hyer, lectures her highly attentive class on tolerating the aberrant lives of great artists is simply laughable. "If I had known Poe, I would undoubtedly been repelled by his drinking," she tells a room full of nicely pressed students, "but I would have tried to understand."

In fact, there are few subjects that Hollywood treats as poorly as it does the classroom or the intellectual world in general. The pretense of what comprises the "intellectual world" begs for satire, as academic satirists from Kingsley Amis to David Lodge have proven, and the ephemerality of what an "intellectual" actually is tends to render hilarious groping efforts of Hollywood to answer that question.

But when Hollywood chooses to satirize the intellectual we are off to the races. The great moments in which intellectuals are lampooned in Hollywood are too many to enumerate. Think of Mischa Auer's Italian poet Carlo, in Gregory La-Cava's *My Man Godfrey*, for example, pet and protégé to Alice Brady's sublimely ditzy society matron. Carlo is prone, when the family argues over money matters, to dramatic, Anna Pavlova–like poses in the corner of the room and to mournful soliloquies ("Oh! Money, money, money! The *Frankenstein* monster that destroys souls.") that he abandons instantly when trays of hors d'oeuvres appear. Brady's character, Mrs. Bullock, is, of course, a sucker for his angst. "Please don't say anything more," she chastises her family in that loony trill that was her forte. "You're upsetting Carlo." But, in the tradition of scatterbrain screwball mothers, she is just as likely to turn from benevolent protectress to condescending tyrant, as, for example, when she insists that Carlo do his hilariously accurate imitation of a gorilla for her daughter (Carol Lombard) who is throwing a tantrum and needs distraction (Photo 9). At this point, the resident poet becomes resident fool and reveals his position in the house as one step up from domestic staff, a clown who has to sing for his supper. Of course, character great Eugene Pallette, playing, as usual, the long-suffering father, is there to witness the whole sorry spectacle, aghast at what happens when wealth meets high culture.

Or, think of the scene where Gary Cooper takes his fists to Capra's fictional version of the Algonquin Round Table in *Mr. Deeds Goes to Town*. Deeds, a greeting card poet freshly arrived in New York, has gone to Tullio's, a restaurant where you can "eat with the literati," in hopes of rubbing elbows with what he perceives, in his charming innocence, as fellow writers. A gaggle of famous writers sitting at a "big round table" do indeed invite Deeds over to their table but only to mock his commercial jingles. When Deeds catches on to their true intent, he does what Cooper's normally exceedingly good-natured characters do when they are confronted with exasperating and inexplicable cruelty—he starts swinging. Much to our satisfaction, he decks two of the writers.

Photo 9. Mocking intellectuals was one of Hollywood's strong suits. Here the poet Carlo (Mischa Auer) is forced to do his imitation of a gorilla to earn his keep with the wealthy family in Gregory LaCava's *My Man Godfrey*. Courtesy of Photofest.

As early as 1928, King Vidor was already teasing Hollywood for its inferiority complex vis-à-vis "serious subject matter" in *Show People*, in which Marion Davies plays an aspiring actress who finds she has a gift for film comedy, and taking pies in the kisser, but wants only to work at the "High Arts" studio. Preston Sturges would make the same film 13 years later, with a film director instead of an actress. Joel McCrea's Sullivan, a highly successful comic director in Sturges' *Sullivan's Travels*, wants to make a real film about the social troubles of America. Its bloated title alone, "Oh Brother, Where Art Thou?" (with an emphasis on the first two words), tells us what Sturges thinks of that enterprise.

Many of the best jokes in the film are at the expense of Sullivan's high-mindedness and self-seriousness, for example, when Sturges regular Porter Hall, playing Mr. Hadrian, one of the two producers to whom Sullivan pitches his project, lays into Sullivan. "These are troublous times," intones McCrea, his antique diction mirroring his high-flown attitude. Hall responds with his trademark nasal drone and biting terrier intensity and in one of those bits of staccato dialogue typical of Sturges:

"What do you know of trouble?"
"What do I know about trouble?"

"Yes, what do you know about trouble?"

"What do you mean, what do I know about trouble?"

"Just what I'm saying, you want to make a picture about garbage cans. What do you know about garbage cans? When did you eat your last meal out of one?... You want to make an epic about misery. You want to show hungry people sleeping in doorways. You want to grind 10,000 feet of hard luck, and all I'm asking is what you know about hard luck?"

Sullivan, of course has no answer to this question, leaving Hall to sniff, conclusively, "people always like what they don't know anything about."

Sullivan's greatest deflation of pomposity, though, occurs at the hands of his gentle and highly civilized butler, Burroughs (played with gracious gentility by Sturges regular, Robert Grieg, perhaps Hollywood's greatest butler). "If you permit me to say so, Sir," says Burroughs, referring to poverty, "the subject is not an interesting one. The poor know all about poverty, and only the morbid rich find it glamorous." "But," Sullivan responds, "I'm doing it for the poor. Don't you understand?" Burroughs comes back at Sullivan with one those speeches that pop up now and then in Sturges's films and which always surprise us, coming, as they do, from the character we least expect them to. The poor, Burroughs says, "rather resent the invasion of their privacy," adding, "I believe quite properly sir... You see, Sir, rich people and theorists, who are usually rich people, think of poverty in the negative, as the lack of riches, as disease might be called the lack of health. But it isn't sir. Poverty is not the lack of anything but a positive plague—with filth, criminality, vice, and despair as only a few of its symptoms. It is to be stayed away from even for the purpose of study. It is," Burroughs says, finishing with a flourish, "to be shunned." Burroughs rightly suspects Sullivan of being interested in glorifying poverty, not doing anything about it. And in his own small way, he makes the point that Marxist critics have about film for years, that it allows a pleasant catharsis for audiences by allowing them to dabble in the world's ills without troubling them to actually do anything about those ills.

It's part of Sturges's unique way of blending tones that he films this scene with a kind of mock elevation of tone, even segueing to a dramatic close-up of Burroughs delivering his final lines, and yet we know he agrees with Burroughs's every word. Sullivan, crestfallen and a little peeved, responds with a wisecrack ("Well *you* seem to have made quite a study of it") that only sets up more effectively Burroughs's final riposte: "Not willingly, Sir." Burroughs's gentility and eloquence strike us as that much more touching, now that we know that he sprang from poverty, and Sullivan's interest in poverty that much more juvenile.

Hollywood is on firm ground when it is slinging mud at intellectuals, not when it is trying to invoke them. And their satire here should not be dismissed as an irresponsible anti-intellectualism, the kind of which is often decried in America. Because, if the best Hollywood films were often anti-intellectual, they were not so because they were unintelligent or because they have a hidden fear of the intellectual. Rather they aimed for an intelligence without pretensions and one that expressed itself in creatively realized scenes and dialogue, in ingenious business, not in explicit messages or ponderous speeches. Sullivan's films, the producer Hadrian tells him, were great because they "didn't stink with messages." The potshots Hollywood took at intellectuals had a certain resonance because they were backed up by an ability to be significant and resonant without being pretentious, didactic, or obfuscatory.

A POPULIST COMEDY

If Hollywood tended to embarrass itself when it took itself seriously, when it played the intellectual, it excelled when it found its inspiration in the streets. Hollywood's language flows from all sorts of populist tributaries: from the asides and wisecracks of Jewish comic traditions and Vaudeville; from mob culture and crime fiction; from Mark Twain's cynical humor and uniquely American diction that, in turn, filtered through the slang of Damon Runyon and Ring Lardner and finally through the wisecracks of the Algonquin Table and the tough lingo of Hemingway and detective fiction. And all of these influences can be perceived in the patois of the journalists, like Ben Hecht, Billy Wilder, and Charles MacArthur, who turned out to be among Hollywood's best screenwriters, the newspapermen who had a better feel for the energetic rhythms and populist feel Hollywood was looking for in its language than many of the literati that Hollywood was importing to gin up its scripts at the same time.

But it's not just the journalists who created this language because much of this new dialogue, just as rapid and sophisticated as that of a Noel Coward play but slangier and more street-oriented, came from film people themselves—Darryl Zanuck at Warner Brothers and Frank Capra and Robert Riskin at Columbia, Howard Hawks at Columbia and other studios—and none of these guys were journalists. They were Hollywood pros, which meant they kept their audience in mind and aimed for a language that was as familiar and accessible to the audience as it was lively and inventive, a language with a zippy energy that made certain the audience's attention would not flag. Just as Hawks and Capra were discovering that speeding the tempo of comedy up made it work on the big screen, their writers were learning to master dialogue that kept pace and crackled with energy. Hawks was instrumental here with his excited, overlapping dialogue and his continued search for language that was intelligent but naturalistic and unpretentious. Hawks and his cohorts (which included news reporters) wrote the hepped up way intelligent Americans liked to think they spoke, a kind of Hemingway lingo, equal parts perception and slang.

In the end, Hollywood's propensity for creative slang and the scrappy language of the street, found its place in screwball comedy, which became an amalgam of the old sophisticated comedy of manners and the new, more democratic street-wise prose. Light and sophisticated comedy (in the manner of Wilde, Shaw, and Maugham or their underlings Coward and Phillip Barry) had been a good fit for Hollywood. The airy banter of these comedies didn't intrude too much on the entertainment focus of the medium. The breezy asides and concise epigrams of sophisticated, light comedy fit nicely in film, not taking up too much room in a medium that, at its best, emphasized the visual as much as, or more than, the verbal. Hollywood could do sophisticated comedy passably well. It's pleasant to watch, for example, Norma Shearer and Robert Montgomery giving it their all in MGM's version of Noel Coward's *Private Lives*, even if we suspect that the milieu is a little too sophisticated for them and note that Norma Shearer emotes too manically in her slightly off-key portrayal of the flighty rich.

And the banter of sophisticated comedy is as much an ingredient of Hollywood comic language as its more populist influences. "Agatha might commit a sin, but she'd never commit a faux pas," says Lowell Sherman in his 1931 comedy *Bachelor Apartment*. We love Hollywood for its many daffy, Wildesque lines like this. Hollywood's large stable of excessively effete character actors imported from Britain feasted on this kind of language even long after Capra and Hawks had set off the mania for a more American kind of diction. "Shall I tell you how I glittered through the South Seas like a silver scimitar," asks the supremely British Reginald Gardnier in *The Man Who Came to Dinner*; "I tell you, if I didn't have such a splendid education, I'd yield to the animal in me," says the mild-mannered Charles Ruggles—a small fidgety man about as far removed from the animal kingdom as the male specimen can get—in *Bringing Up Baby*.

But as numerous and memorable as lines like these are and as big a part as they are of the Hollywood dialogue tradition, we always have a sense that Hollywood is borrowing, in these witty asides, from the sophisticated theatrical comedy that preceded it. Hollywood really hit its verbal stride and created something of its own when Hawks and Capra came along, with Billy Wilder and Preston Sturges in their wake, with Columbia comedies like Capra's *Platinum Blonde* and Hawks's *His Girl Friday* and *Ball of Fire*, and with Sturges's comedies for Paramount. Here we have all the wit, sophistication, and ellipticalness of a British comedy of manners but in a new American incarnation; the energy is greater, the dialogue plainer and slangier. There's a little bit of Wilde's daft inventiveness but none of his effeteness in William Powell's "I need you as much as I need a giraffe" in *The Ex-Mrs. Bradford* and Barbara Stanwyck's "I need him like the axe needs the turkey" in *The Lady Eve*. There's a coarse, slangy inventiveness, a chaotic freedom to screwball diction. "If I ever lay my two eyes on you again, I'm gonna walk right up to you and hammer on that monkey skull of yours 'til it rings like a Chinese gong," Rosalind Russell's Hildy Johnson says to Cary Grant's Walter Burns in *His Girl Friday*. There's a kind anarchic glee, a thrill of inventiveness in language like this.

Of course the first thing we notice about this kind of language is that it is steeped in slang. But it is striking for more than its slang. If Hollywood dialogue were only about energetic slang, then it would represent little more than an extended version of the scenes in the Andy Hardy films in which Judge Hardy shakes his head at the new generation's new lingo. When Howard Hawks and Ben Hecht seek a replacement for the line "Oh you're just in love" and find it in the line "You've broken out in monkey bites," they are not just seeking to translate that line into slang; they are trying to have some fun with it, take the time to express their idea with more zing and poetry. In this sense they are just doing, in the dialogue, what Hawks, and other great directors do throughout the film, and what I talked about in Chapter 7, filling the film with "business," styling it, taking the time to find more inventive, memorable ways of getting their ideas across rather than just blurting them out. It's slangy but also highly inventive and literate.

They're also investing their films with greater energy. As different as the street language of the gangster, detective, or newspaper film is from the high society chatter of the screwball comedy, all these genres are characterized by a rapid-fire delivery, a lovely zippy rhythm. In all cases, it is a cinema that has a buoyant energy and expresses that energy in a rapid, clever, excited use of language. There is a love of language here that seems to reflect a love of life.

And even though it spoke in this new zippy slang, Hollywood was still capable of churning out the bon mots with the steady regularity of the most sophisticated comic traditions. "Mack, you ever been in love," Henry Fonda asks J. Farrell MacDonald in *My Darling Clementine*. "No," MacDonald responds. "I been a bartender all ma life." We get in Hollywood the same penchant for tight little pithy epigrams of sophisticated comedy but epigrams that are tougher, closer to the street. "Johnny's such a hard name to remember and so easy to forget," says Rita Hayworth to Glen Ford in *Gilda*; "She tried to sit on my lap while I was standing up," says Humphrey Bogart in *The Big Sleep*; "I've seen women I'd look at quicker but never one I'd look at longer" Gable says to Lana Turner in *Honky Tonk*; "Why don't you get a divorce and settle down," Oscar Levant asks Joan Crawford in *Humoresque*.

All of these lines resemble the mental palindromes, the little games with parallels, inversions, and reversals that fill Wilde's plays, except they have a tougher, grittier context; they're a little more uncouth. British comedy segued into American screwball so seamlessly that it's not always easy to separate the two. " "Have a drink," says Noel Coward, himself, in *The Scoundrel*, "just a little one to lessen the difference in our characters." The line seems pure Coward until we remember it was written by newspapermen Ben Hecht and Charles MacArthur. Sturges is one of the great virtuosi of rapid, slangy American diction, and yet his films are also chock-full of nattering effete characters specializing in the urbane diction of sophisticated comedy. "That's one of the tragedies of this life," says Rudy Vallee of Claudette Colbert's husband in *The Palm Beach Story*, to give just one example, "that the men who are most in need of a beating up are always enormous."

SIMPLE, TOUGH TRUTHS

And Hollywood's inventiveness in dialogue is not limited to the domain of comedy, though at times it seems as though its accomplishments in comic language are its greatest. Hollywood writers were also good at taking certain essential truths and framing them in plain colloquial language, rendering them quiet and unpretentious. Capra, for example, for all of his speechifying, was capable in his best films of a kind of poetic plainspokenness or understated folksy expression that could steer clear of cliché and be quite touching. When Gary Cooper, for example, finally realizes that the intellectual writers are mocking him for his greeting card poetry, in *Mr. Deeds Goes to Town*, the simplicity of his response is eloquent next to their smarmy irony: "Maybe it is comical to write poems for postcards," he concedes, "but a lot of people like them. Anyway it's the best I can do." Many of Hollywood's greatest actors were effective, not because they were good orators, but because they weren't. Henry Fonda or John Wayne's characters tend to be very reluctant to talk for too long or lack confidence in their ability to deal with the important aspects of life in words. When they do speak, it tends to be when they have to, and the words are selected for their simplicity, their sincerity, and their lack of affectation, and for their enduring wisdom. These are guys who made their career playing men who don't talk much but when they do are worth listening to.

If Hollywood had a stable of effete comics, like Reginald Gardiner and Eric Blore, to deliver its sophisticated comedy, it also had a stable of streetwise, life-toughened types, like Thelma Ritter, to straighten out those who think too much. "When a man and a woman see each other and like each other, they ought to come together—wham!—like two taxis on Broadway, not sit around analyzing each other like two specimens in a bottle," says Ritter's character, Stella the insurance nurse, in *Rear Window*, to Jimmy Stewart's L.B. Jefferies, who she thinks has been pathetically slow in his pursuit of Grace Kelly. "Listen Joe," James Gleason says to Robert Walker's young GI, who has expressed doubts as to whether a GI should marry before he goes off to war, in Vincent Minnelli's *The Clock*, "if people thought about everything that could happen they'd never do anything."

To be sure, these homespun philosophers are not particularly strong proponents of rationalism. Hollywood's philosophy matches its aesthetic. These are films that are determined to not be weighed down by ideas. When they do express ideas, they tend to be brief, tersely expressed, and successful in their simplicity, not their elaboration. But if Hollywood is weak in ratiocination it is proportionally rich in succinct, epigrammatic truths and refreshingly devoid of windbaggery.

The ending of *The Clock*, for example, is notable for the way it skirts around large ideas and heavy sentiment. The morning after his 2-day whirlwind romance and one-night honeymoon with Judy Garland, Robert Walker, preparing to leave for Europe, broaches the subject of the danger he's heading to, but Garland cuts him off with the film's only words on the subject: "Two days ago you came to this city, and you didn't know anybody. You didn't know me, and I didn't know you. And now we're married, and we both know that that was meant to be. So don't you see whoever makes the arrangements for people is doing pretty well for us? That's all we need to know."

Now, no one is going to confuse this with high literature. But it's not bad either. It's not particularly original or poetic in its insights. It's good more for what it doesn't do than what it does. It doesn't resort to speeches just because the moment is dramatic. It steers clear of piety. It deftly moves around the big subjects, getting past them with the maximum of wisdom and the minimum of words. It follows the Hollywood dictum of shutting up when things get serious. It recognizes the inferiority of words to images in conveying the most serious moments in the film.

Eric Rohmer appreciated "the character of universality of themes" in American films. "Of course," he wrote, "you will say most of them are no more than platitudes. But I prefer ideas that are as old as the hills, and unashamedly so, to the flat echo of the turn-of-the-century writing that Europe is wont to take as its inspiration."[9] Certain French intellectuals' affection for Hollywood was tied to their fatigue with the trendy negations of modernism. Rohmer was the most traditional of the French film critics, the most classically educated and the most conscious of film's relation to the art that preceded it. He is the one French critic to applaud Hollywood for its "morality," by which he means, not the ideas it spits out, but the way it doesn't shy away from embodying certain universal truths, its monumental simplicity. Classic Hollywood traffics in tried and true ideas but, at the same time, is careful to deliver those ideas with few words and little pomposity.

Hollywood is rich in a more acidic expression of truths as well. Noir films of the 1940s, with their acute sense of the traps and ironies of life, and their savaged heroes, were particularly replete in a kind of tough, wise wisdom, expressed in terse, acute aphorisms. "I hate big league blondes," says Anne Shirley in *Murder, My Sweet*, "All bubble bath and dewy morning and moonlight. And inside, blue steel . . . cold . . . cold . . . only not so clean." Raymond Chandler's language sets the keynote for noir dialogue. Billy Wilder said he "learned what real dialogue was" from Chandler. There is a tough wisdom to the language of hard-boiled detective fiction that gives Hollywood films some philosophical breadth, a strong dash of cynicism to counterbalance their often inspiring but also at times relentless optimism. "Alligators have it right," says Eve Arden in *Mildred Pierce*, a film on crime fiction writer James Cain's novel, "they eat their young."

Humphrey Bogart found his comfort zone in this kind of language and after toiling away in futility playing weak heavies in Warner Brothers gangster films carved out a distinct niche for himself through his genius for bitter sarcasm, for a frustration with life that expressed itself in vicious wisecracks. "Go ahead, put Christmas in your eyes, and keep your voice low," he tells Lizabeth Scott in *Dead Reckoning*. "Tell me about paradise and all the things I'm missing." "I don't mind if you don't like my manners," he says in *The Big Sleep*. "I don't like 'em myself. They're pretty bad. I grieve over them long winter evenings." Lines like these are cathartic when Bogart delivers them. Few actors have seethed and relished bitter anger so satisfyingly. The intensity of Bogart's anger is a big part of why such an unlikely leading man found a cult following in the 1960s and 1970s. He sneers better than anyone in Hollywood. And his anger moves us because we know that lying just underneath it is tremendous vulnerability. Hawks wisely emphasized Bogart's shaking hands during the climax of *To Have and Have Not*, when he turns on the Vichy police who have been beating up his sad-sack friend, Eddie. We identify with Bogart's anger so much because it wells from an almost tearful frustration with life. We always sense enormous suffering and vulnerability within his sarcasm.

At the same time it would be a mistake to associate the toughness and cynicism of Hollywood dialogue only with film noir. "The only difference between men is the color of their ties," says Helen Broderick in *Top Hat*, a film that represents Hollywood at its most charmingly upbeat. Cynicism, particularly about men, women, and love is at the heart of Hollywood dialogue from the outset of talkies. A Warner Brother musical like *42nd Street* or a Hawks comedy like *Ball of Fire* are both a great deal breezier than any film noir but would give noir a run for its money in the quantity of their cynical asides and in the darkness of their world view. And, more than 60 years later, *His Girl Friday* still makes our jaw drop in its numerous moments of cynicism and cruelty. Think only of Cary Grant, playing Walter Burns, outraged that a reporter would choose to marry a woman rather than file a report. Asking to talk to the woman in question, he sets new standards for ungallantry, "Oh, good evening, Madam. Now listen, you 10-cent glamor girl. You can't keep Butch away from his duty.... What's that? ... You say that again, and I'll come over there and kick you in the teeth! ... Say, what kind of language is that?"

Hollywood writing had always been rich in cynical asides, tough wisecracks. "A smart quip," writes Rosemary Jarski, "a pithy putdown, a snappy comeback—whatever shape it takes is the perfect humerus soundbite," and succinct soundbites are what Hollywood was looking for from its writers, who had to work around the major bulk of a film—its sounds and images. The wisecrack is perfect for Hollywood—brief, unaffected, close to the street, entertaining, but, like the films themselves, not devoid of meaning, a contentless way of including content. The wisecrack, as Jarski notes, is inherently democratic, "sharp and sardonic, perfectly tuned for exposing hypocrisy and dissing authority." And though the wisecrack has "no pretensions to profundity or posterity," it is nevertheless capable of conveying a good deal of wisdom.[10]

Though it aimed at filmmaking that did not get bogged down with ideas (or perhaps because it did), Hollywood nevertheless arrived at a treasure trove of memorable aphorisms—little hard-bitten bits of wisdom that rival the work of great epigrammatists. Orson Welles was one of Hollywood's best at reeling off succinct and tough and tired truths. "Making money isn't so difficult," says Mr. Bernstein to the reporter in *Citizen Kane*, "if all you care about is making money," a line that recalls a similar aphorism by G.K. Chesterton: "To be smart enough to make all that money, you need to be dumb enough to want to." After catching Charles Kane in an infidelity that will compromise his political career, Kane's opponent, Governor Gettys (played by Ray Collins), summarizes human intransigence tidily: "If it were any other man," says Gettys, "I'd say you've learned your lesson. But you're going to need a lot of lessons. And you're going to get a lot of lessons." Billy Wilder too, schooled in Raymond Chandler lines like "There's nothing emptier than an empty swimming pool," had a talent for sad, terse summaries of life. "They treat you oh-so-gently once you're dead," Joe Gillis notes, as we watch his body being fished out of Norma Desmond's pool in *Sunset Blvd.* And Wilder set the standard for economic summaries of the decline of American cinema in Norma Desmond's famous line from the same film: "I'm still big; it's the pictures that got small."

Welles and Wilder were masters of aphorism, but really it was a talent of all Hollywood writers. "How extravagant you are, throwing away women like that," Claude Rains says to Humphrey Bogart in the Epstein brothers' script for *Casablanca.* "Someday they may be scarce." These are the kind of lines Hollywood specializes in, hard and pithy, memorable because they are as simply written as they are essential in their truth. If Hollywood found that it was inexpert, to the point of embarrassing itself at translating "serious literature" to the screen, it also found that it had quite a knack for the more modest art of wisecracks, aphorisms, exit lines, asides, bon mots, and witticisms. Classic Hollywood writing works in the margins of the film. Spare, allusive, highly stylized, it has more in common with poetry than it does with the novel. That film dialogue is a kind of poetry is apparent in filmmakers' work outside of Hollywood as well. Jean-Luc Godard, for example, is something of a modern day La Rochefoucauld, his films spill out with so many aphorisms. But classic Hollywood's slangy, energetic dialogue represents a peculiarly populist kind of poetry. As accessible as it was creative, as noteworthy for its ingenuity as it was for its lack of pretension, Hollywood writing often set itself the lofty goal of translating the oldest of truths in the simplest of language, the furthest thing possible from the modernist complexities that were going on in the field of literature at the time.

THREE-CUSHIONED DIALOGUE

If one crucial ingredient of Hollywood is its crisp, slangy, energetic diction, another has to be its deftness and discretion, its reluctance to say things directly and explicitly, its tendency, on the contrary, to express its point by circuitous and elliptical means. Here, as in talking about story construction, it is difficult to separate the scenarist's influence from that of the director. With word and image alike, the key in Hollywood was to avoid the message, to avoid saying things in easy and direct ways and instead to uphold the silent film tradition of putting your audience to work, talking around your subject, so that the audience had to do a little pleasureful sleuthing to get your point. One doesn't often think of Emily Dickinson and Hollywood at the same time, but Dickinson's advice to "Tell all the truth but tell it slant / Success in circuit lies" is an apt summary of the Hollywood writing technique.

It has become something of a cliché to praise Hollywood for its discretion, its ability to suggest sexuality or allude to violence without explicit statement. But Hollywood's discretion vis-à-vis sex and violence can also be seen, not just as a reaction to the code, but as a subset of a larger ethic that always emphasized to writers and directors alike that the more serious the business in a film, the more it called for ingenious and original treatment. Erotic suggestiveness is only one aspect of an aesthetic belief in Hollywood, that the closer a film got to any serious situation, the more careful it had to be, the more incumbent it was upon the film to express itself with grace and suggestiveness, not to translate the sacred into hard, boring words. This not only went for sex and violence but also for anything that by its nature was so large or serious that it threatened to overwhelm a film; love, friendship, piety, patriotism, strong emotion are all qualities that if not handled gingerly can represent too strong an ingredient in a film. Hollywood filmmakers, with their cult of an invisible style and with their determination to avoid explicit statements and messages, took it as a point of pride to handle "serious" themes lightly. Conversely, the best tended to be at their most cautious when things got to be too serious.

King Vidor, for example, felt that John Gilbert's career was ruined, not, as tradition holds, because his voice was too nasal for sound film, but simply because his kind of Lothario role translated poorly into sound cinema: "When sound films first came in and the audience heard a great lover, like John Gilbert, say 'darling' or something, it got a laugh. The minute you say 'I love you,' it sort of gets humorous."[11] Hollywood quickly learned that silent film could tolerate a more operatic approach to its material, and the challenge in sound cinema was to take the mickey out of clichéd dialogue.

This was a task Howard Hawks (Photo 10) set himself to. He often referred, in his interviews, to the kind of writing he favored as "three-cushioned dialogue," where "you say almost the opposite of what you mean. Hemingway used it a great deal. Noel Coward used it a lot . . . All it means is saying something by going around the bush—not being direct—and it seems to be liked. It leaves the audience to make their own interpretation of the thing. Also, they don't feel as if they're hearing the same thing all over again."[12] "Three-cushioned dialogue" has several advantages. It allows you to escape clichés and the obvious. It involves the audience. Hawks isn't quite exact when he says that the audience can make its own interpretation; the interpretation is usually dictated by the references in the dialogue. But it allows the audience to figure out the joke, to put the coordinates together, and to experience that pleasure of having pieced the idea together for itself.

Cary Grant and Ingrid Bergman's love scene in Hitchcock's *Notorious*, penned by Hawks alum Ben Hecht, is a pretty good example of three-cushioned dialogue. This scene represents the first time in the film that Devlin (Grant) and Alicia (Bergman) have gotten past their misunderstandings about her "notorious" past and have succumbed to their passion for one another. They lock in an embrace on the windswept balcony of a hotel in Rio de Janeiro, and Hitchcock shoots their kisses in sumptuous, soft-focus close-up. The scene begs for romantic dialogue and delivers it, in a way, but, oddly enough, via a discussion about what the couple is going to have for dinner that night. "It's nice out here," Alicia whispers between kisses. "Let's not go out for dinner; let's stay in." "We have to eat," Devlin playfully objects. "We can eat at home. I'll cook," says Alicia. "I thought you didn't like to cook," Devlin teases again. "No," Alicia says, with contentment, as she settles in cozily for another kiss. "I don't like to cook."

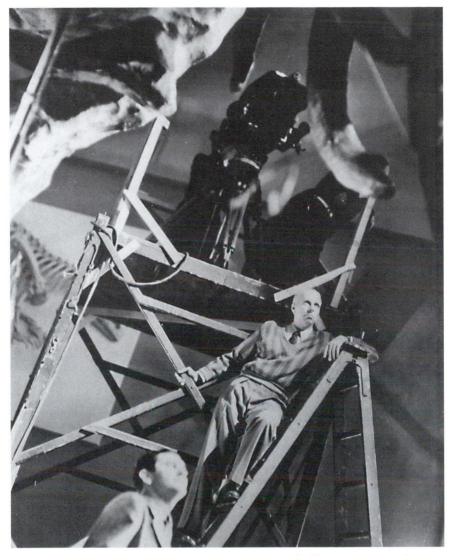

Photo 10. Howard Hawks worked with great writers and did more, perhaps, than any director to soften film dialogue and make it more natural. Courtesy of Photofest.

Now, this is three-cushioned dialogue but of a pretty transparent sort. It's obvious why Alicia wants to stay in and that it doesn't have a thing to do with dinner. But as the conversation continues, the food metaphor is extended and becomes a little more oblique. "No, I don't want to cook," is only the first part of a sentence that continues after the kiss, "but I have a chicken in the oven, and you're going to eat it." "What about the washing up afterwards?" Devlin asks.

"We'll eat with our fingers."

"Don't we need any plates?"

"Yes, one for you and one for me."

"Do you mind if I have dinner with you tonight?"

"I'd be delighted."

In this latter part of the conversation, the allusions are not so crystal clear. We know that Hitchcock liked to play games with the censors and that one of his favorite ways to convey sex was through food metaphors, so the dialogue allows him to contemplate the sexual activities of night, without being explicit. With this knowledge in mind, "I have a chicken in the oven, and you're going to eat it," suddenly strikes us as vaguely obscene, though we might be hard-pressed to explain why. The rest of the dialogue is probably open to sexual parallels as well. Hitchcock had a famously lascivious sense of humor, and as with Shakespeare, if you think you see a dirty joke in his work, you're probably right.

But the hand of Ben Hecht is here as well as Hitchcock's, and we can see other goals in this kind of writing beyond sexual innuendo. One is to avoid clichés. As Hawks said, three-cushioned dialogue saves you from "saying the same thing over and over again." It saves you from that literal rendering of love feelings that Vidor noticed rendered the first sound films laughable. The most important aspect of three-cushioned dialogue may be what it doesn't to do. It doesn't resort to familiar romantic phrases. In fact, it avoids them like the plague. The goal here is to reinvent the wheel, to convey romance effectively without recourse to tired traditions and bloated passions. Hecht wants to find a clever way of expressing his couple's passion, not a moony one.

And why shouldn't a couple be clever when they make love? Why must they wrap themselves in Wagnerian pathos? Hecht's notion is that a couple charged in love *would* be playful, *would* be verbally dexterous. The fun they have with language reflects the fun they have with each other. It's an approach to romance that emphasizes humor and cleverness rather than grand drama. It wants to avoid cliché, but even more, it aims for cool. A scene like this reminds us of the paradox that I've cited often in this book, that though Hollywood has a reputation for an almost childlike innocence, it often seems more notable for its adult, sophisticated attitude to love. Here, as is so often the case in Hollywood, sex and humor mingle. Hollywood could be lushly romantic (witness Hitchcock's famous technique in this scene, where the camera fluidly revolves around the lovers, as though a member of a three-way dance), but at the same time the best Hollywood films drew short of gushing, puerile expression—pure shots of intense feeling. They danced around their passion, played with it, and treated it with humor and irony.

Now, as the example from *Notorious* confirms, three-cushioned dialogue is always going to breed a good deal of sexual innuendo. Hawks was as good as anyone at slipping dirty jokes and double entendres into his films. Witty double entendre is often a sign of a good Hollywood film. It suggests the kind of gamesmanship and inventiveness that bodes well for a film in general, the determination to be clever on the smallest level. And so some of the best dirty jokes seem to find themselves in the work of the best filmmakers. "Shall we drink to a blitzkrieg," Stanley Ridges asks Carole Lombard in Lubitsch's *To Be or Not to Be*. "I prefer a slow encirclement," responds Carole Lombard. "Would you care to come in and see Emma," Henry Fonda asks Barbara Stanwyck outside his stateroom, in Preston Sturges's *The Lady Eve*, referring to his pet snake. "That's a new one, isn't it?" responds Stanwyck. "The Mayor's wife, what was her name?" asks Hildy Johnson, in Hawks's *His Girl Friday*. "You mean the one with the wart," responds Walter Burns. "Right" says Hildy. "Fanny" says Burns. "The characters you meet," says Shirley MacLaine's character Fran, an elevator operator who often has to frequently defend herself against passes in Billy Wilder's *The Apartment*. "Something happens to men in elevators. Must be the change of altitude. The blood rushes to their head or something."

Some of these lines are jaw-dropping in their explicitness while at the same time, paradoxically, quite allusive. They remind one of Hedda Gabler's description of her erotic conversations with Lovborg in *Hedda Gabler*: "frank but in a roundabout way," a banter that is healthily coarse and dancingly fey at the same time. This inventive eroticism is due in part to the code but even more to the aesthetics of Hollywood that took great pleasure in implying things. Time and time again Hollywood is drawn to, and deals best with, situations in which things are so serious they can't quite be said. Ford's heroes, for example are often charming in their struggle to express themselves despite not being wordsmiths and despite their deep suspicion of empty chatter. The aristocrats in screwball comedy see it as bad taste to express themselves directly and are always up to the challenge to say things wittily, suggestively. Gangster, detective, and newspaper films are peopled with tight-lipped, no-nonsense types, deeply suspicious of intellectual falderal and of other people and, for both reasons, highly reluctant to commit their true feelings to words. The hard-boiled detective of film noir was soft inside, the biggest sucker for feminine wiles in the film. His tough lingo implied corresponding soft feelings that he could not articulate. Hollywood's scenarists were, paradoxically, at their most expressive when their characters were at their least, when those characters fumbled, deferred, dissembled, and landed on red herrings. These scenarios provide the opportunity for dialogue that was subtle and elliptical, that made the audience discern emotion rather than take it down the funnel of their ears, a verbal equivalent to what silent film asked of us, that we read the text, work a little at figuring it out, a game the best directors knew we always liked to play.

FAILURES

Needless to say, Hollywood was not always up to its own demands. Even some of Hollywood's best films have moments where they spit out their meaning rather than dance around it gracefully. *The Philadelphia Story*, for example, is one of Hollywood's great treasures. It sparkles with MGM's glittering visual sophistication and represents a superb assemblage of director, actors, and technicians. MGM often realized its fullest potential when George Cukor was at the helm. The film's dialogue (by Donald Ogden Stewart, from a Phillip Barry play) is mostly excellent as well. But it falters awfully from time to time, and that faltering occurs when it tries to explain itself, tie up its film neatly in one thesis.

The thesis here is that Tracey Lord is "an ice princess" who needs melting—a thesis, as has been often noted, with uncanny correlation to Katharine Hepburn's relationship with the American public at the time. And this thesis is often hammered away at far too directly, as, for example, when Cary Grant's C.K. Dexter Haven lectures Hepburn's Tracey Lord about how his alcoholism and philandering in their previous marriage was due to her being coldly judgmental, a scene that annoys us for its political incorrectness but even more for casting Cary Grant as a humorless, hectoring, ungenerous husband. Cary Grant exists to save women from men like this.

The ludicrousness of the film's "thesis" is particularly apparent in the scene in which Seth Lord, Tracey's father, goes one better than C.K. Dexter Haven and suggests to Tracey that if she had been a warmer daughter he might not have been driven to the well-publicized affairs that are proving an embarrassment to Tracey's upcoming wedding. Tracey's father points to the example of his long-patient wife, suggesting to Tracey that if her mother quietly suffers his indiscretion with great nobility and discretion, how difficult could it be for Tracey to show a little patience and understanding?

Again, our frustration with the scene is less with its whopping political incorrectness and extraordinary lack of logic than with its grating didacticism, its hectoring tone, and, even more, the way it makes this otherwise fleet-of-foot film grind to a halt. Hollywood movies, like undergraduate essays, are most prone to mistakes when they gnaw away at theses, when they feel compelled to bottle a film's light and energy in some routine or ill-considered "idea." The more Hollywood dances, like a Symbolist poem, elliptically around an idea, the nimbler it is, the more it expresses itself enigmatically, the more elegant it is. It's at moments like the one in which Seth Lord lectures his daughter on the duties of a daughter that the fairy-tale magic of *The Philadelphia Story* dissolves and reveals the underlying hardware of its aging New York dinner theater source. If not used sparingly, ideas, like special effects and other things that stick out glaringly, can age a film badly.

Even the greatest filmmakers failed as often as they succeeded in treating their subjects elliptically, in writing around a point rather than blurting it out. Hitchcock and Ben Hecht found a neat way of conveying Alicia Huberman's patriotism in *Notorious* by having Cary Grant's government agent, Devlin, play a recording that captured her making patriotic statements that previously she had not owned up to. This idea saves Alicia's character from the self-glorification of the patriotic speech. In fact, she is caught trying to hide her virtue from the world. That's a nice way of elegantly sidestepping an opportunity for stentorian bombast. But Hitchcock and John Steinbeck were not always able to stay clear of a kind of smug, self-satisfied patriotism in *Lifeboat*. "Aren't you going to kill me?" the German boy who has comes aboard the lifeboat asks. "'Aren't you going to kill me?'"

John Hodiak repeats disgustedly. "What are you going to do with people like that?" Here, Hodiak's character expresses a sense of the superiority of his race that makes him queasily similar to his object of disgust.

Hawks often lost his touch for subtle, naturalistic, intelligent banter in the male bonding scenes that were sometimes a little more moving to him than to his audience. Ford often couldn't contain his drunken sentimentality. Capra's weakest moments are when he spits out his populist message rather than expressing it in his energetic frames and his and Robert Riskin's crackling dialogue. The ability to deal deftly and elliptically with the most serious subjects and truths is one of the key ways of separating the wheat from the chaff in Hollywood. It separates the good films from the bad and the stronger efforts of great filmmakers from their weaker ones. It was in this matter of how much to say that Hollywood often defined its greatness. The less said, the better. Hollywood writing was an art of working around an idea, finding the most creative way of getting it across, avoiding at all costs saying it straight out, leaving room for a great deal of thought by not hogging it all to yourself.

13

Hollywood and Rhythm

The ties between literature and film have often been overemphasized. Language is only one ingredient in film and one that should, and often does, take a background to image and sound. A film that does not have something to "say" in words can still be a great film; the masterpieces of silent cinema, particularly those of Murnau and Chaplin, in which there was an emphasis on using the minimum number of title cards, prove that. And in the post–silent film era, a dependable (though not infallible) barometer of filmmakers' success is how much they wean themselves of a dependence on words and convey their meaning more subtly through sound and image.

Hollywood's relationship to the visual arts can be exaggerated too. Certainly, many of Hollywood's greatest directors (Hitchcock, Ford, Murnau, Welles, just to name a few) were stunning visual stylists. Moreover, Hollywood's mantra was to show rather than tell, to take full advantage of the new medium's ability to communicate visually as well as verbally, and to create works that avoided stagy speechifying. Also, one of the glories of Hollywood is its professionalism when it comes to blocking a shot. One of the first things that attract us to the classic Hollywood film is the care taken, even in its least efforts, to carefully compose a shot. And in the best films shots are arranged not only to be painterly and attractive but also to be significant, to say something in their arrangement.

That said, Hollywood is not particularly revolutionary in its shot arrangement. Most of its directors are not a great deal more conversant in great works of art than they are in great works of literature. Hollywood defined itself by a rigidly conservative visual aesthetic, based on the most general Renaissance principles, and tended to suppress innovation in shot composition. Directors like Murnau and Hitchcock, who had Expressionist tendencies in shot arrangement, had to suppress those tendencies, to use them rarely and efficiently in order to work in Hollywood. For all of its professional insistence on attractive and well thought-out composition even on the most menial level, Hollywood was suspicious of any shot that was too expressive or artistic. Visuals were to be subordinate to the general purpose of the film. They were not to impede with an easy apprehension, and the smooth flow, of the story. "I never heard anybody walk out of the theater and say, 'Wasn't that a great camera angle,'" exclaimed Mervyn LeRoy in defending Hollywood's classical aesthetic. "Never."[1] LeRoy's comments are apt to make us chuckle a little. Shot analysis is all too common among cinephiles exiting theaters today. But for the Hollywood of LeRoy's day, striking shots were a low priority.

The art form to which Hollywood (and film in general) may be most closely allied is the one that is often the least emphasized: music. A sturdy, musical rhythm is the most necessary ingredient of a good film. A film can survive without particularly artistic shots. Preston Sturges, Billy Wilder, and Ernst Lubitsch are just three examples of grade A Hollywood filmmakers who are not particularly notable for their visual style. But no film is successful without a sense of musical rhythm. And a successful and sophisticated sense of musical rhythm exists in the most disparate variety of film success, whether it is the abrupt meter changes of Godard's artsy films or the quick, charming rhythms of classic Hollywood screwball comedy.

Certainly, I am not the first to emphasize the musical nature of film. But there is still a stubborn tendency in the most erudite as well as the most popular film criticism to read films in literary ways, to look for content, meanings that we might pull out of the film as we do objects from a box. It is easier to talk about a film in terms of content, in terms of something that can practically be held in one's hand than in the more ephemeral language of musical criticism. And yet many of the greatest Hollywood films justify themselves not in terms of what they say but in how they say it, the satisfying ride they give us, their uncanny ability to keep the ball in the air for 90 minutes, the sense we have, after seeing them, of having existed for an hour or two in a world of quick grace and vivacity.

There is in film criticism a reluctance to recognize the complexity and sophistication that goes into films that masquerade as lighter fare, films whose virtues are not in the volume of their drama or the seriousness of their message or the massiveness of their images but in the musicality of their rhythm. Hence the long history in Hollywood, in the classical era and today, of ignoring comedy and handing out awards to its stuffiest and most message-laden films and to the actors most polished at mimicking the nervous tics of the mentally handicapped. And hence the tendency sometimes to value the visual power in a few striking sequences over the careful craftsmanship of a film as a whole.

QUASIMUSICALS

Needless to say, the best examples of how film is a musical medium are musicals themselves. And, in many ways, musicals are the favorite genre of the Hollywood purists, because musicals represent such an abstract experiment in the pure musicality of film. They make the fewest concessions to the literary requirements

Photo 11. Many of Hollywood's greatest films, like Hawks's *To Have and Have Not*, had a musical rhythm even if they weren't overt "musicals." Courtesy of Photofest.

of realism, plausibility, or depth of character. They most approach that Jamesian ideal of a work of sublime beauty that is about nothing. They are also, by consequence, quite difficult to pull off. They most easily fall into patterns of burlesque and melodrama; their structure is often too weak to hold up the edifice of the film.

In some ways, the films that most deftly take advantage of the musicality of film are those films that deftly weave musical elements into a film that otherwise represents a fairly typical classical narrative, operating within the pseudorealistic laws of space and time that classical films require. Andrew Sarris, for example, notes that Josef von Sternberg's early films with Dietrich are often overlooked in studies of musicals, "and yet their songs advance the feelings and actions of the characters more dramatically than do most musicals." That's a pattern that continues with the films Dietrich makes with other directors as well. When Dietrich was signed to a film, she often brought a package of songs with her, and those songs were significant in establishing the rhythm of the film. *Casablanca* and *To Have and Have Not* (Photo 11), Sarris notes, are also rarely treated as musical, "even though the rhythms of these films' action seem to flow out of the piano more than the moviola."[2]

Sarris describes films here that are resolutely musical but that weave their music in and out of a realistic narrative with ease and elegance. It is striking, in cataloguing the great films of Hollywood, how many of them have found a means of drawing music into their narrative, some trick for making their films more musical or rhythmic. Preston Sturges's *Unfaithfully Yours* is another accomplishment in integrating large quantities of music into a naturalistic narrative, with its story of an orchestra conductor who suspects his wife of infidelity and who, while performing, fantasizes about how he might respond to her unfaithfulness. His fantasies correspond to the music he is conducting: overtures from Rossini's *Semiramide*, Wagner's "*Tannhauser*," and Tchaikovsky's "Francesca da Rimini." During the Rossini piece, for example, he indulges in a fantasy of gleeful and sadistic revenge, while during the Wagner pieces he plays, in his mind's eye, the role of the touchingly magnanimous, all-forgiving husband.

Sturges is, of course, only making explicit in this film the musical rhythm that is an essential aspect of *all* his films. Sturges often finds clever ways of sneaking music into his narrative to give shape and coherence to a scene. For example, in *The Palm Beach Story*, Rudy Vallee sets himself up outside Claudette Colbert's window, serenading her with his trademark song, "Goodnight Ladies." The music then becomes the backdrop to those scenes where Colbert and Joel McCrea, housed in adjoining rooms, try to fight off their attraction to one another. In the end, the music is too much for them. Vallee's romantic serenade drives them into each other's arms and dashes his own romantic aspirations. Sturges's films have such a strong musical thrust that, at certain climactic points in the narrative, they often abandon language altogether, as the characters run around manically, and the musical accompaniment assumes the function of language—providing parallel sounds for screams, pratfalls, and expressions of horror and amazement.

Hitchcock's *Rear Window* is a good example of how a Hollywood film can be resolutely musical from beginning to end without being overtly "a musical." Hitchcock set himself the challenge here of making a film that proves to be very musical without any artificially imposed, or outside, soundtrack. Everything we hear in this film, all the sounds and music in the film, are incidental or diegetic; they come from the apartment complex in which the film is set. A composer who lives nearby works out a theme on his piano, slowly improving it as the films goes. A neighbor, Miss Torso, dances to loud jazz. An opera singer practices her scales. The film takes place during a heat wave in Greenwich village, so all the neighbors have thrown open their windows, and a variety of pop tune snippets of music emanate from their radios and record players.

Hitchcock loves to capitalize on the incongruity of music and image. For example, during the scenes in which the murderous husband, Lars Thorwald, carries out sections of his dead wife's body in his jewelry salesman's display case, we are treated to a lugubrious bit of organ music, both morbid and comic, which adds a strange carnival effect that contrasts sharply with the gruesomeness of Thorwald's chore. The sound of hootenanny music accompanies Jeff's nauseating realization that Thorwald is coming to get him the night he becomes aware of Jeff's presence.

Other times, the music is hilariously appropriate, such as when the lonely neighborhood spinster, Miss Lonelyhearts, desperate for romance, acts out an imaginary dinner date with an imaginary suitor, while a recording of Bing Crosby's "To See You Is to Love You" plays somewhere in the apartment complex she shares with Stewart's character, Jeff. The music touchingly expresses her loneliness and romantic desire but at the same time mocks her, referring, as it does ("to see you is to love you"), to the delusional nature of what she is doing.

The rather lengthy sequence in which Miss Lonelyhearts pantomimes an imaginary date represents a kind of musical video within the film. Jeff and Lisa (Jimmy Stewart and Grace Kelly) have just finished a quarrel about Jeff's unwillingness to commit to a relationship, when we hear the first distant strains of the Crosby recording. As Lisa goes off to make Jeff dinner, Jeff (who has acquired the habit of spying on his neighbors while recovering from a broken leg), turns his attention to Miss Lonelyhearts's window. She, like Lisa, is also preparing dinner and also unhappy in love. (Hitchcock traffics in such parallels between his central couple and the neighbors throughout the film.)

The Miss Lonelyhearts sequence is cued to start and finish to the words in Crosby's song. Jeff turns his attention to her, and she is "set in motion" with the first words of the song, "To see you is to love you." She crumples in despair at her dining room table to the final words of the song, "In the same old dream tonight." After Miss Lonelyhearts's pantomime sequence, however, an instrumental portion of the song continues, providing a backdrop for the continuation of the scenes during which Jeff and Lisa return to their conversation on love and commitment. While the music plays, Jeff and Lisa survey other neighbors across the courtyard, speculating on the neighbors' lives, comparing those lives to their own. Jeff somewhat insultingly compares Lisa to a neighbor he calls "Miss Torso," a dancer Jeff likes to peep on, who is, at that moment, flirting with several men in her apartment. Lisa defends Miss Torso as simply "juggling wolves" and asserts that she doesn't love the one man she has singled out for kisses on her balcony. "How do you know," asks Jeff. "You said it resembled my apartment, didn't you?" Lisa answers, returning to the kitchen.

Lisa's answer, emphasizing that she too has to juggle wolves but remains faithful to Jeff, represents the exit line of the sequence. It shuts Jeff up and is timed to coincide with the winding down of the Crosby record, both the line and the end of the music underlining the end of the scene. The Crosby song is continuing to shape the rhythmic contours of the scene. Hitchcock stops, however, to squeeze in one final bit of business just as the music slows to its final notes. Jeff turns his attention to the window (shades closed) where we know a newlywed couple resides and who we know (as Hitchcock has made it abundantly clear) is making love at that moment. The very final moments of the Crosby record, then, coincide with a comic reaction shot of Jeff's wry contemplation of what's going on behind those shades. This final comic note, combined with the final notes of the song, represents the coda to a sequence that had begun several minutes earlier with the beginning of the song cued to Miss Lonelyhearts's pantomime.

The Miss Lonelyhearts sequence is an example of the way the best Hollywood directors will find a musical excuse to give some rhythm and shape to a scene. Scenes like this are highly stylized and reminiscent of set pieces in operas that are so structured, such works of their own, that they call for an audience's applause.

And they point to one of the glories of classic Hollywood—its tendency, in its best films, to take the smallest sequence of a film seriously, to pace it and give it a sure rhythm, a beginning, a middle, and an end, a solid structure. Sequences like this are the rhythmic parallel to Hollywood's devotion to well-composed shots, testimonies to Hollywood professionalism, its sound structure on even the smallest level. Sequences like this are also so stylized that they remind us that even a film like *Rear Window*, which gives its due to plausibility and which operates within Hollywood's realistic depiction of time and space, prides itself on its artifice, its artistic flourish, its musicality.

In between these overtly musical passages in *Rear Window* are all sorts of stops and starts of music that Hitchcock and composer Franz Waxman use to punctuate the film, to wake us up, to lull us, to jumpstart the narrative, to comment ironically on what we are seeing. And in between these bits of music are bits of noise, used equally for rhythmic effects, a musique concrete of children's cries in the street, muted conversations from nearby apartments, distant foghorns from the river. Hitchcock often spoke of voices in his film being just as important for their sound as they are for the words they express. The distant, often indiscernible, sounds of the neighbors' conversation often represent just one more sound introduced into the pattern of the film's soundtrack, as voices do in Jacques Tati's films, where the nattering of his characters is prized for how it sounds, not what it says.

Ironically, this film would never be considered a "musical," and yet it has a greater rhythm, a more consistent musicality than many "musicals" that interrupt their narrative with unwarranted musical numbers that are wholly divested from plot and do little to advance the themes of the film. There is, in Hollywood, a relentless pull toward the musical, toward scenes that are strong in structure and rhythm. These films offer us the best of both worlds, the seamless realism of the classical Hollywood narrative and a lyrical rhythm that gives that narrative a greater style and resonance. These films embody the Hollywood paradox of quiet, invisible structure that at times gives way to elegant style.

NONMUSICAL RHYTHM

Of course there are great Hollywood films, and scenes within those films, that have little musical content. But even these, if they truly belong among Hollywood's greatest films, tend to have a complex or impressive rhythm. Orson Welles's films provide good examples of rhythm that is not dependent on music as well. Coming from radio, Welles had a particularly strong sense of the rhythmic nature of sound and dialogue. "I judge a scene by how it sounds," he told Bogdanovich. "I almost prefer to turn away from the actors. I think the sound is the key to what makes it right. If it sounds right, it's gotta look right." It is striking how often the greatest films of any era sound good as well as look good. A film that has a solid rhythm is not jarring when you hear it from another room. It's short on discordant sounds and irrelevant musical bombast. Welles's greatest frustration with *The Lady from Shanghai* was the soundtrack that Columbia producer Harry Cohn superimposed on the film. Welles planned, for example, that the mirror scene at the end of the film would be silent, "except for the crashing glass and ricocheting bullets. Like that it was terrifying. All that was lost of course, with that corny string choir snoring away under it." Welles likewise complained in a memo to Harry Cohn that poor scoring had destroyed "the character of Michael's run down the pier. From the gunshot through to the phone call, a careful pattern of voices had been built up with the expenditure of much time and effort."[3]

Welles often expressed frustration that he was renowned for his Expressionist visual style, which was not really new to him, rather than for the complex rhythms of his soundtrack—its carnival barking rhythms, spot-on timing, and overlapping dialogue—which he took pride in pioneering. In response to Peter Bogdanovich's suggestion that "from the technical point of view, the most important thing in *Kane* perhaps is the use of soundtrack," Welles said, "Yeah, but nobody followed that. They can't. They don't know how. That's a particular trick and it hasn't influenced anybody. They could learn to do it, but they don't. You can't just say 'Now let's do the overlapping thing.' . . . You have to drill them so that the right syllable comes at the right moment. It's exactly like conducting an orchestra. You have to say, 'Can't' comes in now. Once again.' Because the operative word is 'can't' and you come in under there. It's very, very mechanical. It's cold as hell, ice cold—exactly like conducting."

Welles's comments are interesting here for a couple of reasons. First, Welles emphasizes that good dialogue needs to be arranged musically. He agrees with Hitchcock that words are important for how they sound as well as what they communicate, that there is a rhythmic, poetic quality to film dialogue at its best. Second, the frustration in his remarks emphasizes that there is a bias toward the visual in film appreciation, an ease in discerning visual tricks and a deafness to the possibilities and accomplishments in sound and rhythm, which are more ineffable, less obvious to the eye, harder to get hold of.

Howard Hawks was the director who came as close to innovating as Welles did with dialogue. Hawks, too, is famous for overlapping dialogue that is impressive in its calculated timing, though Hawks's overlapping dialogue is not as coldly mechanical, or as virtuosic, as that of Welles. Hawks uses dialogue to softer effect, reflecting his penchant for an understated, naturalistic feel to his dialogue and the freedom he would accord to the improvisational timing of the actors. In the pressroom scenes of *His Girl Friday*, Hawks plants his reporters in several parts of the room and creates a kind of round-robin of voices. The effect is almost the aural equivalent of the way Ford will place several candles and lamps in his scene to create variety of light and smoke effects in the various tiers of his visual composition. Hawks's dialogue has the same multitiered quality in dialogue that Ford's does in image. One voice takes over just where the other leaves off; in another pair, one overlaps the other at just the right moment; in a third pair, one person's conversation offers ironic contrast to another's. All this is interspersed with the seemingly irrelevant words and sounds of a poker game, which nevertheless offers its own contribution to the timing of the scene. "Will anyone take that?" complains one reporter about a ringing phone. "I'll take two," says another reporter playing cards. The effect is one of easy rhythm and conveys the sense that Hawks wanted to get across, that these professional newsman spend so much time in this room that everything moves with a rhythmic regularity, the aural equivalent of a well-feathered nest.

Hawks also brings a certain rhythm to his scripts by the repeated use of phrases, little phrases, and snippets of dialogue that operate like poetic refrains. Hawks loved to repeat his lines, to use them over and over again, to play with them, to work variations off them, and to develop them consistently with the growth of his characters. The more important a relationship between two characters in a Hawks film, the more their conversation is governed by these repetitions, until, as in the case of Bogart and Bacall in *To Have and Have Not*, they no longer directly converse with one another but instead slyly and elliptically refer to a private, shared symbolism. Think of the lines that float through *To Have and Have Not*, accumulating new significance with each use: 'Was you ever bit by a dead bee?'; 'You're not sore, are you?"; "Sometimes you make me so . . . "; "I'd walk if there wasn't so much water"; "Got a match?" Hawks was able to give such simple and unpretentious lines a notable resonance by playing with them deftly and musically throughout his film.

Take, for example, the short history of the line "I'd walk if there wasn't so much water." When Lauren Bacall's character, Slim, lets these words slip for the first time, Humphrey Bogart's character, Steve, understands that though Slim acts like a loose woman, she actually hates the life she leads and would like to return to a life of normalcy in America. Later, Steve, feeling duped by Slim, repeats the words sarcastically, expressing his disgust for women and their false sincerity, an attitude he had well before Slim showed up on the scene. Steve refers to the line a third time after he has come to trust Slim and has paid for her plane ticket home. "I wouldn't want your feet to get wet." Here, he teases her a little for her lack of innocence and also conveys to her that he believes in her and wants her to start over. He also makes it clear that he has made the decision that she won't stay with him. If she's going to start anew, she'd better avoid hard-boiled types like himself.

The dialogue is poetic on two counts; first, it is wonderfully allusive. Hawks and his gang of writers were masters, as we have seen, of this "three-cushioned" form of writing, where the characters talk around their feelings rather than spit them out. Once they land on a line they both like and understand, they tend to stick with it. Second, the language is repetitive: lines keep resurfacing, taking on new resonance and shapes, gathering more history and deepening with each use. Hollywood writing was, in a way, inherently musical because it looked at a story as a complex system of recurrent motifs. Instead of stating its idea overtly, the best Hollywood film is likely to tuck its ideas into a repeated visual motif, to show rather than tell. And rather than indulge in tons of expository material, it is likely to develop a character through a repeated motif, a telling physical detail or gesture, a repeated phrase. Story construction in Hollywood, then, is an arrangement of a kind of score, a rhythmic arrangement of motifs, something of closer kinship to the musical allusiveness of poetry than the lengthy elucidations of narrative prose.

Of course, musical dialogue and story construction that is as rhythmic and tight as a musical score is the provenance of theater as well as film. And, in truth, when Hollywood is at its best, it often reveals its debt to the theater of the well-made play, from which it derived so many of its ideas about story construction, or to the verbal dexterity of the best turn-of-the-century light comedy: Shaw, Wilde, Maugham, Coward.

But as Rouben Mamoulian (who described rhythm as "the greatest force in nature") noted, "You only have one movement on the stage, that of the actors. But this is not the case on the screen, where you have three movements—the movement of actors, the movement of the camera, the movement in cutting."[4] Mamoulian saw the director as a kind of conductor integrating these different movements. The complex rhythms of film are evident in a sequence like the one described earlier from *Rear Window*, where the rhythm of the sequence is established not just from the music and dialogue but also from Hitchcock's ingenious shot selection and his delicate darting from window to window, for example. Hitchcock was fond of talking about shot selection in musical terms and, like Welles and Mamoulian, liked to cast the director in the role of symphony conductor: "Don't put a great big close-up there because its loud brass," Hitchcock said, for example, "and you mustn't use a loud note unless it's vital."[5] Like Sturges, Hitchcock took the opportunity to set a major portion of one of his films, *The Man Who Knew Too Much*, to an orchestral piece that found its source within the action of the film.

Movies achieve a complex musical effect all their own. The movement of an actor pulls in one direction, the camera in another, the music playing in yet a third. The result is a sense of being pulled apart, an exhilaration that occurs as we try to balance several contrasting but balanced stimuli at the same time. The effect is very similar to that of listening to a well-arranged tercet or quartet in an opera, where we experience an exquisite frustration in following several emotions at once. And indeed opera sometimes seems, of all the art forms, closest to cinema in the way it combines music, drama, language, and movement. Opera seems particularly close to classic Hollywood, where the sentiments are idealized and the technique stylized, leading to an art form of great musicality and also one of great simplicity and heightened emotion.

A director's sense of rhythm is of such importance that one is tempted to say that it is the signature trait of the Hollywood director, as the painter's stroke is his. We have a tendency to associate filmmakers with their visual style. This works when the filmmaker has a strong visual flair, as Hitchcock, Welles, and Ford do. It's less satisfactory for those filmmakers whose greatness does not lie in their visual extravagance, Lubitsch, for example, Wilder, Sturges, and Hawks, in fact the vast majority of Hollywood directors.

But all the best directors have a strong rhythmic signature, even the visual stylists. Laconic Ford's films take their time, while Hitchcock's meticulous set pieces are sprung with diabolical exactitude. Visually, Welles and Sturges have little in common, but rhythmically Sturges seems Welles's only match in terms of a pace that hurls forward audaciously. It seems inevitable that Sturges would finally edit his film to Rossini as he does in *Unfaithfully Yours* because all of his films seem to rush forward with the chaotic charm of Rossini. And for musical frenzy, there is no surpassing those montage sequences in Sturges in which things start to spin wildly out of control, as, for example, in the honeymoon sequence in *The Lady Eve* in which Henry Fonda's increasing surprise and horror at what he learns about his wife's amorous past is timed to the accumulating energy of a speeding locomotive.

Capra's screwball rhythms were born from his observation that action slowed down on a cinema screen. Scenes that seemed quickly paced while filming were slower in the projection room and even slower in the cinema. Capra once said, "I'd see my films on Moviola or in a small projection room and they'd look fine. But I'd go to the theater, and the audience always seemed to be a little ahead of the film. Those beautiful lap dissolves would come on, and they'd go for the popcorn. All this ego-massaging stuff that we had—we called it fine camera work—it means absolutely nothing. It just interfered with the story."[6] Again, we see, in Capra's comments, the primacy of the Hollywood filmmaker's quest for successful rhythm coupled with his inherent distrust of visual effects that are too striking or arty.

Capra's success may owe something to his background in the sciences. (He had a degree in chemical engineering from California Institute of Technology.) Rather than complain about previews of his films, he tended to approach them empirically. He had noted that "you can send ten people to see the same preview and they'll all have different opinions," so he struck on the idea of taping the reactions of a preview audience, measuring the lengths, lapses, and durations of their laughter: "You'd be surprised how you can absolutely tell what the audience is doing by the sound, by the stillness, by the laughs. You can tell by the popcorn, how the paper begins to rattle. And it is completely objective; the truth is there."[7] Capra's approach testifies to Hollywood's art being one of timing as much as one of artistic expression, as it is understood in the world of literature and art. The result of Capra's experiments was a new kind of speeded-up tempo, a new kind of comedy that would transform Hollywood's comic nature from European-based to more purely American. Capra's emphasis on speeded-up tempo became a truism in Hollywood. Director Robert Wise cites one of the most valuable bits of advice that he ever got as coming from director Richard Wallace who told him, "[I]f it seems a little slow on the set, it will be twice as slow in the projection room." "And, oh man," said Wise, "have I ever found that to be true."[8]

But Capra emphasized that his rhythm wasn't for everyone. He cites George Stevens as a director who went the opposite direction with tempo. Stevens, Capra said, would follow a girl out of a doctor's office "and his camera would stay on her back as she walked down street over to another street and got onto a bus. By being on her so long you began to wonder, 'What's on her mind?' And she became fascinating. He got his effects by slowing down."[9] Most of Hollywood's greatest directors shot little excess footage because the studios made them extremely conscious of budgetary concerns and because they knew the less the footage available, the less tinkering the studio could do in the editing phase of the process. Stevens, though, shot a good deal of coverage and spent eons in the editing room, where he managed to arrive a rhythm that not only tolerated but also thrived on long, silent passages that tended to pique his audience's curiosity rather than fatigue it.

There is, then, no single kind of rhythm to Hollywood, but there does seem to be a proportional relationship between Hollywood's greatest directors and a discernible, signature rhythm. Of course we don't want to oversimplify a director's musical signature anymore than we do any other aspect of the Hollywood art. A director's rhythm is subject to the vicissitudes of the studio system. Lubitsch's latter work isn't as thick with the feel of the Viennese waltz as his earlier work is—a result, to some degree, of Capra's Americanization of comedy. A director's rhythm will be determined to some degree by the genre he's working with. Screwball certainly comes with its own rhythmic determination. Genres, studios, editors, writers, composers, and the amount of freedom a director is allowed—all of these things are going to qualify, often neutralize, a filmmaker's particular rhythmic signature. But we can say this: very few of the great Hollywood directors are rich visual stylists; even fewer are notable for their literary content; but all of them, when they are at their best, are masters of rhythm.

SOUNDTRACKS THAT COMPLICATE

If we argue that Hollywood's great quality is its musicality we must, at the same time, admit that Hollywood is responsible for a great many abuses of music and atrocious soundtracks. In fact, an unimaginative soundtrack is probably more common in Hollywood than a subtle or innovative one. One of the signal traits in separating the greater Hollywood films from the weaker ones is this issue of music. There is a proportional relationship in Hollywood between the quality of the film and the subtlety of the approach to music, both in terms of the film's score and the general musicality of the film. Bombastic soundtracks which overamplify the obvious are all too common in Hollywood, and the better directors often found themselves fighting a studio-imposed soundtracks that stepped all over the subtle rhythms of their film, as happened to Orson Welles in the filming of *The Lady from Shanghai*. The damage inflicted on films by studio soundtracks argues against the notion that studio restrictions were always to a film's benefit. Rather, the greatest soundtracks in Hollywood seem to occur in the films of those directors who were able to exercise some artistic control and escape the dictates of the studio.

In general, when one lists Hollywood's virtues, the film's background scores do not rate high on the list; in fact, the background scores often seemed to stampede over more subtly expressed images. Editor and director Robert Parrish said that John Ford thought of musicians and sound effect cutters as he did film editors, "necessary evils." He recalled Ford calling the editors and composers together on the last day of shooting one picture (he doesn't say which) and saying to them, "Look, the picture's finished now. I know you're going to try to louse it up—you're going to put in too much music, or over-cut or under-cut it or something—but try not to spoil this for me because I think it's a good picture." Ford often spoke of his distaste for the musical scores that were layered over his films. He didn't like the music for *Cheyenne Autumn*, for example. "I thought it was a bad score," he said, "and there was too much of it—didn't need it. Just like in *The Searchers*: with that music they should have been Cossacks instead of Indians."[10]

The worst soundtracks are either, like the ones Ford disdains, too bombastic or oversimplified, announcing loud musical coordinates to the emotions we are supposed to experience in a scene. They are excessively literal, coming up with an exact correlation to what we are seeing and do not, as Hitchcock or Welles might, find music that is at odds, in interesting ways, with what we see. Orson Welles, for example, described Heinz Reimhold, the composer Harry Cohn brought in to touch up *The Lady from Shanghai*, as "an ardent devotee of an old-fashioned type of scoring now referred to in our business as 'Disney.' In other words, if somebody falls down, he makes a falling down sound in the orchestra, etc." Welles complained that the "big musical outburst" Reimhold added after Grisby's line "I want you to kill him" rendered the line "absurd," adding, "[T]here is nothing in the fact of Rita's diving to warrant a big orchestral crescendo. . . . What does matter is Rita's beauty . . . the evil overtones suggested by Grisby's character, and Michael's bewilderment. Any or all of these items might have inspired the music. Instead the dive is treated as though it were a major climax or some antic moment in a *Silly Symphony*."[11]

A good soundtrack, Welles suggests, searches for the quieter, more hidden emotions in a scene and avoids coordinating literally with what is on the screen. Hitchcock learned early in film that if you were showing one thing, your audience needn't be listening to the same thing. You could visit offscreen locales aurally and cover two spaces within one scene, enriching the film moment. Similarly, he was loath to use musical effects that "matched" a scene. Rather, music was an opportunity to complicate what we were seeing, as in the famous assassination scene in the second *The Man Who Knew Too Much*, where the gun's muzzle slowly emerges from the side of the screen accompanied by strains in Bernard Herrman's composition that would seem more appropriate for a torrid love scene. Hitchcock liked to confuse our conventional expectations, in this case touching on one of his favorite paradoxes, the close relationship between love and violence.

Moreover, many of the greatest musical moments in film history occur when the director finds ways of including the music in a scene that are at once innovative and natural. Most of the examples of music in film that I've examined in this chapter are examples of source music, where the director found some excuse in his narrative or environment to include some music. In this manner, the filmmaker avoided the artificiality of superimposed music summoned from out of the blue and arrived at a relaxed, natural introduction of music to the scene.

Billy Wilder, for example, uses the love song "Fascination" as the central theme to *Love in the Afternoon*. With its lush and melancholy melody, it is an obvious choice for a love story, but it also runs the risk of being a little too saccharine and predictable. By making the song part of the repertory of the gypsy band that Gary Cooper has hired to follow him around and help him seduce young ladies, Wilder adds a note of sarcasm to the piece, softens it with a bit of irony, saves it from bald-faced melodrama. Rudy Vallee's signature song, "Goodnight Ladies," is a lyrical bit of hokum, its inclusion in *The Palm Beach Story* typical of the way Hollywood studios were always trying to jam popular radio acts in their film. But with Sturges, the song represents a lovely bit of self-parody, with Vallee assembling a full orchestra outside Colbert's window for his midnight serenade and clumsily reading his score upside down, a gag that asks the audience to chuckle privately at this teasing reference to Vallee's real career. Hitchcock pulls Bing Crosby's "To See You Is to Love You" out of the Paramount vaults for *Rear Window* but makes it a cruelly clever commentary on Miss Lonelyhearts's delusional state (entertaining a make-believe suitor only she can see) and the energy Jeff puts into voyeurism rather than the actual romance with Lisa whom he has at hand.

Franz Waxman's original theme for *Rear Window*, "Lisa's Theme," is a likeable if fairly predictably sappy love theme, but Hitchcock is innovative in how he uses the melody. He introduces it as a piece of music one of Jeff's neighbors is composing in an apartment nearby. This little trick allows Hitchcock not only to make the music incidental and thus more natural in its inclusion in the film but also to create a parallel between the development of the film and the development of its score, the musician's piece. Hitchcock, incidentally, places his cameo in the musician's apartment, where he is winding a clock, seeming to discuss the composer's music with him. (He mouths the words "B, B flat.") Hitchcock seemed to want to associate himself with the artist surrogate in the film, his fictional coordinate in setting the tempo for the film.

In all of these films, the directors arrived at ways of including music that were naturalistic, incidental to the action of the film and ways of playing with the music, moving the songs away from the obvious, and finding little ironic means to complicate the songs' purpose in the films.

Conclusion

My intention in writing this book has been to offer an elucidation of the classic Hollywood film. I mean it as an aid to those who are interested in the studio era films but sometimes unsure as to what makes these films artful or why they are taken as seriously as they are. I do not intend the book as a screed in defense of the art of Hollywood. That said, a book with these intentions is, by necessity, going to have to confront certain biases not only against classic Hollywood but also against a certain kind of art in general that classic Hollywood represents. The classic Hollywood film stands for a great deal that the world of modern art doesn't respect. It's a disturbingly commercial product, produced, often, by people who knew little about and cared little for art. It was determined to be profitable. It represents light, breezy entertainment, offering little of the content many of us associate with serious art.

Of course, the classic Hollywood film is not the first example of art that has suffered, in reputation, for being too close to the mainstream or for having been too popular. Kipling and Tennyson's jingoism has so strongly annoyed postcolonial criticism that their proponents have had to work overtime to maintain the two writers' deserved places in the British literary canon. A careful study of Maupassant's work suggests one of the most austere and thoughtful prose stylists of the nineteenth century, a writer of extraordinary feeling, restraint, and perception. But because he managed, at the same time, to write in an accessible language and reach a wide audience and because his aesthetic disavowed the need to express opinion, he still fights a reputation, in the United States at least, as a young person's writer, bereft of any serious ideas. Despite Puccini's opulent orchestration and gift for harmonic invention, he has always paid dearly for his popularity, often condescended to as the emotional panderer to opera's least musically literate. In many ways, the problems classic Hollywood presents, to those who want to explain why they take these films seriously, are the same problems critics have always encountered when they have defended art that was too popular and hence perceived as too shallow.

And yet it is the classic Hollywood film's lack of content, not its serious import, that often accounts for its greatness. Andrew Sarris has noted the "middlebrow reflex" to esteem serious films over comic ones and suggests that one of the reasons modern audiences are sometimes slow to warm up to classic Hollywood is that the "new generations of the sixties, seventies, eighties, and nineties seem to have been attuned more to emotional intensity than intellectual irony."[1] Hollywood, in its best efforts, doesn't take itself too seriously. It has a light touch that contrasts favorably with the turgid self-analysis that characterizes much of both the art and commercial cinema of the post-Hollywood and postpsychoanalytic era.

If, as Andrei Tarkovsky says, "personal bias must always be hidden" for a film to be successful, then Hollywood's refusal to weight its films with content, a refusal that was born as much from financial concerns as artistic ones, turns out to have been fortuitous. A display of ideas, Tarkovsky writes, "may give a film immediate topical relevance, but its meaning will be contained to that passing usefulness. If it is to last, art has to draw deep on its own essence."[2] The essence of Hollywood is not its ideas but its craft, its tight structure, its musical rhythm, its light but engaged spirit, its timeless classical construction. If Hollywood sought to express ideas, it did so most successfully when it dealt with simple, universal themes, those "old as the hills" ideas that Eric Rohmer found to be a respite from the "flat echo" of European modernism, ideas that transcended differences in cultures and, it turns out, wore well with time.[3]

Even Hollywood's ties to commerce seem, in the long run, to have been to its benefit. As we have seen, there was much to recommend the Hollywood producer. Hollywood directors came, in hindsight in particular, to respect the studio boss for his ability to green-light a project quickly, his willingness to trust and finance his talent. Before the studios divested of their theater holdings, when they still controlled their own market, they had the freedom to gamble more on artistic or adventurous projects. And the sheer quantity of films the market demanded in the studio era made the studios busy hives of creative energy, often compared to Renaissance era art studios. But it's not wholly accurate to describe classic Hollywood as the fruit of the marketplace. Hollywood actually blossomed under protectionism. While studios had a monopoly on theater holdings, they had the resources to gamble and innovate. When they had to play by the rules of the free market, they were forced to weigh their costs more carefully. The energy and the craft of the industry (as well as the number of films) diminished. Free trade, in this sense, was death to the Hollywood film.

Almost all the qualities that critics of Hollywood decry are the very same ones that are close to the heart of the Hollywood aficionado. For example, it is undeniable that Hollywood was guilty of excesses in its expression of innocence, sentiment, and optimism. A cursory glance at any number of B film series will attest to that, as well as some A level craft like MGM melodramas from the 1930s and Warner Brothers melodramas and propaganda films from the 1940s. That said, Hollywood's greatest sentimentalists—Ford, Capra, and Chaplin, for example— knew how to cut the sweetness of their treacle. Each of these directors was expert at representing certain gruff realities of the human condition that offset idealism. They achieved a balance of emotions and ideas that paralleled the balance they arrived at in shot arrangement and story construction. And these films had the added benefit of having aimed high. Hollywood's idealism is one of its cardinal virtues. It was not scared of sentiment, and it didn't cave in to the puerile morbidity, the easy negations, and the romantic poses that infested much of the cinema, both American and European, that came in its wake.

Of course, it's important not to overidealize the classical era of Hollywood. In its compulsion to spit out product at dizzying rates, Hollywood created a good many awful and mediocre films, perhaps far more mediocre films than great ones. And even Hollywood's best films are often scarred by the rushed process of the studio system.

Moreover, while the production of a film in the Hollywood studio was well organized in terms of production, it was a mess in terms of assigning authorship. The studio film process resists the idea of a single work of art by a single artist. Even those who have been most often accorded the title of "artist" in Hollywood, the directors, bridle at the word, preferring to see themselves as professionals, craftsmen, good workers. Hollywood, as Hawks said, was not art, it was "business, fun."

Also, the art of classic Hollywood is a quiet, subterranean thing. Hollywood's filmmakers expressed themselves implicitly, through their mise-en-scène, not overtly through the explicit statement of ideas. And the art of Hollywood is diffused across a great many films, some less excellent than others. Sometimes, the circumstances and collaboration of a film provided the perfect environment for the art of Hollywood to clearly manifest itself. More often, the rushed, com- mercial nature of the process obscured and qualified the film's artistry. Some films are nearly perfect; many more have, as the directors were fond of saying, "a lot of good things in them."

For all these reasons, the art of Hollywood can be truly said to be hidden, not overtly apparent. Nevertheless, when we examine, as a whole, this teeming produce that the films of the studio era represents, it is undeniable that there are a good many films within this mass that represent a kind of pure product, the height of what Hollywood could accomplish. These films continue to astound us by the carefulness of their craft, their attention to detail, their healthy spirit, the subtlety of their expression, their sound construction, their understanding of the possibilities of cinema. They are characterized by a level of craftsmanship that is, ironically, often unmatched by films that have emerged from latter, more technologically sophisticated eras and from milieus that would seem to foster greater freedom in artistic expression. Though they were originally intended to entertain and turn a profit, they have turned out, even to their creators' surprise, to be worthy of study. As Godard said, these films have "the kind of simplicity which brings depth."

A FINAL QUESTION

When we reflect on the art of the Hollywood studio film, it's hard not to ask ourselves whether it is still possible to make the kind of film in which classic Hollywood specialized. The answer, it seems to me, is ambiguous. On the one hand, the answer has to be no. The unique circumstances of the studio era finished with the divestiture of the studio's theater holdings and the advent of television. The era has passed into history. Hollywood doesn't make as many films as it did then; nor does it make them at one studio (or nearly as much within a studio in general) or with that same feverish pace that rendered the Hollywood studio a hotbed of creative energy, an artist's studio of sorts. Gone with that feverish energy is a certain upbeat playfulness that spilled over from the artistic process into the very energy of the films.

Moreover, when contemporary filmmakers have tried to recreate the atmosphere of a Hollywood film, they have found it difficult to do so without arriving at a certain condescending nostalgia. Hollywood's light-spirited optimism is played like childish naiveté, or its film noir style is exhibited with a self-satisfied smirk. These films are falsified by an excessive self-consciousness that suggests the classical Hollywood film is a thing of the past, inextricably linked to its times.

That said, the Hollywood film is not just an historical occurrence; it's also a composite of virtues. And there is nothing to stop contemporary filmmakers from arriving at those virtues in their films. A film that is highly reminiscent of the classic Hollywood films can be created any time someone makes a film that has a strong sense of unity, a film that holds together as a whole, a film that is rich in, and deft at, characterization, a film that speaks in images and avoids spelling out its ideas, a film that avoids ponderous explanations of both its characters' motivations and the film as a whole. A film is strongly reminiscent of the Hollywood film if its entire attack is based on the classical notion of balance—if it is balanced in shot composition and arrangement and also in its ideas, offering an ingenious dialectic of optimism and pessimism. It has to be both subtle, asking its audience to actively read its cleverly arranged clues, and accessible, smart as it is entertaining. It will not only involve us during the first viewing but also provide a wealth of quiet detail and subtle expression that rewards repeat visits. It won't fear sentiment but will avoid mawkish emotions and morbid self-analysis. It will move briskly but not become subject to the depleted craft that occurs when rapid pacing is all that is considered. It will be idealistic but earthy as well, insistently moral but well versed in human evil and the ambiguities of the human situation. It will be artful but avoid artiness like the plague. Its supreme values will be its humility, its lack of pretension, its light touch, its playful sense of its craft, its sense of humor about itself.

I suspect that this kind of film is being created here and there, all over the globe. In many ways, the classical Hollywood film can be seen as a blueprint for good classical filmmaking in general. It falls outside the confines of this study to examine where, and how much, the art of the classical Hollywood film is still with us. From my cursory view, a film that is characterized by the careful craft and measured emotions of a classic Hollywood film is as likely to appear in a foreign cinema as it is in American's independent scene or in Hollywood's contemporary commercial cinema. Sergio Leone felt that he was the legitimate heir to the Hollywood Western in the 1970s and warned American filmmakers that if they couldn't nurse and cultivate their own cinematic traditions, it would be up to filmmakers from other countries to do so. In fact, today's Hollywood, with what Sarris describes as its "contemporary sloppiness of construction brought on by the blind worship of 'energy,'" may be the environment least conducive to classic Hollywood's quiet charms. But no book on classic Hollywood should finish with a bitter sense of a lost golden era. Classic Hollywood represents a template for a certain type of good filmmaking that, though too often ignored, is unlikely to ever disappear.

Notes

INTRODUCTION

1. Ty Burr, "Once Upon a Classic," *The Boston Globe*, reprinted on Web site, ptanderson.com, May 24, 2005, 1–8.

CHAPTER 1

1. David Bordwell, Janet Staiger, and Kristin Thompson, *The Classical Hollywood Cinema: Film Style and Mode of Production to 1960* (New York: Columbia University Press, 1985), 157.

2. Robert Sklar, *Movie-Made America: A Cultural History of American Movies* (New York: Vintage Books, 1975), 155.

3. George Stevens, *The Great Moviemakers of Hollywood's Golden Age* (New York: Alfred A. Knopf, 2006), 97–98.

4. Ronald L. Davis, *Just Making Movies: Company Directors on the Studio System* (Jackson, MI: University Press of Mississippi, 2005), 208.

5. Ibid., 66.

6. George Stevens, *The Great Moviemakers of Hollywood's Golden Age*, 135, 193.

7. Peter Bogdanovich, *Who the Devil Made It?* (New York: Alfred A. Knopf, 1997), 370.

8. George Stevens, *The Great Moviemakers of Hollywood's Golden Age*, 289–290.

9. Ronald L. Davis, *Just Making Movies*, 10, 44, 145, 76.

10. Ethan Mordenn, *The Hollywood Studios: Their Unique Styles During the Golden Age of Movies* (New York: Fireside Books, 1988), 15.

11. "The Secret Society of Old Hollywood," Cobblestone Entertainment Book Publishers, June 14, 2006, http://www.cobbles.com/news.

12. Peter Bogdanovich, *John Ford* (Berkeley, CA: University of California Press, 1967), 91.

13. George Stevens, *The Great Moviemakers of Hollywood's Golden Age*, 323.

14. Ibid., 53.

15. Ibid., 44.

16. Ibid., 65.

17. Ibid., 80.

18. Ibid., 117.

19. Ronald. L. Davis, *Just Making Movies*, 107.

20. Ibid., 146.

21. George Stevens, *The Great Moviemakers of Hollywood's Golden Age*, 117.

22. Peter Bogdanovich, *John Ford*, 91.

23. George Stevens, *The Great Moviemakers of Hollywood's Golden Age*, 53.

24. Gerald Mast, *A Short History of the Movies* (New York: Macmillan, 1986), 287.

25. Ibid., 289.

26. Ethan Mordden, *The Hollywood Studios*, 368.

27. Ronald L. Davis, *Just Making Movies*, 168.

28. George Stevens, *The Great Moviemakers of Hollywood's Golden Age*, 126.

29. "Sept hommes a debattre," *Cahiers du Cinema*, 150–151 (December 1963–January 1964): 20.

30. Andrew Sarris, *You Ain't Heard Nothing Yet: The American Talking Film, History and Memory, 1927–1949* (Oxford: Oxford University Press, 1998), 104.

31. Thomas Schatz, *The Genius of the System: Hollywood Filmmaking in the Studio Era* (New York: Metropolitan Books, 1988), 491.

32. David Bordwell, Janet Staiger, and Kristin Thompson, *The Classical Hollywood Cinema*, 367–378.

33. George Stevens, *The Great Moviemakers of Hollywood's Golden Age*, 82.

CHAPTER 2

1. Stanley Cavell, *The World Viewed* (Cambridge, MA: Harvard University Press, 1979), 7.

2. Joseph McBride, *Frank Capra: The Catastrophe of Success* (New York: Simon & Schuster, 1992).

3. Thomas Schatz, *The Genius of the System: Hollywood Filmmaking in the Studio Era* (New York: Henry Holt & Co., 1996).

4. Ethan Mordden, *The Hollywood Studios: Their Unique Styles During the Golden Age of Movies* (New York: Fireside Books, 1989), 14.

5. Cameron Crowe, *Conversations with Billy Wilder* (New York: Alfred A. Knopf, 1999), 100.

6. Peter Bogdanovich, *This is Orson Welles* (New York: HarperCollins, 1992), 263.

7. George Stevens, *Conversations with the Great Moviemakers of Hollywood's Golden Age* (New York: Alfred A. Knopf, 2006), 411.

8. Ibid., 81.

9. Ronald L. Davis, *Just Making Movies* (Jackson, MI: University Press of Mississippi, 2005), 22.

10. Peter Bogdanovich, *Who the Devil Made It* (New York: Alfred A. Knopf, 1997), 104.

11. George Stevens, *Conversations with the Great Moviemakers of Hollywood's Golden Age*, 50.

12. Ibid., 199.

13. Steven C. Smith, *A Heart at Fire's Center: The Life and Music of Bernard Herrman* (Berkeley, CA: University of California Press, 2002), 192.

CHAPTER 3

1. Ethan Mordden, *The Hollywood Studios: Their Unique Styles During the Golden Age of Movies* (New York: Fireside Books, 1988), 11.

2. Ibid., 132.

3. Andrew Sarris, *The American Cinema: Directors and Directions, 1929–1968* (Chicago, IL: University of Chicago Press, 1968), 23.

4. Ibid., 24.

5. David Thomson, *The New Biographical Dictionary of Film* (New York: Alfred A. Knopf, 2002), 520.

6. Andrew Sarris, *The American Cinema*, 29.

7. Scott Eyman, *Ernst Lubitsch: Laughter in Paradise* (New York: Simon & Schuster, 1993), 85.

CHAPTER 4

1. Jim Hiller, ed., *Cahiers du Cinema: The 1950s; Neo-Realism, Hollywood, New Wave* (Cambridge, MA: Harvard University Press, 1985), 6.

2. Ibid., 78.

3. Peter Bogdanovich, *Who the Devil Made It* (New York: Alfred A. Knopf, 1997), 375, 376.

4. Todd McCarthy, *Howard Hawks: The Grey Fox of Hollywood* (New York: Grove Press, 1997), 611.

5. Peter Bogdanovich, *Who the Devil Made It*, 373.

6. Cameron Crowe, *Conversations with Wilder* (New York: Alfred A. Knopf, 2001), 100.

7. Andrew Sarris, *You Ain't Heard Nothing Yet: The American Talking Film, History and Memory, 1927–1949* (Oxford: Oxford University Press, 1998), 56–57.

8. Ronald L. Davis, *Just Making Movies: Company Directors on the Studio System* (Jackson, MI: University Press of Mississippi, 2005), 92–93.

9. George Stevens, *Conversations with the Great Moviemakers of Hollywood's Golden Age* (New York: Alfred A. Knopf, 2006), 263.

10. Tom Milne, *Godard on Godard* (New York: Da Capo, 1972), 188.

11. Jim Hiller, *Cahiers du Cinema*, 9.

12. Ibid., 10.

13. George Stevens, *Conversations with the Great Moviemakers of Hollywood's Golden Age*, 128.

14. Ibid., 340.

15. Richard Schickel, *The Men Who Made the Movies* (Chicago, IL: Ivan R. Dee, 1975), 215.

16. George Stevens, *Conversations with the Great Moviemakers of Hollywood's Golden Age*, 36–37.

CHAPTER 5

1. David Bordwell, Janet Staiger, and Kristin Thompson, *The Classical Hollywood Cinema: Film Style* (New York: Columbia University Press, 1985), 4–5.

2. Cameron Crowe, *Conversations with Wilder* (New York: Alfred A. Knopf, 1999), 66.

3. David Bordwell, Janet Staiger, and Kristin Thompson, *The Classical Hollywood Cinema*, 235.

4. Peter Bogdanovich, *Who the Devil Made It* (New York: Alfred A. Knopf, 1997), 250.

5. Cameron Crowe, *Conversations with Wilder*, 69, 66.

6. Ibid., 325.

7. Ibid., 315.

8. David Bordwell, Janet Staiger, and Kristin Thompson, *The Classical Hollywood Cinema*, 169.

9. George Stevens, *Conversations with the Great Moviemakers of Hollywood's Golden Age* (New York: Alfred A. Knopf, 2006), 213.

10. Joseph McBride, *Orson Welles* (New York: Da Capo Press, 1996), 115.

11. Max Wilk, *Schumucks with Underwoods* (New York: Applause Theater and Cinema Books, 2004), 71–72.

12. Peter Bogdanovich, *This is Orson Welles* (New York: HarperCollins, 1992), 61, 82.

13. David Bordwell, Janet Staiger, and Kristin Thompson, *The Classical Hollywood Cinema*, 3, 168–69.

14. George Stevens, *Conversations with the Great Moviemakers of Hollywood's Golden Age*, 341, 346.

15. Ibid., 159.

16. Ibid., 213.

17. Ronald L. Davis, *Just Making Movies: Company Directors on the Studio System* (Jackson, MI: University Press of Mississippi, 2005), 182.

18. Peter Bogdanovich, *John Ford* (Los Angeles, CA: University of California Press, 1978), 99.

19. George Stevens, *Conversations with the Great Moviemakers of Hollywood's Golden Age*, 319.

20. Ronald L. Davis, *Just Making Movies*, 120.

21. George Stevens, *Conversations with the Great Moviemakers of Hollywood's Golden Age*, 319.

22. Ibid., 329.

23. Peter Bogdanovich, *Who the Devil*, 324.

24. George Stevens, *Conversations with the Great Moviemakers of Hollywood's Golden Age*, 319.

25. Peter Bogdanovich, *John Ford*, 99.

26. Richard Schickel, *The Men Who Made the Movies* (Chicago, IL: Ivan R. Dee, 1975), 214–215.

27. Ronald L. Davis, *Just Making Movies*, 38, 90.

28. Peter Bogdanovich, *Who the Devil Made It*, 445, 449.

CHAPTER 6

1. George Stevens, *The Great Moviemakers of Hollywood's Golden Age* (New York: Alfred A. Knopf, 2006), 36.

2. Francois Truffaut, *Hitchcock* (New York: Simon & Schuster, 1985), 283.

3. Peter Bogdanovich, *Who the Devil Made It* (New York: Alfred A. Knopf, 1997), 71.

4. George Stevens, *The Great Moviemakers of Hollywood's Golden Age*, 320.

5. Peter Bogdanovich, *Who the Devil Made It*, 71.

6. George Stevens, *The Great Moviemakers of Hollywood's Golden Age*, 103.

7. Stanley Cavell, *The World Viewed* (Cambridge, MA: Harvard University Press, 1974), 152.

8. Peter Bogdanovich, *John Ford* (Los Angeles, CA: University of California Press, 1978), 99.

9. George Stevens, *The Great Moviemakers of Hollywood's Golden Age*, 265.

10. Ibid., 171.

11. Robert Bresson, *Notes on the Cinematographer* (London: Quartet, 1975), 67.

CHAPTER 7

1. David Bordwell, Janet Staiger, and Kristin Thompson, *The Classical Hollywood Cinema* (New York: Columbia University Press, 1985), 73.

2. David Bordwell, Janet Staiger, and Kristin Thompson, *The Classical Hollywood Cinema*, 81.

3. Peter Bogdanovich, *Who the Devil Made It* (New York: Alfred A. Knopf, 1997), 450.

4. Charles Thomas Samuels, *Encountering Directors* (New York: De Capo Press, 1972), 324.

5. Peter Bogdanovich, *Who the Devil Made It*, 449.

6. Andrew Sarris, *You Ain't Heard Nothin' Yet* (Oxford: Oxford University Press, 1998), 316.

7. George Stevens, *The Great Moviemakers of Hollywood's Golden Age* (New York: Alfred A. Knopf, 2006), 11.

8. Ibid., 103.

9. *Billy Wilder Speaks*, directed by Volker Schlorndorff and Gisela Grischow, produced by Bioskop film, distributed by Kino International, 2006.

10. Peter Bogdanovich, *Who the Devil Made It*, 332–334, 356.

11. Peter Bogdanovich, *John Ford* (Los Angeles, CA: University of California Press, 1978), 107.

12. Peter Bogdanovich, *Who the Devil Made It*, 245.

13. Peter Bogdanovich, *This is Orson Welles* (New York: HarperCollins, 1992), 186, 126.

14. George Stevens, *The Great Moviemakers of Hollywood's Golden Age*, 258.

15. Ibid. 415.

16. Christopher Frayling, *Something to Do with Death* (New York: Faber and Faber, 2000), 182.

17. Andrew Sarris, *You Ain't Heard Nothin' Yet*, 204.

18. Todd McCarthy, *Howard Hawks: The Grey Fox of Hollywood* (New York: Grove, 1997), 200.

19. George Stevens, *The Great Moviemakers of Hollywood's Golden Age*, 120.

20. Max Wilk, *Schmucks with Underwoods* (New York: Applause Theater and Cinema Books, 2004), 254,

21. Todd McCarthy, *Howard Hawks*, 372.

22. Max Wilk, *Schmucks with Underwoods*, 284.

23. Todd McCarthy, *Howard Hawks*, 361.

24. Ronald L. Davis, *Just Making Movies: Company Directors on the Studio System* (Jackson MI: University Press of Mississippi, 2005), 65–66, 69.

25. Donald Spoto, *The Dark Side of Genius: The Life of Alfred Hitchcock* (New York: Ballantine, 1983), 378.

CHAPTER 8

1. George Stevens, *The Great Moviemakers of Hollywood's Golden Age* (New York: Alfred A. Knopf, 2006), 82.

2. Robert Sklar, *Movie-Made America: A Cultural History of Making Movies* (New York: Vintage, 1975), 280.

3. Scott Eyman, *Ernst Lubitsch: Laughter in Paradise* (New York: Simon & Schuster, 1993), 197.

4. David Bordwell, Janet Staiger, Kristin Thompson, *The Classical Hollywood Cinema: Film Style and Mode of Production to 1960* (New York: Columbia University Press, 1985), 19.

5. Francois Truffaut, *Hitchcock* (New York: Simon & Schuster, 1985), 99.

6. Peter Bogdanovich, *The Cinema of Alfred Hitchcock* (New York: Museum of Modern Art, 1963), 16.

7. Scott Eyman, *Ernst Lubitsch*, 204.

8. Peter Bogdanovich, *Who the Devil Made It* (New York: Alfred A. Knopf, 1997), 444.

9. David Thomson, *The New Biographical Dictionary of Film* (New York: Alfred A. Knopf, 2002), 556.

10. Ethan Mordden, *The Hollywood Studios: Their Unique Styles During the Golden Age of Movies* (New York: Fireside, 1988), 85.

CHAPTER 9

1. Scott Eyman, *Ernst Lubitsch: Laughter in Paradise* (New York: Simon & Schuster, 1993), 150.

2. Peter Bogdanovich, *Who the Devil Made It* (New York: Alfred A. Knopf, 1997), 466.

3. Scott Eyman, *Ernst Lubitsch*, 243.

4. Charles Higham, *Warner Brothers* (New York: Charles Scribner's Sons, 1975), 104.

5. Ethan Mordden, *The Hollywood Studios* (New York: Simon & Schuster, 1988), 161.

6. Andrew Sarris, *You Ain't Heard Nothin' Yet* (New York: Oxford University Press, 1998), 356.

7. Ibid., 356.

8. Sergio Leone, "John Ford," *Cahiers du Cinema* 422 (July–August 1989), 14–15. Translations are mine.

9. Ibid., 14–15.

10. Ethan Mordden, *The Hollywood Studios*, 153.

11. David Thomson, *The New Biographical Dictionary of Film* (New York: Alfred A. Knopf, 2002), 98.

12. Jim Hiller, ed., *Cahiers du Cinema: The 1950s; Neo-Realism, Hollywood, New Wave* (Cambridge, MA: Harvard University Press, 1985), 88.

CHAPTER 10

1. Donald Spoto, *The Dark Side of Genius: The Life of Alfred Hitchcock* (New York: Ballantine, 1983), 291.

2. Peter Bogdanovich, *The Cinema of Alfred Hitchcock* (New York: Museum of Modern Art, 1963), 31.

3. Francois Truffaut, *Hitchcock* (New York: Simon & Schuster, 1985), 313.

4. Donald Spoto, *The Dark Side of Genius*, 439.

5. Peter Bogdanovich, *Who the Devil Made It* (New York: Alfred A. Knopf, 1997), 268.

6. Ibid., 314.

7. Peter Bogdanovich, *This is Orson Welles* (New York: HarperCollins, 1992), 15.

8. Robert Bresson, *Notes on the Cinematographer* (London: Quartet Books, 1986), 112.

9. Oreste de Fornari, *Sergio Leone: The Great Italian Dream of Legendary America* (Rome: Gremese, 1997), 143.

10. Robert Bresson, *Notes on the Cinematographer*, 74.

11. Ibid., 20.

12. George Stevens, *The Great Moviemakers of Hollywood's Golden Age* (New York: Alfred A. Knopf, 2006), 181.

13. Peter Bogdanovich, *Who the Devil Made It*, 276.

14. Ibid., 341.

15. Sessue Hayakawa, "Hayakawa, Japanese Screen Star," *Literary Digest* 55 (November 3, 1917), 70–72.

16. Jim Hiller, ed., *Cahiers du Cinema: The 1950s; Neo-Realism, Hollywood, New Wave* (Cambridge, MA: Harvard University Press, 1985), 89–90.

CHAPTER 11

1. Frank Capra, *The Name above the Title: An Autobiography* (New York: Vintage, 1971), 247.

2. Andrew Sarris, *You Ain't Heard Nothin' Yet* (New York: Oxford University Press, 1998), 320.

3. Ronald L. Davis, *Just Making Movies: Company Directors on the Studio System* (Jackson, MI: University Press of Mississippi, 2005), 31.

4. Donald Spoto, *The Dark Side of Genius: The Life of Alfred Hitchcock* (New York: Ballantine, 1983), 392.

5. Peter Bogdanovich, *This is Orson Welles* (New York: HarperCollins, 1992), 220–221.

CHAPTER 12

1. Andrew Sarris, *You Ain't Heard Nuthin' Yet: The American Talking Film, History and Memory, 1927–1949* (Oxford: Oxford University Press, 1998), 24.

2. David Bordwell, Janet Staiger, and Kristin Thompson, *The Classical Hollywood Cinema: Film Style and Mode of Production to 1960* (New York: Columbia University Press, 1985), 165–169.

3. Thomas Schatz, *The Genius of the System: Hollywood Filmmaking in the Studio Era* (New York: Metropolitan Books, 1988), 104–105.

4. David Bordwell, Janet Staiger, and Kristin Thompson, *The Classical Hollywood Cinema*, 173.

5. Thomas Schatz, *The Genius of the System*, 105.

6. George Stevens, *The Great Moviemakers of Hollywood's Golden Age* (New York: Alfred A. Knopf, 2006), 271.

7. Jim Hillier, ed. *Cahiers du Cinema: The 1950s; Neo-Realism, Hollywood, New Wave* (Cambridge, MA: Harvard University Press, 1985), 38.

8. Max Wilk, *Schmucks with Underwoods* (New York: Applause Theatre and Cinema Books, 2005), 131–132.

9. Jim Hillier, *Cahiers du Cinema*, 90.

10. Rosemarie Jarski, *Wisecracks: Great Lines from the Classic Hollywood Era* (Chicago: Contemporary Books, 1999), x.

11. George Stevens, *The Great Moviemakers of Hollywood's Golden Age*, 36.

12. Peter Bogdanovich, *Who the Devil Made It* (New York: Alfred A. Knopf, 1997), 363.

CHAPTER 13

1. George Stevens, *The Great Moviemakers of Hollywood's Golden Age* (New York: Alfred A. Knopf, 2006), 159.

2. Andrew Sarris, *You Ain't Heard Nuthin' Yet: The American Talking Film, History and Memory, 1927–1949* (Oxford: Oxford University Press, 1998), 37.

3. Peter Bogdanovich, *This is Orson Welles* (New York: HarperCollins, 1992), 310, 89.

4. George Stevens, *The Great Moviemakers of Hollywood's Golden Age*, 175–176.

5. Charles Thomas Samuels, *Encountering Directors* (New York: Da Capo Press, 1972), 234.

6. George Stevens, *The Great Moviemakers of Hollywood's Golden Age*, 95.

7. Ibid., 86.

8. Ibid., 461.

9. Ibid., 95–96.

10. Peter Bogdanovich, *John Ford* (Berkeley, CA: University of California Press, 1978), 9, 106.

11. Peter Bogdanovich, *This is Orson Welles*, 195–196.

CONCLUSION

1. Andrew Sarris, *You Ain't Seen Nothin' Yet* (Oxford: Oxford University Press, 1998), 335, 361.

2. Andrey Tarkovsky, *Sculpting in Time* (New York: Alfred A. Knopf, 1986), 184.

3. Jim Hillier, ed., *Cahiers du Cinema: The 1950s; Neo-Realism, Hollywood, New Wave* (Cambridge, MA: Harvard University Press, 1985), 90.

Bibliography

Aberdeen, J.A. *Hollywood Renegades: The Society of Independent Motion Picture Produc-ers*. Los Angeles, CA: Cobblestone Entertainment, 2000.

Anderson, Christopher. *Hollywood TV: The Studio System in the Fifties*. Austin, TX: University of Texas Press, 1978.

Bainbridge, John. *Garbo*. New York: Holt, Rinehart & Winston, 1971.

Berg, A. Scott. *Goldwyn: A Biography*. New York: Ballantine, 1989.

Blake, Michael. *Lon Chaney: The Man Behind the Thousand Faces*. Lanham, MD: Vestal Press, 1993.

Bogdanovich, Peter. *The Cinema of Alfred Hitchcock*. New York: Museum of Modern Art, 1963.

———. *John Ford*. Berkeley, CA: University of California Press, 1967.

———. *This is Orson Welles*. New York: HarperCollins, 1992.

———. *Who the Devil Made It?* New York: Alfred A. Knopf, 1997.

Bordwell, David, Janet Staiger, and Kristen Thompson, *The Classical Hollywood Cinema: Film Style and Mode of Production to 1960*. New York: Columbia University Press, 1985.

Bresson, Robert. *Notes on the Cinematographer*. London: Quartet Books, 1986.

Bronlow, Kevin. *Behind the Mast of Innocence*. New York: Alfred A. Knopf, 1990.

Buscombe, Edward, ed. *The BFI Companion to the Western*. New York: Atheneum, 1988.

Callow, Simon. *Orson Welles: The Road to Xanadu*. New York: Viking Press, 1995.

Capra, Frank. *The Name Above the Title: An Autobiography*. New York: Vintage, 1971.

Cavell, Stanley. *The World Viewed: Reflections on the Ontology of Film*. Cambridge, MA: Harvard University Press, 1979.

Chaplin, Charles. *My Autobiography*. New York: Simon & Schuster, 1964.

Chierichetti, David. *Hollywood Costume Design*. New York: Harmony, 1976.

Coursedon, Jean-Pierre, and Pierre Sauvage, eds. *American Directors*. Volume 1. New York: McGraw-Hill, 1983.

Crafton, Donald. *The Talkies*. New York: Charles Scribner's Sons, 1997.

Crowe, Cameron. *Conversations with Billy Wilder*. New York: Alfred A. Knopf, 1999.

Custen, George F. *Twentieth Century's Fox*. New York: Basic, 1997.

Davis, Ronald L. *Just Making Movies: Company Directors on the Studio System*. Jackson, MI: University Press of Mississippi, 2005.

De Fornari, Oreste. *Sergio Leone: The Great Italian Dream of Legendary America*. Rome: Gremese International, 1997.

Deutelbaum, Marshall, and Leland Poague, eds. *A Hitchcock Reader*. Ames, IA: Iowa State University Press, 1986.

Doherty, Thomas. *Pre-Code Hollywood*. New York: Columbia University Press, 1999.

Eyman, Scott. *Ernst Lubitsch: Laughter in Paradise*. New York: Simon & Schuster, 1993.

———. *Lion of Hollywood: The Life and Legend of Louis B. Mayer*. New York: Simon & Schuster, 2005.

Finler, Joel. *The Hollywood Story*. New York: Crown, 1988.

Fitzgerald, F. Scott, au., and Matthew J. Burccoli, ed. *A Life in Letters*. New York: Charles Scribner's Sons, 1994.

Frayling, Christopher. *Something to Do with Death*. New York: Faber & Faber, 2000.

Freedland, Michael. *The Warner Brothers*. New York: St. Martin's Press, 1983.

Gallagher, Tag. *John Ford: The Man and His Films*. Berkeley, CA: University of California Press, 1986.

Gomery, Douglas. *The Hollywood Studio System*. New York: St. Martin, 1986.

Grobel, Lawrence. *The Hustons*. New York: Charles Scribner's Sons, 1989.

Gutner, Howard. *Gowns by Adrian*. New York: Abrams, 2001.

Hamilton, Ian. *Writers in Hollywood, 1915–1951*. London: Heinemann, 1990.

Harvey, James. *Romantic Comedy in Hollywood from Lubitsch to Sturges*. New York: Alfred A. Knopf, 1987.

Harvey, Stephen. *Directed by Vincente Minnelli*. New York: Harper & Row, 1989.

Hay, Peter. *MGM: When the Lion Roars*. Atlanta, GA: Turner, 1991.

Hayakawa, Sessue. "Hayakawa, Japanese Screen Star." *Literary Digest* 55 (November 3, 1917): 70–72.

Hecht, Ben. *A Child of the Century*. New York: Simon & Schuster, 1954.

Heisner, Beverly. *Hollywood Art*. Jefferson, NC: McFarland, 1990.

Higham, Charles. *Warner Brothers*. New York: Charles Scribner's Sons, 1975.

Hiller, James, ed. *Cahiers du Cinema: The 1950s; Neo-Realism, Hollywood, New Wave*. Cambridge, MA: Harvard University Press, 1985.

Jarski, Rosemarie. *Wisecracks: Great Lines from the Classic Hollywood Era*. Chicago, IL: Contemporary Books, 1999.

LaSalle, Mick. *Complicated Women: Sex and Power in Pre-Code Hollywood*. New York: St. Martin's, 2000.

Lasky, Betty. *RKO: The Biggest Little Major of Them All*. Englewood Cliffs, NJ: Prentice Hall, 1984.

Leff, Leonard J. *Hitchcock and Selznick: The Rich and Strange Collaboration of Alfred Hitchcock and David O. Selznick*. New York: Weidenfeld and Nicholson, 1987.

Leff, Leonard J., and Jerold L. Simmons. *The Dame in the Kimono: Hollywood, Censorship, and the Production Code from the 1920s to the 1960s*. New York: Grove Weidenfeld, 1990.

Leone, Sergio. "John Ford." *Cahiers du Cinema* 422 (July–August, 1989): 14–15.

Levy, Emanuel. *George Cukor: Master of Elegance*. New York: St. Martin's, 1996.

Mast, Gerald. *The Comic Mind*. Second edition. Chicago, IL: University of Chicago Press, 1979.

————. *Howard Hawks: Storyteller*. Oxford: Oxford University Press, 1982.

————. *A Short History of the Movies*. New York: Macmillan, 1986.

McBride, Joseph. *Frank Capra: The Catastrophe of Success*. New York: Simon & Schuster, 1992.

————. *Orson Welles*. New York: Da Capo Press, 1996.

McCarthy, Todd. *Howard Hawks: The Grey Fox of Hollywood*. New York: Grove Press, 1997.

McClelland, Doug. *Forties Film Talk*. Jefferson, NC: McFarland, 1992.

McDonald, Paul. *The Star System: Hollywood's Production of Popular Identities*. London: Wallflower, 2000.

McGilligan, Patrick. *Backstory: Interviews with Screenwriters of Hollywood's Golden Age*. Berkeley, CA: University of California Press, 1986.

————. *Film Crazy: Interviews with Hollywood Legends*. New York: St. Martin's, 2000.

————. *George Cukor: A Double Life*. New York: St. Martin's Press, 1991.

Milne, Tom. *Godard on Godard*. New York: Da Capo, 1972.

Mordenn, Ethan. *The Hollywood Studios: Their Unique Styles during the Olden Age of Movies*. New York: Fireside Books, 1988.

Naremore, James. *Acting in Cinema*. Berkeley, CA: University of California Press, 1988.

Parish, James Robert. *Hollywood Character Actors*. New Rochelle, New York: Arlington House, 1978.

Peary, Gerald, and Roger Shatzkin, eds. *The Modern American Novel and the Movies*. New York: Frederick Ungar, 1978.

Phillips, Gene. *Alfred Hitchcock*. Boston, MA: Twayne, 1984.

Pickard, Roy. *The Hollywood Studios*. London: Frederick Muller, 1978.

Ross, Lillian. *Picture*. Cambridge, MA: De Capo Press, 1992.

Samuels, Charles Thomas. *Encountering Directors*. New York: De Capo Press, 1972.

Sanders, James. *Celluloid Skyline*. New York: Alfred A. Knopf, 2001.

Sarris, Andrew. *The American Cinema: Directors and Directions, 1929–1968*. Chicago, IL: University of Chicago Press, 1968.

————. *The Films of Josef von Sternberg*. New York: Museum of Modern Art, 1966.

————, ed. *Interviews with Film Directors*. New York: Avon, 1969.

————. *You Ain't Heard Nothing Yet: The American Talking Film, History and Memory, 1927–1949*. Oxford: Oxford University Press, 1998.

Schatz, Thomas. *The Genius of the System: Hollywood Filmmaking in the Studio Era*. New York: Metropolitan Books, 1988.

Schickel, Richard. *The Men Who Made the Movies*. Chicago: Ivan R. Dee, 1975.

Sennett, Robert S. *Setting the Scene: The Great Hollywood Art Directors*. New York: Abrams, 1994.

Silvester, Christopher, ed. *The Grove Book of Hollywood*. New York: Grove Press 1998.

Sinyard, Neil. *Silent Movies*. New York: St. Martin's Press, 1982.

Sklar, Robert. *Movie-Made America: A Cultural History of American Movies*. New York: Vintage Books, 1975.

Smith, Steven C. *A Heart at Fire's Center: The Life and Music of Bernard Herrman*. Berkeley, CA: University of California Press, 2002.

Sperling, Cass Warner, Cork Millner, and Jack Warner. *Hollywood Be Thy Name: The Warner Brothers Story*. Lexington, KY: University Press of Kentucky, 1998.

Spoto, Donald. *The Dark Side of Genius: The Life of Alfred Hitchcock*. New York: Ballantine, 1983.

Stevens, George. *The Great Moviemakers of Hollywood's Golden Age*. New York: Alfred A. Knopf, 2006.

Sturges, Preston, au., and Sandy Sturges, ed. *Preston Sturges*. New York: Simon & Schuster, 1990.

Tarkovsky, Andrey. *Sculpting in Time*. New York: Alfred A. Knopf, 1987.

Thomas, Bob. *Thalberg: Life and Legend*. Beverly Hills, CA: New Millennium Press, 2000.

Thomson, David. *The New Biographical Dictionary of Film*. New York: Alfred A. Knopf, 2002.

Truffaut, Francois. *Hitchcock*. New York: Simon & Schuster, 1985.

————. *Les Films de Ma Vie*. Paris: Flammarion, 1975.

Vidor, King. *On Filmmaking*. New York: David McKay, 1972.

Vieira, Mark. *Sin in Soft Focus*. New York: Abrams, 1999.

Von Sternberg, Josef. *Fun in a Chinese Laundry*. New York: Macmillan, 1965.

Walker, Joseph, and Juanita Walker. *The Light on Her Face*. Hollywood: The ASC Press, 1984.

Weis, Elisabeth, and John Belton, eds. *Film Sound: Theory and Practice*. New York: Columbia University Press, 1985.

Wilk, Max. *Schmucks with Underwoods*. New York: Applause Theater and Cinema Books, 2004.

Zollo, Paul. *Hollywood Remembered*. New York: Cooper Square, 2002.

Index

About the Author

JOHN FAWELL is associate professor at Boston University. He has written two books, *Hitchcock's Rear Window: The Well-Made Film* and *The Art of Sergio Leone's Once upon a Time in the West*, as well as a variety of articles on the nature of film, Hollywood, French Cinema, and literature (Tolstoy, Valery, Tennyson, Maupassant.)